SHARING
THE SECRETS

SHARING
THE SECRETS

Open Source Intelligence and the War on Drugs

J. F. Holden-Rhodes

PRAEGER

Westport, Connecticut
London

Library of Congress Cataloging-in-Publication Data

Holden-Rhodes, J. F.
    Sharing the secrets : open source intelligence and the war on
drugs / J. F. Holden-Rhodes.
        p.   cm.
    Includes bibliographical references and index.
    ISBN 0–275–95454–4 (alk. paper)
    1. Narcotics, Control of—United States.   2. Drug traffic—United
States—Investigation.   3. Intelligence service—United States.
I. Title.
HV5825.H65   1997
363.4'5'0973—dc20   95–40090

British Library Cataloguing in Publication Data is available.

Library of Congress Catalog Card Number: 95–40090
ISBN: 0–275–95454–4

First published in 1997

Praeger Publishers, 88 Post Road West, Westport, CT 06881
An imprint of Greenwood Publishing Group, Inc.

Printed in the United States of America

The paper used in this book complies with the
Permanent Paper Standard issued by the National
Information Standards Organization (Z39.48–1984).

10 9 8 7 6 5 4 3 2 1

Copyright Acknowledgments

The author and the publisher gratefully acknowledge permission to use
the following:

Excerpts from Kent, Sherman. *Strategic Intelligence for American World
Policy*. Copyright renewed © 1949 by Princeton University Press. Re-
printed by permission of Princeton University Press.

For Gavin Holden Rhodes, artist, musician, scholar,
his father's son, a leader for the next generation

Contents

Preface

We are pilgrims, Master; we shall go
Always a little further.
—J. F. Flecker, inscription on the Clock, Bradbury Lines, Hereford, U.K.
Home of the Special Air Service Regiment (SAS)

Even as I began the outline that would serve as the framework for this book, the title, *Sharing the Secrets* came to mind. I knew that those words best described the essence of what it was that I wanted to write about. The title, and really the idea for such a work, had their genesis some 25 years earlier in Vietnam. There as a Lieutenant, and later as a Captain of Marines, I learned the art of reconnaissance and the craft of intelligence as a platoon leader and S-2 (Intelligence Officer) with the 3rd Force Reconnaissance Company and as the commander of Company D, 3rd Reconnaissance Battalion, 3rd Marine Division. Later, with Company 3-3, 3rd Combined Action Group, 3rd Marine Division, operating along *la rue sans joie* (the Street without Joy) Route 1—the war-scarred highway that ran between Hue, Quang Tri, and Danang—I learned an entirely new aspect of intelligence. It was here that I learned about drug trafficking. In the aftermath of the Tet Offensive, it amazed me that opium still flowed from the Golden Triangle—the world's largest poppy growing area along the China, Burma, Thailand border—unslowed by war.

In 1980, now with the Army as the Latin America and Caribbean Team Chief, 9001st Military Intelligence Detachment (Terrorism Counteraction), I experienced the same amazement as we watched cocaine flow from the Andean Ridge toward the United States, seemingly unrecognized and certainly unchecked. By the time cocaine and then "crack" were at last discovered, long after we and others had sounded an unheeded warning and we had coined the term "narco-terrorism," I was "hooked" on the drug business. What struck me early on, however, was the inadequacy of intelligence in dealing with drug trafficking issues. Something was missing.

The obsession with classification, slavish attention to technical aspects, and a corporate lockstep mindset had robbed intelligence of its soul. What was missing was the belief that the creation of intelligence is an art form, something supported, not dominated, by science. Analysis, really gifted analysis, had all but been extinguished. Intelligence had stopped thinking.

In 1989, I began work at Los Alamos National Laboratory as a graduate research assistant and doctoral candidate at the University of New Mexico. Upon completion of my doctoral studies I was appointed as a Post Doctoral Fellow and selected as the Counter Drug (CD) Intelligence Team leader. The role of the CD Intelligence Team was to serve as a special—but unofficial—staff section for the US Southern Command (SOUTHCOM). Our mission was to provide modeling and simulation support which would serve as the basis for "predictive, actionable, counter drug intelligence" to SOUTHCOM. In addition, we were to serve as an adversarial "Red Team," i.e., to think, act, operate, and present our intelligence products as "narcotraficantes." Our intelligence products were developed and executed as though we were a drug trafficking organization.

As the research, crafting, and eventually completion of this book took place, the title seemed to fit even better. Only as the final pages were being smoothed out did the impact of the title hit home. The concept of sharing the secrets is the classic exemplar of an oxymoron. What had seemed intuitively correct at the onset of the research—that only by sharing the secrets could intelligence have any impact on the wars on drugs—was still untested theory. I continued to wonder if all the pieces really fit and if my concept would work in the real world. I argued for and received permission to perform our work for SOUTHCOM in an unclassified, open source mode. Thus, the opportunity to test and evaluate theory in a real-world laboratory came to pass. Early on, it became strikingly clear what the "missing" element was. Traditional intelligence wasn't good enough. What was needed was a new intelligence. Because of the nature of drug trafficking, I sensed that a more multifaceted approach—a melding of classic strategic, military, and certain elements of what passed for law enforcement intelligence—was needed. But what would be the "grist" to feed the new intelligence?

In the 9001st Military Intelligence Detachment, we had worked with the fledgling concept of Open Source Intelligence (OSINT) and had developed a real skill for getting to the "heart of the beast" solely through the use of unclassified information. I seized upon the concept of OSINT as the basis for counter drug intelligence (CDI). Over a three-year time-frame I had the opportunity to design, test, and evaluate OSINT methodology and products. During that time, I had the opportunity to talk or work with nearly every agency involved in the war on drugs. From Panama to Mexico, from the South West Border (La Frontera), to Washington, and from Aqua Prieta and Guzman Mountain along the "boot-heel" of the New Mexico/Mexico border, to Joint Task Force 4, 5, and 6 (the multi-service military organizations formed to provide support to law enforcement agencies), I had the opportunity to use OSINT to develop counter drug intelligence products.

This is the story of that journey, a pilgrimage that has just begun.

Acknowledgments

A work such as this depends on the assistance of many people, both those who believed and those who tried to stop the secrets from being shared. The former made the road easier, the latter, through their obstacles, ensured that there would be no quarter asked—and certainly none given.

To Terry Bearce, who opened the door; to Peter Lupsha, mentor and fellow predator; to Bob Himmerich y Valencia, fellow "Jarhead" and scholar who believed in me; to Greg Gleason, scholar/entrepreneur who also believed; to Commander Jerry Kasner, my adopted father who taught me the art and passion of writing; to Professor Dick Ellis, who championed my cause; to Hank Marsden of ONDCP, a mentor who made me see that it could be done; to Marie Harper, LANL, friend and librarian extraordinaire, without whose knowledge and guidance I would not have been able to find the secrets; to Lieutenant Colonel Jim Nicholson, comrade in arms and analyst par excellance; to Colonel John Miller of the US Naval Instutute Proceedings and Anne Collier of the Naval Institute Press, who believed that I had something important to say; to Admiral John Linnon, USCG, a sea-dog of the first order who was not afraid to tell the truth at the highest level; to Russ Holland and Randy Layland, the best maritime analysts in the business; to Major General John Pickler; who understood how the military could support law enforcement; to Doug Ball, former Director, National Drug Intelligence Center, who sacrificed his career in order that counter drug intelligence might become a reality.

My thanks to Tina Skinner and Deborah Ross who took a difficult manuscript and made it come together.

To Mog-Ur and the blind mice at the Snake-Pit—the Systems Research Division, Sandia National Laboratories, where smoke and mirrors still passes for Intelligence—time is running out.

To the narcotraficante, who made it over the fence just as my cross-hairs centered on his back, good hunting, we'll meet again.

For all those who risked their careers to provide me with information in the hope that the truth might lead to a realistic national drug policy, here is my promise fulfilled.

Above all others, this is for Karen-Marie who knows the meaning of Semper Fidelis. And for Jo-Anne.

SHARING
THE SECRETS

Introduction

We ought to be seeking tentative answers to fundamental questions, rather than definitive answers to trivial ones.
                                                                    —James H. Billington

The last decade of the 20th century and on into the early years of the 21st will be a time of great turmoil and violent change. As the United States faces the uncertainty and violence of a postcolonial, multitribal world, it is abundantly clear that American Intelligence will have to be rethought and rebuilt.[1] *Sharing the Secrets: Open Source Intelligence and the Wars on Drugs*, is about the design, testing, and evaluation of a new "Intelligence" for today and the future. It is an attempt to provide grist for the thinking and debate that must pave the way for the rebuilding of American Intelligence. Intelligence designed to focus upon drug trafficking is but one of the facets of the new American intelligence requirements.

As an intelligence primer, this book provides a foundation for the belief that intelligence work and its products do not have to be classified. It makes the case for a new unclassified intelligence. Constructed from the vast knowledge produced by the information and communication revolutions, it is an intelligence that can provide the evaluated information that American decision makers require. Its distinguishing characteristic is that it is intelligence that can be shared. As a policy formulation and evaluation tool, this new intelligence is directed towards an "exhaustive examination of a situation for which a policy is required"— drug trafficking and a National Drug Control Strategy—and "the objective and impartial exploration of all the alternative solutions which the policy problem offers."[2]

The setting for *Sharing the Secrets* is cocaine trafficking in the western hemisphere. It is clear that the scourge of drugs is a serious threat to our national well-being. Drug problems have been a recurring concern in American life since the turn of the century. What is new, in this the "fifth round" of drug wars, is the depth to which drugs have permeated American life; and, the astonishing world-wide growth, power, and wealth of the drug business. The richest, most powerful multi-national business conglomerate in the world, the drug industry has reached into and impacted our quality of life in a manner never before experienced. The actual number of yearly deaths attributed to drugs is relatively small in the overall scale of things. But the unimaginable amounts of money, the violence of an unprec-edented nature, and corruption of unknown depths that the drug business spawns has forced the United States to embrace a siege mentality. As we continue to floun-der, it is readily apparent that we still don't understand the nature of drug traffick-ing. If it is true that knowledge is power, then we as a nation continue to be power-less as we face a problem against which we have directed billions of dollars with no apparent results. The crux of any problem is to be able to define it, to search for "the heart within the beast."[3] Only then can one work towards potential solutions. This is where intelligence comes into play.

The concept of intelligence is best explained by Sherman Kent, one of the founding fathers of American Intelligence:

Although there is a good deal of understandable mystery about it, Intelligence is a simple and self-evident thing. As an activity it is the pursuit of a certain kind of knowledge; as a phenomenon it is the resulting knowledge. In a small way it is what we all do every day. No matter whether done instinctively or with skillful conscious mental effort intelligence work is in essence nothing more than the search for the single best answer.[4]

One suspects, however, that most Americans see Intelligence in a different light then that portrayed by Sherman Kent. For them, and sadly for most decision-makers, Intelligence is seen through images of spies and intrigue. But the truth of the matter is that Intelligence work remains the simple, natural endeavor to get the sort of knowledge upon which a successful course of action can be rested.[5]

Kent argued that the special knowledge upon which our nation's foreign poli-cies and strategies must rest should be considered as strategic intelligence.[6] This intelligence should be "high-level foreign positive intelligence," the "kind of knowl-edge our state must possess regarding other states in order to assure itself that its cause would not suffer nor its undertakings fail because its statesmen and soldiers plan and act in ignorance."[7] Kent also argued that if foreign policy is the shield of the republic, then strategic intelligence is the thing that gets the shield to the right place at the right time. With great prescience, Sherman Kent understood that it is intelligence that stands ready to guide the sword.[8]

As Sherman Kent sought to create an intellectual structure for American Intel-ligence for the world of his time, so have I attempted to define and craft the struc-ture of a new element of American Intelligence—Open Source Intelligence (OSINT). Open Source Intelligence is the search for the single best answer. It is both process and result. It is knowledge crafted from information drawn from the widest possible range of focused sources. These sources are open in the fullest sense and no clandestine collection methods are used in their acquisition.

The collected information is not subject to proprietary constraints with the exception of copyright related concerns. The information that is the grist for OSINT is analyzed, evaluated, and crafted into an intelligence product through the functioning of the Intelligence Production Cycle: direction, collection, analysis, and production. The ultimate OSINT product may be strategic, operational, or tactical in nature, not necessarily in a military sense, but as it relates to the subject to which it is applied. Open Source Intelligence is derived from a research methodology which is marked by sound reasoning ability, judgment, intellectual honesty, and objectivity. Driven by these attributes, the OSINT research process reexamines what has been looked at before and, of equal importance, the product(s) of new exploration. The OSINT research process is purposeful, systematic, contributes new knowledge, and is ultimately aimed toward some type of action. Because the information to which the OSINT process is applied may be virtually anything, Open Source Intelligence is uniquely suited to function in almost any subject matter environment and is constrained only by the nature of the subject, the availability of information, cost, and the skill of the persons crafting the information into an Intelligence product.[9]

In applying the concept of Open Source Intelligence to drug trafficking, I used Sherman Kent's definition of the function of intelligence to guide my work:

Intelligence is not the formulator of objectives; it is not the drafter of policy; it is not the maker of plans; it is not the carrier out of operations. Intelligence is ancillary to these; to use the dreadful cliché, it performs a service function. Its job is to see that the doers are generally well informed; its job is to stand behind them with the book opened at the right page, to call their attention to the stubborn fact they may be neglecting, and—at their request— to analyze alternative courses without indicating choice.[10]

In *Sharing the Secrets*, I have attempted to call to the attention of the doers the stubborn facts that they may be neglecting in the drug trafficking arena. The key for this exercise is Open Source Intelligence. Drawing further from Kent, I echo his argument that "intelligence must not be the apologist for policy, but this does not mean that intelligence has no role in policy formulation."[11] Rather, intelligence should be used to conduct an "exhaustive examination of the situation for which a policy is required." Here that examination is directed towards the National Drug Control Strategy and the efforts of the counter drug community.[12]

In building upon George Pettee's belief that, "the United States cannot have a national policy comparable to its commitments unless it has the means to form such a policy and to base it upon the best possible knowledge of facts and circumstances," I use OSINT to produce the "facts and circumstances." The end result is that *Sharing the Secrets* is "a body of descriptive material which will enable serious public discussion to begin" on national drug policy and strategy.[13] Tying all the pieces together, I have crafted an intelligence methodology that enables the Intelligence Community to share the secrets with each other and policymakers, and most importantly, the American people.

Sharing the Secrets is directed to a three-tiered audience: the American public, who have yet to be told the truth about the drug wars; to academics who have failed to come to grips with drug issues; and, to decision makers in federal, state, and local governments, who have failed to demand from the Intelligence and Law Enforcement communities, facts and alternatives with which a realistic national drug policy and strategy might be designed and implemented.

I believe that the majority of the Americans have been directly effected by the impact of drugs. They will actively participate in efforts to stem the impact of drugs—if they are told the truth about what is possible, and the real cost of those efforts. To them, this book offers an opportunity to understand where their fears begin, i.e., in the drug producing and transiting countries. And, while they might not care to sort through history and theory, they can find sections within this book that will provide a clear definition of the drug threat and what their government has done, and not done, to counter, drug trafficking. This knowledge will enable them to frame questions that they should place before their elected representatives in order to get to the heart of the matter. Ultimately, it is the individual American alone, who will turn the tide.

For the academics who have refused to dirty their hands in the squalid back-alleys of the drug world, this text is a primer which provides the tools with which to understand the supply-side issues and to reflect upon how supply issues affect demand issues, thus forming the basis for coherent policy recommendations. To academia goes the challenge of responding to the wars on drugs as their predecessors did some fifty years earlier, when it was American academics who filled the ranks of the fledgling intelligence services at the start of World War II, and who played a major role in shaping post-war American Intelligence.

For the decisionmakers—federal, state, and local—who have yet to come to grips with the realities of the wars on drugs; and, who have been remiss in not holding the feet of the military, law enforcement and intelligence communities to the fire, I have attempted to open the book to the right page and have provided the stubborn facts that they may have been neglecting.

Lastly, for the Intelligence Community, I offer a case study in the application of Open Source Intelligence. Field-tested and forged in the heat of the war on drugs, OSINT is a useful tool with which to refocus and redirect their efforts toward rebuilding American Intelligence.

THE SEARCH FOR TENTATIVE ANSWERS TO FUNDAMENTAL QUESTIONS

The designers of the *National Drug Control Strategy* (NDCS) gave Intelligence the highest priority as they attempted to chart a course that would lead the nation out of the scourge of drugs. The much heralded NDCS stated that, "the war against drugs cannot be fought—much less won—without good intelligence." The drafters of the NDCS recognized that intelligence in the counter drug arena was different from traditional Intelligence in that it consisted of both "traditional" intelligence and law enforcement intelligence. What was unclear was how this undefined "new" Intelligence would be created, and how it would be applied.[14]

My search to define and apply Open Source Intelligence was done in an evolutionary manner. Because of the nature of the subject, my work is multidisciplinary. It touches upon policy issues both domestic and foreign; international relations; national and regional strategies and tactics. My analytical framework rests upon the learned foundation provided by those who set the standards for thinking about and understanding American intelligence. I sought to absorb the essence of their work so as to understand primary Intelligence theory and issues prior to moving towards the crafting of OSINT. In part, in intelligence jargon, they have provided the theoretical basis for my "sources and methods."

I used as the framework for the intellectual foundation of my study, the works of George S. Pettee and Sherman Kent. Their tomes are the collective genius and genesis of thinking about US Intelligence immediately following World War II. *The Future of American Secret Intelligence,* and *Strategic Intelligence For American World Policy* are as applicable today as they were almost fifty years ago. I drew heavily from Angelo Codevilla's, *Informing Statecraft: Intelligence For A New Century.* I share his affinity for American Intelligence and concur with his picture of the shortcomings of traditional Intelligence and his prescriptions for "getting it right." I relied on Colin S. Gray's, *War, Peace, and Victory: Strategy and Statecraft for the Next Century,* for the understanding of what strategy is and for the basis of a strategic framework to which to apply intelligence products as the essence of sound policy and effective strategy.

As Harry Howe Ransom sought to explore the then "unknown ground" of American government and the national intelligence community in *The Intelligence Establishment,* I seek to expand the search beyond the confines of the traditional national intelligence community to the point where intelligence touches foreign shores and reaches down to the state and local level. To fail to reach in this manner will ensure that the effort to scope and craft a national drug policy and strategy will fall short of the mark.

The primary works that I have drawn upon each have a common thread—an inquiry into the nature, structure, and utility of American Intelligence. Open Source Intelligence is perhaps more "strategic" in nature then any other Intelligence in our history. Berkowitz and Goodman define strategic Intelligence as "analysis produced in a process clearly separate from that used to develop policy, based on combined sources of information, and intended to go beyond simple descriptions of military deployments or political events."[15] It is my belief that OSINT expands the definition of strategic to include not only high level or far-flung events and information, but also to mean strategic on a small scale and in a narrowly defined setting. Thus, in a setting at the state or local level, strategic as applied to drug trafficking implies all those activities—be they in Colombia, Mexico, or just down the interstate, that impact the trafficking activities in that specific locale.

For the intelligence requirements of his time, Kent argued that two elements should be left out of the new intelligence: "knowledge of our own domestic scene and all knowledge of the sort which lies behind police functions."[16] Kent left these elements out of his intelligence equation for good reason. The world had just emerged from the throes of W.W. II and the excess of Nazi Germany. As an historian, he was acutely aware of the constitutional concerns about authoritarian rule. The National Security Act of 1947, subsequent legislation, amendments, oversights, and Executive Orders, have sought to keep police powers separate from intelligence. Today, because of the depth to which drug trafficking has permeated American society stressing to the breaking point its social fabric and its police functions; intelligence directed toward drugs requires the inclusion and melding of federal, state, and local police information.

Abram N. Shulsky argues that "intelligence is primarily about the discovery and protection of secrets."[17] While counter drug intelligence must have the capability to discover and protect those secrets, above all else, it must have the capability of sharing the secrets within the national intelligence community, the military departments, and state and local law enforcement agencies. In turn the Law enforcement "trinity"—Federal, State, and Local— must distill the information gathered, evaluate it, and provide decisionmakers at each level with the truth.

Sharing the Secrets is descriptive, proscriptive, and prescriptive. After setting the stage in my introduction, I have developed six case study chapters. Each study is a link in a chain, capable of standing alone but serving the purpose of joining together the issues so as to set the stage for my findings and conclusions.

In Chapter 1, "The New Intelligence Environment," I begin with an overview of American Intelligence from 1946 through 1989, and then into the future. I address this time frame in terms of "eras"—1941–1946, 1947–1989, 1989 and beyond. I discuss key events and issues to show the evolution of intelligence and describe the new challenges that intelligence must address as it enters the 3rd Era. Critical to understanding the new environment is an appreciation of the "Gray Area Phenomena," the advent of non-state actors and the lessening role of nation-states.

In Chapter 2, "In Search of a Common Ground: The Quest for Counter Drug Intelligence," I set the stage by tracing the history of the still-continuing search for the basis for an intelligence that might be used in the drug trafficking arena.

Chapter 3, "The National Drug Control Strategy: The Intelligence Agenda," deals with drugs, national security and the attempt to create a national drug control policy and strategy. Emphasis here is directed toward the Intelligence Agenda of the NDCS. I provide an historical review of the American experience with drugs since the turn of the century. I also trace the evolution of drug policy and growth of the present day counter drug intelligence agencies, showing the lack of a unified effort among the 48 federal agencies that has resulted in as many drug "wars" as there are agencies involved.

Chapter 4, "The Threat," deals with a study of the cocaine trafficking industry from the production countries, through "El Conducto"—the conduit through the transiting countries—and on to Mexico, the linch-pin in the drug arena.

Chapter 5, "The Militarization of the War on Drugs," provides a detailed examination of the reasons why the military establishment was directed to join the wars on drugs, the refusal of the military to "fight," the belated entry of the military, and the role of the military to date.

Chapter 6, "The South West Border: La Frontera," is an examination of the intelligence aspects of the wars on drugs. It is a first-hand account and analysis of the evolution and performance of federal, state, and local law enforcement agencies and the military at a place where all the elements of the drug war are supposed to fit together.

The final chapter, "Getting It Right: Opening the Book to the Right Page," deals with the total picture of the war against cocaine today. Drawing together the links provided by the previous case study chapters, I sculpt a comprehensive picture of the supply-side in the war on drugs using Open Source Intelligence to open the book to the right page and call attention to the stubborn facts that are being overlooked. The result is an exhaustive examination of the situation for which a policy is required and the exploration and presentation of an alternative solution.

Chapter 1

The New Intelligence Environment

> Intelligence is the kind of knowledge a state must possess regarding other states in order to assure itself that its cause will not suffer nor its undertakings fail because its statesmen and soldiers plan and act in ignorance.
>
> —Sherman Kent
> *Strategic Intelligence for American World Policy*

THE FIRST INTELLIGENCE ERA, 1941–1946

In the closing days of World War II, the American Intelligence Community (IC) found itself in a dilemma. Barely five years old, the IC was faced with a war-ravaged world and the new threat of communism. Founded and forged in the crucible of war, the IC had learned its trade "on the job." It was clear, however, that there was much still to be learned and that the experiences of the first era—both good and bad—would shape the framework for the future. One thing was certain, however: there would be the requirement for "a first class intelligence service to support our national objectives."[1]

In 1946, George S. Pettee published *The Future of American Secret Intelligence*. Pettee focused his work on the "faults and errors of strategic intelligence during the war." To do this he built an analytical "fault-tree" with which to look at the shortcomings of intelligence during the war. Lastly, he applied the "fault-tree" to address future applications of strategic intelligence. His "template" is as valuable today as it was in the postwar period.

1. The shortcomings of intelligence work were due in large part to growing pains. Within a period of five years, the American intelligence establishment grew from virtually nothing to a worldwide operation. The intelligence community learned its job as the war progressed. With the war over, the structure of American Intelligence would have to be formalized and refocused.

2. The worldwide intelligence effort had been administered by officials with little or no direct intelligence experience. Because there was no US intelligence community prior to the war, there was little or no direct experience in government intelligence, which Pettee explained was the reason for the direction of intelligence by inexperienced officials, with the results of their efforts being almost exclusively produced by trial and error.

3. The administration of intelligence was partly backwards because the administration of research was generally backward. Pettee argued that the research process in the creation of intelligence was critical. Unless one asks the right questions and then proceeds with a series of definite operations (I interpret this to mean that the research activity is purposeful, that it is performed in a systematic manner, and that it contributes new knowledge), the intelligence product will not be of high quality.

4. Lastly, he argued that the location of the intelligence establishment within the government must be resolved in such a way that things will happen in the government which ought to happen in a modern government as the consequence of modern intelligence.

With the United States now six years into the throes of its fifth drug war, the Pettee "fault-tree" takes on new utility. Almost 50 years later, Pettee's work still has great value as it provides a diagnostic framework by which to evaluate our national drug policy and strategy.

Sherman Kent's classic text, *Strategic Intelligence for American World Policy* followed in 1949. Acknowledging Pettee's "trail-breaking work in strategic intelligence" Kent's book provided an overview of the current intelligence issues of the time and his own prescriptions for the future. He wrote that intelligence "is the knowledge which our highly placed civilians and military men must have to safeguard the national welfare."[2]

In retrospect, it is not surprising that it was scholar-spies and analysts who were the first to articulate what the shape of the new intelligence environment might look like and to define future intelligence requirements. Pressed into service to staff wartime intelligence prior to the creation of centralized intelligence, American academics helped to shape World War II intelligence activities. Ray Cline suggests that the joining of scholars and the application of their skills provided the new Central Intelligence Agency (CIA) with superior intellectual skills, causing it to be ranked amongst the top such organizations in the world.[3] R. W. Jones, in his classic work *The Wizard War*, also argued that it was academics who helped to shape the wartime intelligence and greatly influenced the postwar years.

Pettee and Kent spawned a generation of works that took the discussion of American Intelligence to new heights. *Central Intelligence and National Security* by Harry Rowe Ransom, *Strategic Intelligence and National Decisions* by Roger Hilsman, *Strategic Intelligence for American National Security*, by Bruce D. Berkowitz and Allen E. Goodman, *A World of Secrets: The Uses and Limits of Intelligence,* by Walter Laqueur, and *Informing Statecraft: Intelligence for a New Century*, by Angelo Codevilla are examples of the genre. These books serve as the underpinnings for discussions of strategic intelligence and helped to frame the primary issues of American intelligence in the postwar world.

The legacy of George S. Pettee and Sherman Kent was twofold. First, their work ensured the institutionalization of American strategic intelligence thinking. Secondly, they set the stage for the shaping of the American intelligence community by framing arguments for the issue of centralized versus decentralized intelligence.

Pettee argued that to "conduct strategic intelligence without consolidating all intelligence in a single organization must mean a sort of subcontracting system, with many suppliers of parts, and a parent firm making parts itself which none can supply, and assembling the complete product."[4] His argument for centralized intelligence was built around the concept that a central intelligence agency must be more than an "inter-departmental committee." It must obtain from the other intelligence branches their judgments and combine these to create centralized findings, conclusions, and recommendations. Secondly, it must undertake such work at primary levels, from collection of raw material through the stages of analysis, as necessary only for strategic intelligence, and other work for which it was the prime though not sole customer. Lastly, it must perform the necessary coordinating functions that would ensure the rigorous logical performance of the whole sequence of operations, the sum of which produced strategic intelligence.[5]

In a chapter devoted to the arguments surrounding the centralized intelligence controversy, Sherman Kent noted that the postwar Intelligence Community was split into two camps. On the one hand, some opted for "a very large operating organization," while on the other hand, there were those who wanted central intelligence to be a "kind of holding and management organization."[6] Kent was quick to note in the strongest terms that "centralization violates what to me is the single most important principle of successful intelligence, i.e., closeness of intelligence producers to intelligence users or consumers."[7] With that thought foremost in mind, he stated that centralized intelligence should consist of "some sort of oversight" over the work of other intelligence departments.[8]

Today, unrecognized by most players within the drug intelligence community, this debate rages on. At present, it is the centralized, federally dominated approach that holds the upper hand. It is this dominance that continues to ensure that the melding of the "big I" of federal centralized drug intelligence and the "little i" of state and local drug intelligence, will not take place. Without the ability to share the secrets, the goal of decentralized drug intelligence, and the promise of some modicum of success in the war on drugs will not be realized.

THE SECOND INTELLIGENCE ERA, 1947–1989

The 1947 National Security Act was a direct response to the emerging Cold War which would shape US intelligence policy for the next decade. Section 102 of that document also established "under the National Security Council a Central Intelligence Agency [and] a Director of Central Intelligence." From this evolved the present American intelligence community of which the CIA is the linchpin and over which the Director of Central Intelligence (DCI) presides as the president's primary advisor on national foreign intelligence. In addition to the CIA, the Intelligence Community now encompasses the Defense Intelligence Agency (DIA); the foreign intelligence and counter intelligence components of the Army, Navy, Air Force, and Marine Corps; the National Security Agency; several Defense

Department offices that collect specialized intelligence through reconnaissance programs; the intelligence components of the State Department, the Treasury, and the Department of Energy; and the counterintelligence components of the Federal Bureau of Investigation.

Separate from Cold War threats, US intelligence responded to three major national security issues during this period:

1. Where and under what circumstances should the United States employ its own military forces in Third World conflicts?
2. What should be the degree and duration of the US military commitment to such conflicts?
3. How should the United States respond to "gray area" challenges that lack a clear-cut threat to US vital interests?

It was the last issue which caused the greatest consternation for the Intelligence Community. However, in light of the urgency of the first two issues, "gray area" challenges received short shrift.

During the years from 1965 to 1975, it seemed that the Soviet Union might well be moving toward a position of world dominance. In 1975, a year that many considered to be the nadir of US influence in world affairs, it seemed as though the bottom had fallen out. Rod Paschal argued that

there are few single years that can be pointed to as periods of great change, but 1975 was one of them. It was a year when all the old assumptions, all the usual notions, and all the parameters that defined the relationship between nations changed. Those relationships had been shaped by the fundamental global political structure. The year had begun as a mere continuation of events that were either caused or heavily influenced by the world's bipolar arrangement.... The year ended with a decided shift in favor of Moscow. On the surface, the events of 1975 appeared to represent the beginning of the final triumph of Marxism in the Third World. By the end of 1975, the Khmer Rouge had sounded the death knell for Phnom Phenh; Cambodia and South Vietnam had fallen; Angola and Mozambique had been seized by communist forces; and within the following four years, Nicaragua, Ethiopia, and Afghanistan had succumbed to Marxist forces.[9]

Iran fell in 1979. The failure at Desert One of the disjointed US attempt to rescue American hostages in Tehran in 1980 placed US credibility at the lowest ebb since North Vietnamese tanks crashed through the gates of the Presidential Palace in Saigon. Pax Americana appeared to have ended. The upside of Desert One was the rethinking and limited change of CIA and military assets which resulted in the eventual creation of the Special Operations Command. This process also resulted in a review of strategic intelligence requirements and methods for the future. Unfortunately, little was accomplished by the time of the invasion of Grenada in 1983. US forces stormed ashore with virtually no knowledge of the island.

The Grenada operation came within a hairsbreadth of being a military disaster. That it succeeded as well as it did was due primarily to incredibly good luck. The intelligence situation was a debacle of the first order. Nothing was known about the 400 or so students outside True Blue Campus. There were no proper maps, despite Grenada's having been the center of communist activity for over four years.

The imposition of stringent security did not achieve tactical surprise but served only to ensure that participating units planned in isolation and fought in ignorance of what others were doing. Grenada was indicative of the continuing refusal or failure by decisionmakers to recognize "gray area threats" and the outright failure of intelligence.

The US military resurgence, dramatically advanced by the Reagan administrations, caused US intelligence to focus even more closely on Cold War threats, insuring that "gray areas" would stay just that. With the exception of the unanticipated "flashpoint," events that would later be recognized as fitting the pattern of "gray threats," strategic intelligence remained focused upon a "Red versus Blue" mindset—any conflict between the United States (Blue) and the Soviet Union (Red). This mindset, which overlooked the fact that many of the threats during this time had more of a nationalistic bent, clouded US strategic judgments and ensured that the real issues were never recognized. Even today, US wargaming exercises frequently fall back on a "Red Team/Blue Team" approach that glosses over the "plaid" color of world politics.

THE THIRD INTELLIGENCE ERA, 1989 TO THE PRESENT

The world has never been at peace since the victory celebrations of 1945. Today, approximately 40 countries—excluding the nationalistic, religious, and ethnic goblins released by the collapse of the USSR—are in the grip of war, rebellion, terrorism, economic crisis, or the throes of illegal drugs. In the 80 wars since 1945, 15 to 30 million people have died.[10] The one clear trend that has emerged is that the world has become more violent with each decade since World War II. Alvin Toffler has prophesied that we now face the ultimate political power shift. He suggests that the opportunity exists to redesign democracy for the 21st century or descend into a new Dark Age.[11]

In an address to the Intelligence Community, entitled "The Future of American Intelligence," Robert Gates, former Director of Central Intelligence, spoke to a new world of challenge and threat. He pointed out that "history is not over. It simply has been frozen and now is thawing out with a vengeance Americans will ignore at their peril. We in intelligence thus owe to the government reminders of the past, understanding of the present, and a forecast of the future."[12]

The end of the Cold War raised questions about the shape and structure of American Intelligence. Key to restructuring is the need to redefine the concept of national security from one focused narrowly on defense and global military-strategic issues, to one which is broader yet includes those wider traditional interests of earlier intelligence eras; economic markets and regional political stability. In short, we need to define what constitutes national interests. The end of the Cold War has raised questions about the effectiveness of American strategic intelligence. Writing about US intelligence in an age of uncertainty, Paula L. Scalingi notes that there "is currently an emerging consensus within the congressional committees that oversee intelligence, that the community is not prepared to meet the challenges of the 1990's."[13]

Columnist William Pfaff wrote in early 1991 that impending legislation dealing with intelligence restructuring could be the "most profound reform since 1947." Pfaff foresees momentum building that would create a new intelligence executive to oversee the intelligence community from "outside and above" existing agencies, a position that would set goals and provide formal oversight. The criticism leveled against the IC is that it provides "bland, non-decisive assessments that are blended and bureaucratized" thanks to internal power struggles and precaution taking. Pfaff argues further that within the intelligence bureaucracy, independent thought is not a career enhancing attribute. He ends his argument with the idea of "institutionalizing dissent," so as to ensure that the intelligence product produces arguments for a course of action rather than smooth "facts."[14]

The road to change appears to be a rocky one. Early proposals for US intelligence restructuring submitted by Senator David Boren and Representative David McCurdy received mixed reviews. Both bills would have created a Director of National Intelligence (DNI) with sole budgetary authority over all national intelligence. There would be a Deputy DNI for the Intelligence Community and a Deputy DNI for Estimates and Analysis. The DNI or "intelligence czar" would do what the Director of Central Intelligence was meant to do by the National Security Act of 1947—oversee, coordinate, and synthesize the workings of the nation's several information-gathering elements.

The bills met with resistance, both in the Department of Defense and the CIA. Secretary of Defense Dick Cheney blasted the plan as impeding wartime tactical intelligence and "markedly increasing the costs" of national intelligence. DCI Robert Gates surprised many when he offered his own "evolutionary" reforms including an ombudsman to prevent politicization of estimates and an "A Team/B Team" approach to assure diversity of opinion.[15] To date, no formal restructuring has taken place. Even the revelations of the Ames spy debacle have not moved the monolith of US intelligence.

Writing in the *American Intelligence Journal,* Dr. Roy Godson argues that the proposed reorganization plans may have overlooked several critical questions. Foremost is the issue of defining what we want the intelligence community to do. Godson, a longtime observer of intelligence, suggests that a "clear and seemingly logical intelligence community structure may not be the most effective in practice." "To be blunt," says Godson, "before institutional arrangements are set down in law we need to be clear about the specific missions of the intelligence community and the practices we want to instill for carrying out those missions."[16]

The criticism directed at the intelligence community falls into four areas. First is the failure to forecast the collapse of the Soviet Union—an area that the IC had been primarily focused upon for 40 years—and second is the failure to "call" the Iraqi assault into Kuwait. Third is the continuing series of failures to either recognize or forecast threats in the "gray areas," places in which the United States had national interests that didn't fit the accepted mold. The breakup of the Soviet Union and the restructuring of Russia suddenly cast the "gray area phenomena" (GAP) in a new light. The last area of criticism is the foot dragging by the IC in its efforts to recognize, accept, and apply open source intelligence. Despite efforts in the 1980's by the Open Source Council, sponsored by the Intelligence Community, and follow-up efforts by the Information Handling Committee and the Intelligence Producers Council, OSINT has only of late received serious support within the intelligence community. Except as narrowly defined by the Foreign Broadcast Information Service (FBIS) and other community elements that focused on Soviet scientific and technical literature, the broader, more far-reaching concept of OSINT have neither been understood nor addressed.

Many analysts will testify that their management and their culture are actively biased against the exploitation of open sources. It is much easier for the analyst to seek classified capabilities than to obtain foreign literature, transcripts of foreign video broadcasts, or commercial imagery products. This is the case even though classified sources, by definition, have a narrower focus and restricted production.[17]

The Gulf War, the first major conflict of the third intelligence era, demonstrated just how dependent intelligence agencies had become on certain forms of intelligence. Further, it became clear that not only was intelligence dependent on certain types of sources, but equal or greater emphasis was being placed on the mode in which it was presented. It became painfully clear that the intelligence community had chosen to rely on highly classified, sensitive material which is very narrow in perspective, while ignoring for the most part that information which could have come from the judicious use of open source intelligence.

It appears that the US government responds to only two kinds of intelligence stimuli: either highly classified reports or the morning's edition of the *New York Times*. And the *Times* is only important because it can stir political problems, not because of the intelligence content of the newspaper.[18]

The Gray Area Phenomena and OSINT: Threat and Response

Writing in the autumn 1991 issue of the *American Intelligence Journal*, Robert David Steele noted that it "will continue to be difficult for our senior policy-makers and senior intelligence managers to focus on the need for changed priorities because our intelligence and foreign affairs communities are at least two generations away from fully understanding the Third World and dimensions of change outside the political-military and transnational economic environment."[19]

Those changed priorities are best described as the "Gray Area Phenomena." Defined as threats to the stability of nation-states by non state actors and non governmental processes and organizations, the gray areas appear to be strikingly new and uncomfortably old. Simply put, they are perhaps the most critical issues confronting the world communities at the end of the century.[20] Just beyond the horizon of current events lie two possible political futures, both of which are bleak. The first is a retribalization of large swaths of humankind by war and bloodshed: a Lebanonization of national states in which culture is pitted against culture, people against people, tribe against tribe—a Jihad in the name of a hundred narrowly conceived faiths against every kind of increased globalization and interdependence. The second is being borne by the onrush of technical, economic, and ecological forces that demand increased integration and uniformity. The planet, it appears, is both falling apart and coming reluctantly together at the very same moment. [21]

Gray Area Phenomena are not new. They are typified by the biblical horsemen of the apocalypse, now joined by modern-day riders, each of whom mounts ominous new threats. The end of the Cold War has cleared the fog that kept them shrouded, revealing a veritable Pandora's Box of problems; including the following:

- Ethno-religious-nationalistic conflict
- Weapons proliferation, including conventional, biological, chemical, and nuclear
- Conflict over scarce resources
- AIDS and other infectious diseases
- The globalization of organized crime
- Drug trafficking
- Economic warfare and conflict over technology
- Emigration
- Famine

It is to these threats that the promise of OSINT should be directed. As a first line response, and in many cases as the intelligence of choice, Open Source Intelligence can provide the information that is the grist for solid Intelligence products.

OSINT Prototype

To date, one of the most productive applications of OSINT has been undertaken by the Military Systems Analysis and Simulation Group, A-5, Los Alamos National Laboratory. Responding to a request from US Southern Command in 1991, for support in the areas of detection and monitoring of drug trafficking in Latin America, A-5 set out to model the movement and production of coca leaf from field to finished product and the movement of cocaine hydrochloride (HCL) from the laboratory sites to the United States. While working models were the intermediate goal, the ultimate product was the creation and use of predictive, actionable counter drug intelligence. The decision by the A-5 Intelligence Team to use OSINT was driven by several factors:

1. Past experience with OSINT in the field of terrorism suggested the richness and depth of information available;
2. A prototype study conducted over a ten-year time span of drug trafficking in the Caribbean and Mexico further confirmed such an approach, and the study results compared favorably to classified information;
3. The belief that OSINT "mirroring" techniques—the ability to "look into" a location indirectly through information from another location could provide at least limited access to inaccessible places;
4. The conviction that OSINT could provide the foundation for the counter drug modeling effort.

It was clear that in order to accomplish these goals, a multidisciplinary team would have to be formed. Prior to this project, A-5 staff were a mix of computer scientists and mathematicians. The requirement for team members with drug and counterdrug trafficking backgrounds (as well as political, economic, and a sense of Latin American culture) was met with the addition of several political scientists who were recruited to join the staff. While initial expectations as to the value of librarians assigned to the team were high, what immediately became clear was that without their skill in identifying information sources and rapidly acquiring them, the effort would have failed.

Critical issues and questions concerning the OSINT approach were soon apparent. This was driven by attempting to answer the question "What is it that we are trying to accomplish?"

1. *The availability of sources*: While we had completed an initial source survey, it was still unclear what their availability was.
2. *Target collection timeliness*: It was also unclear how long it would take to get the sources.
3. *OSINT production time*: Once the raw data was in hand, we had to work through the information and determine how long it would take to create the intelligence products.
4. *Sources and citations*: Because our work was to be compared and evaluated against classified products, we had to ensure that our sources and citations were precise and accurate. Of perhaps greater importance was the situation that developed after we began production. Our products although developed through sources entirely different from the classified intelligence producers, frequently came up with the same findings. This caused great consternation and we were requested on numerous occasions to classify our products. We fought these requests each time. To classify our products would have defeated the entire purpose of the exercise. What this set of circumstances did, and still does, is to highlight the important question of what should be classified and what should not.
5. *The realm of OSINT*: It was unclear as to the type of intelligence—strategic, operational, or tactical—that OSINT would produce. Our initial guess was that the OSINT products would fall into the strategic and operational categories. We felt that tactical/real-time intelligence would not be possible because of the delivery times on journals and newspapers that we relied upon. This proved to be true. While we could not produce in real time, we did find that information that would support certain tactical operations could be produced.
6. *Quantification of information for the modeling exercises*: This was initially the area of greatest concern. To build the algorithms for the modeling and simulations, we had to quantify qualitative information for the computer technicians and modelers. This took a bit of doing, for the methods of operation of the political scientists and of he traditional A-5 players were worlds apart. After some very interesting sparring sessions, the desire to build something that had never been attempted overcome the cultural differences and we were soon able to craft a realistic product.
7. *The acceptability of OSINT products to Southern Command and the Intelligence Community*: There was no way to know if our OSINT products would be accepted. Thus, we sought to produce superior products and then present them for review. The "selling" of the products would be done strictly on their merits.
8. *Realistic measures of effectiveness for the OSINT products*: Initially, it was felt that the value of the OSINT products was how they would stand up in comparison to the classified products. However, as time passed it became clear that measuring OSINT products against classified products was not the answer for two reasons. The OSINT products equaled or surpassed classified products. And, from a law enforcement standpoint, OSINT and classified products, if not admissible in a court of law, were simply of no use. What became clear to us was that the only real measure of effectiveness must be the utility of intelligence to the customer.[22]

9. *The Sharing of Secrets*: Our initial thoughts were that OSINT driven end products would produce predictive actionable intelligence that could be shared.

THE OSINT PRODUCTION CYCLE

In addressing the production of intelligence, George S. Pettee wrote that the "entire intelligence task consists of a series of logical operations producing conclusions in a series of stages, each of which provides in turn the premises for another stage of logical operations."[23] In keeping with his description the OSINT production cycle mirrors the functions of the traditional Intelligence Product Cycle-Direction, Collection, Analysis, and Production (see Figure 1.1). The ultimate products were computer-mounted, expert system driven models and simulations. Interim intelligence reports were also produced.

Direction

Model and simulate: coca growing areas; the movement of pasta basica from the preparation areas to the laboratory sites; the movement of finished product from the laboratory sites through the transit countries to the United States borders.

Collection

The target collection plan was straightforward, being driven by the requirements to model the cocaine production process and the cocaine transshipment process. Following the open source approach, all information had to be "off-the-shelf"

Figure 1.1
Overview of the OSINT Process

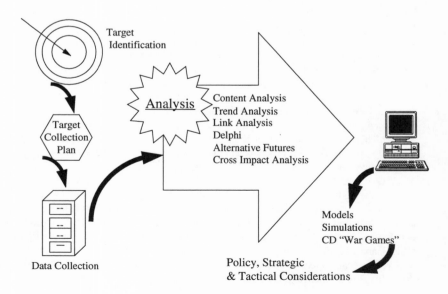

Target Identification

Analysis

Content Analysis
Trend Analysis
Link Analysis
Delphi
Alternative Futures
Cross Impact Analysis

Target Collection Plan

Data Collection

Models
Simulations
CD "War Games"

Policy, Strategic & Tactical Considerations

(see Figure 1.2). In addition to the publications, journals, and magazines mentioned in Figure 1.1 the team had full access to 28 on-line databases. Primary use was made of LEXIS/NEXIS with supplemental use of DIALOG, NEWSNET, and REUTERS. Mead Data Central's products proved to be extremely valuable, with up-to-date information, background information, and pointers for finding "hard to reach" material. Lexis/Nexis also served as a central gateway for access to almost 700 additional databases.

Figure 1.2
Target Collection Plan

1. Search strategy—How, What, Why, Where, When
2. Follow Intelligence Production Cycle
3. Information must be "off-the-shelf," collected from domestic and foreign sources

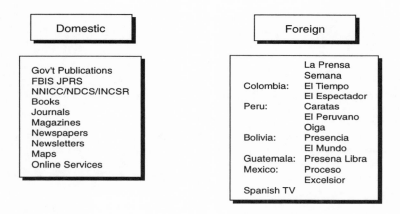

Domestic	Foreign	
Gov't Publications		La Prensa
FBIS JPRS		Semana
NNICC/NDCS/INCSR	Colombia:	El Tiempo
Books		El Espectador
Journals	Peru:	Caratas
Magazines		El Peruvano
Newspapers		Oiga
Newsletters	Bolivia:	Presencia
Maps		El Mundo
Online Services	Guatemala:	Presena Libra
	Mexico:	Proceso
		Excelsior
	Spanish TV	

Analysis

The analysis process followed the time-proven tradition of reading and reading and reading, thinking, sifting, and sorting, identifying the critical pieces, framing the right questions, and ultimately crafting a product. Again, it is important to point out that we were required to go one step beyond and quantify our findings. Early on, we adopted an elitist approach to our work, reflecting the view that "really valuable intelligence is produced by a few talented analysts and estimators."[24]

Production

After two years of producing OSINT products for the US Southern Command, a number of key factors stand out (see Figure 1.3):

1. The requirement for well-crafted search strategies, which was driven by asking the right questions.
2. The richness, depth, and scope of OSINT, and its extremely favorable comparison to classified products.

Figure 1.3
OSINT Production

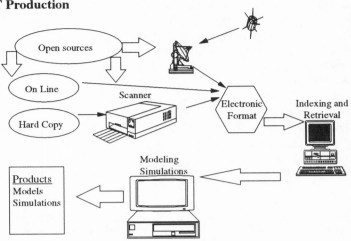

3. The reaffirmation that OSINT like the other types of intelligence is a property of the mind—good people produce good intelligence.
4. The value of a multidisciplinary intelligence production.
5. The importance of a simple, sophisticated information entry and retrieval system.
6. The absolute necessity of method(s) to communicate the intelligence product to consumers.
7. The initial, albeit grudging, acceptance of OSINT by the intelligence community.[25]

1996

Today, almost three years after completion of the work for US Southern Command, it is of some interest to review the status of open source intelligence. While the OSINT-driven model remains at US Southern Command, it is clear that SOUTHCOM is attempting to rapidly distance itself from the drug interdiction business. Los Alamos National Laboratory has adapted the model for the purpose of attempting to track the movement of illegally acquired strategic nuclear materials. While the Department of Energy initiated a program that attempted to use an OSINT-oriented methodology, the program was quickly subverted by DOE "dinosaurs" who interpreted OSINT as an excuse to collect everything on all subjects. Today the "collection of collections" collects dust at the Forrestal Building.[26]

The OSINT methodology that was developed for US Southern Command in 1991 has been refined and further tested from that time forward to the completion of *Sharing the Secrets* in early 1996. The principles of open source intelligence production that were developed early on hold true today. A state of mind rather than a mindset, OSINT is not a rejection of classified information but a reaffirmation that the very nature of intelligence has changed. Going a step further, OSINT is the only tool that will enable intelligence producers to move beyond the consensus products that are bland and of little value—something that has been the norm. Present-day intelligence products, in the main, reflect a porridge-like gruel which is the result of the sharp edges of knowledge and forecasting having been removed by a fetish for consensus. In blunting the elite edge of analysis, the resulting plebian product serves no one well.

OSINT is the power of knowledge at a cost that nearly anyone can afford. This holds true for both the "good guys" and the "bad guys." In an era when major intelligence systems are costly, open source intelligence can draw from a wide range of sources at reasonable cost, providing currency and context that even the most expensive national intelligence platforms can begin to equal. OSINT is the intelligence of first choice. Easily "turned on," it has an advantage over many types of intelligence because of the fact that the grist of it can be drawn from many sources thus overcoming a narrowness of analysis that is part and parcel of intelligence drawn from a limited information base. It is most certainly strategic in nature, but with a fine tuning of sources, it can support operational intelligence with great accuracy and timeliness. When combined with the wide range of readily available information sources and the breadth of communications channels with which to draw out that information, OSINT takes on a forward looking, proactive stance.

OSINT is both "big I"—intelligence at the national level and "little i"—intelligence found at the state and local level. In an all-source intelligence setting, it is both the outer pieces of the puzzle and a "joiner" intelligence whose span and depth provide context for the all-source product. OSINT will continue to be a source of controversy. Damned as "something that we have always done" on the one hand, and "not the thing that real intelligence analysts use" on the other, OSINT is the recognition that intelligence is an elitist undertaking—an art that is best practiced by that small group of people who have the gift of discerning substance and direction from information that others simply offer up in shopping list form.

As the Intelligence Community goes through the throes of fighting changes that are now being demanded of it, OSINT still awaits a champion. Today, both the definition and application of OSINT is slowly making its way into day-to-day use in the Intelligence Community. Dr. Joseph Markowitz, director of the Community Open Source Program Office (COSPO) argues that OSINT is defined as publicly available information that any member of the public can have access to, without the requirement that the information be widely distributed. The second part of the definition is more unique in that the information has to be such that it can be used in an unclassified intelligence context. Here, Markowitz, suggests that it has to be information which is acquired in a very straight forward way "that we're not embarrassed about, and so it doesn't betray a source or a method."[27]

Markowitz argues that OSINT—in the form of the Open Source Information System (OSIS)—should serve as the unclassified outer-most layer of Intelink (an on-line intelligence system found within the Intelligence Community in the Washington area). He went on to note that "we are moving toward a common set of standards and a common look and the capability of moving data across the boundary from the areas of lesser classification in OSIS into replicating that information into areas of higher classification on Intelink."[28]

Markowitz went on to describe an OSINT "node" at the joint analysis center at Molsworth, European Command. There, incorporated into the analysis center, OSINT is an element in producing finished all-source intelligence products for US forces deployed in Bosnia.[29]

The process and products of OSINT have been proved beyond a reasonable doubt; but until the present generation of classified intelligence producers are forced from control in the US intelligence arena, the full promise of OSINT as a integral tool in the overall intelligence arena will not be fully recognized.

Chapter 2

In Search of a Common Ground:
The Quest for Counter Drug Intelligence

> The need for Federal, State, and local law enforcement to share pertinent
> intelligence information is clear. Unfortunately, the sharing of information
> has been somewhat limited.
> —*National Drug Control Strategy*, 1995[1]

The history of attempts at drug control within the United States during the past two
decades has been marked by a series of continuing skirmishes between the executive and legislative branches. The fact that this interplay is conducted in the rough
and tumble of our political system casts a very public and more often than not
emotional and politicized light upon a subject that reaches deeply into the body
politic. To date, the record suggests that short-term political solutions, driven by
the ever present quest for political reward and renewal, both by the Congress and
the president, have ensured that workable, long-term counter drug programs, have
not been designed and implemented.[2] The first thing to go by the boards was honest intelligence estimates. It soon became apparent to even the dullest agency head
that bold, in-depth, well-researched, thoroughly assessed intelligence products were
not the first order of business. Within this atmosphere, almost all attempts at building a drug intelligence "trinity"— federal, state, and local law enforcement intelligence agencies—were doomed to failure.

THE EVOLUTION OF COUNTER DRUG INTELLIGENCE

The National Drug Policy Board (NDPB) was supposed to oversee all Federal
drug control efforts. But immediate criticism of the selection of the attorney general as chairman of the NDPB was registered early on by members of the intelligence community who argued that the nation's top law enforcement officer would
bias the board too strongly toward enforcement agencies and programs. Bureau-

cratic turfism and mission clash—both common to the fledgling system—quickly raised their heads.

Counter drug intelligence concerns fall under the purview of the National Drug Intelligence Committee (NDIC). In 1987 the NDPB assigned lead agency roles amongst members of the intelligence community within this group. The selection of the Drug Enforcement Administration as the lead agency for drug investigations and intelligence was not well received. The DEA did not then, nor does it now, garner great respect for its intelligence work. Shaken early on by corruption from within, and regarded as "cowboys" in their operations, the DEA still remains a questionable choice.[3]

In this atmosphere, attempts at consensus building within the national drug intelligence community have met with mixed results. Driven by institutional bias, turfism, and fiscal issues, conflicts are legendary. The law enforcement bent of the NDIC raises the further issue of a biased national drug strategy with emphasis placed upon tactical and operational intelligence at the loss of strategic intelligence. Furthermore, preoccupation with the former has clearly driven policy initiatives that seek to produce immediate, short-term prosecution results. The development of strategic intelligence policy has not been properly addressed to date, with the result that "informed evaluation of programs, identification of problem areas, and appropriate resource decisions" have not been achieved.[4]

An example of this is the criticism leveled against the Narcotics Intelligence Estimate (NIE). Once again, members of the Intelligence Community argued that the NIE was colored by law enforcement concerns, including a desire for further funding. The National Security Council's Drug Intelligence Officer suggested that like most NIE's produced by committee, the dilution of judgments to get consensus ensured a product of questionable value.[5]

The Anti-Drug Abuse Act of 1988 set the structure and guidelines for national drug policy as we know it today. This effort at shifting the pieces around to come up with a better product was the third such attempt. This act eliminated the National Drug Policy Board, but its replacement, the Office of National Drug Control Policy (ONDCP), has garnered mixed reviews. Initially, criticism was directed to the lack of cabinet status for the director and the lack of fiscal clout for the agency. In the former case, that criticism has been dispensed with because the position is now cabinet level. In the latter case, the control that might be wielded by ONDCP power of the purse strings is becoming more or less a reality, particularly in the case of the High Intensity Drug Trafficking Areas (HIDTA's).

One of the early results of the 1988 legislation was the elimination of the National Narcotics Border Interdiction System. Like Operation Alliance today, the system was criticized for adding little to the overall drug intelligence effort. In addition, the White House Drug Policy Office was also abolished. Raphael Perl of the Congressional Research Service suggested that the White House office had added little to drug policy enhancement.[6]

Perhaps the classic example of drug intelligence caught in a political crossfire is the creation of the Office of Drug Abuse Law Enforcement (ODALE). In January, 1972, President Nixon established ODALE by executive order. Funding for that agency was not drawn through Congress, and agents to man the new agency were drawn from other federal agencies. The very nature of ODALE—"no-knock" warrants and court-authorized wiretaps—clearly pushed the pale of constitutional propriety. According to Egil Krogh, the White House deputy for law enforcement, the purpose of ODALE was to generate pre-election support for the administration and the presidential platform on drug abuse and crime control by direct federal activity in narcotics enforcement at the local level. After several disastrous raids on the wrong houses in Collinsville and Edwardsville, Illinois, ODALE disappeared in a cloud of media outrage.[7] The very nature of ODALE activities did not bode well for drug intelligence in general and those attributes that separate law enforcement investigations from solid law enforcement intelligence activities— interpretation and forecasting—were clearly missing.

A later example is to be found during the 1987 presidential campaign. Senator Joseph Biden introduced a bill entitled the National Narcotics Leadership Act. The bill proposed to create a drug czar. Eight days later, President Reagan rushed to sign Executive Order 12590, which created the National Drug Policy Board. Recognizing the political value of such a concept, President Bush included the drug czar concept in the 1989 National Drug Control Strategy. It is not overly cynical to note that virtually all the important drug legislation has been passed during the year before or within election years. Given that in recent years the party of the president more often than not has not been the dominant party in the Congress, drug issues and legislation have remained a political sore point. The arena has been marked by White House attempts to gain greater control of the counter drug efforts, with election year rhetoric the rule. Congress on the other hand has attempted to stymie presidential attempts at counter drug legislation by developing their own proposals or by micromanaging executive branch counter drug agencies.[8]

Congressional thwarting of presidential drug control initiatives has often been accomplished by attempts to micromanage them. Two cases stand out in stark relief. The 1986 Anti-Drug Abuse Act, initiated by the president and passed by the Congress, contained in addition to appropriations for domestic drug law enforcement and education, monies for international programs. In an attempt to exert its authority within the confines of presidentially driven legislation, the legislation required that assistance be withheld from drug producing countries pending annual recertification of their counter drug programs. The information that would provide the grist for decisions was to be provided by the State Department, an agency whose views are driven by an entirely different set of guidelines. Simply put, the optimistic pictures of cocaine trafficking activities painted each year by the Department of State belie the truth.

The congressional micromanagement in this case continues to result in a yearly series of charades in which drug producing and transit countries show that they have made progress in stamping out drug trafficking. Crafted from a mindset best described as a willful withdrawal from reality, the certification process is reported each year in an annual review published by the Department of State. Subject to doubt and head-scratching, the International Narcotics Matters (INM) report has frequently been described as a case of "cooking the books," due to a lack of veracity in the reports. For example, the 1992 report stated:

In 1991, for the second year in a row, the USG-led anti-drug effort registered important gains. The most salient progress occurred in the Western hemisphere, where governments stepped up their coordinated campaign against the cocaine cartels. By year's end, several important indicators showed that the effort was paying off: coca cultivation was down, US bound cocaine seizures reached an all-time high, and traffickers came under great pressure.[9]

At the same time that the 1992 INM report was presented, Andean Ridge country reports and independent assessments suggested that the contents of the INM report and "ground-truth" in the production countries were widely divergent. Coca production was up and seizures figures, while "higher," were unclear since there was no base-line against which to compare them. Cooperation by foreign governments was perfunctory—as it always has been. Throughout the early 1990's, the gap between the perceived intelligence of officialdom in Washington and reality in the field widened.

Addressing illicit drug availability, the National Drug Control Strategy of 1995, notes that "[a]n assessment of current potential coca production is not encouraging. By most accounts, current coca cultivation is three times what is necessary to supply needs of the U.S. drug market."[10] This single statement speaks volumes to the inaccuracies of the past five years of INM reporting. Unfortunately, within another paragraph or two, the NDCS goes on to shoot itself in the foot, when the argument is made for more emphasis in eradicating drugs at their source.

A second case, which might be titled " How the State Department got an Air Force," is also illustrative. During the late 1970's, the State Department requested funds to develop and purchase special aircraft for aerial spraying. After the money had been approved and several years had elapsed, the Congress discovered in 1981 that Mexico had misused the aircraft by spraying water and fertilizer on suspected marijuana fields instead of herbicides. This resulted in a congressional mandate that the aircraft titles be retained by the State Department in hopes of keeping the program on a true course. Since then, the INM air force has continued to grow. These events, and the cynicism that they spawn, set up the entire counter drug effort, and drug intelligence in particular, for continuing criticism.

Drug Intelligence Today

With the foregoing in mind, it is not surprising that the phrase that best describes the status, structure, and future of drug intelligence is inefficiency bordering upon chaos. Controversy has been the rule rather than the exception in the development, design, and implementation of a genre of intelligence that might serve the counter drug intelligence arena in the United States. Critics of drug wars intelligence today continue to note the duplication of effort, bureaucratic in-fighting, and an overall lack of coordination of efforts amongst agencies with a counter drug mission. But the real problem is much deeper. Today, there is no drug intelligence "trinity," i.e., a community of national, federal, state, and local law enforcement intelligence agencies. What passes for drug intelligence today is intelligence with a "big I,"—Intelligence at the federal and national level, and "little i," intelligence that is associated with state and local law enforcement intelligence. Counter drug intelligence has neither been "fed" from on high, nor has it been "homegrown" to any extent across the country.

The issues that continue to inhibit the growth of drug intelligence are:

1. The separation of power, checks and balances and concerns about civil liberties. Collecting information on US persons who are suspected of drug trafficking activities is critical in producing drug intelligence. The hurdle to be overcome is that such activities must not be conducted in a manner similar to that which infringed upon civil rights during the late 1960's and early 1970's.
2. Counter drug operations, be they federal, military, or state and local, are, more often than not, driven by operations rather than by intelligence.
3. There continues to be an obsession with quantified intelligence products at the expense of recognizing the value of qualitative intelligence products in the overall CDI equation.
4. There are no effective measures of effectiveness (MOE's) in the drug intelligence arena.
5. The obsession, particularly at the national level, with classified intelligence products has ensured that state and local law enforcement intelligence efforts will never have access to the full spectrum of information from which they might create intelligence.
6. Particularly at the federal level, and to a lesser degree where joint task forces work with state and local law enforcement, a "red versus blue" approach—the residue of Cold War thinking—colors and drives a monolithic intelligence mindset that fails to recognize the complexity of the drug trafficking business.
7. The use of intelligence as an operations and policy evaluation tool has not been seized upon by the drug intelligence community.
8. The continuing growth of data bases overshadows the fact that the bigger the database, the less useful it becomes. The database mindset holds that "everything on everything" must be collected. The focus on collection overshadows the real area of emphasis-analysis. What is needed is the creation of knowledge holdings that are germane to the issues at hand.

High Intensity Drug Trafficking Areas

Section 1005 of the Anti-Drug Abuse Act of 1988 authorizes the Director of the Office of National Drug Control Policy to designate certain localities in the United States as "high intensity drug trafficking areas" (HIDTA's). The statute requires the Director to consider a number of criteria including the extent to which the area is a center of illegal drug production, manufacturing, importation, or distribution. The first five areas selected for HIDTA status were

- New York City (and specified surrounding areas);
- Los Angeles (and specified surrounding areas);
- Miami (and all of South Florida);
- Houston (and specified surrounding areas);
- South West Border (those counties on the US/Mexico border reaching from San Diego to Brownsville, Texas).[11]

The five areas were further designated to become recipients of federal assistance through a variety of programs and federal, state, and local cooperative efforts. ONDCP was also tasked with collecting data to be used to evaluate the effectiveness of the HIDTA concept.

The HIDTA's in the large metropolitan areas were focused on dismantling the most significant drug trafficking and drug money laundering organizations operating at the national, regional, and local levels. HIDTA's along the South West Border and in Puerto Rico and the Virgin Islands concentrated on interdiction systems, which included interdiction operations, intelligence, investigations and prosecutions.

In February 1994, after four years in which the much touted HIDTA's had come under growing criticism, ONDCP launched a new concept called the "distribution HIDTA." One of the drivers for this move was the recommendation by many law enforcement officers that HIDTA efforts, when viewed in isolation from other activities, might well produce immediate but often temporary reductions in drug trafficking. Many believe that the knowledge base of other disciplines must be used to attack the drug problem if lasting results are to be achieved. The relatively new Washington D.C./Baltimore, Maryland, HIDTA—which is just now coming on line—will attempt to address both the drug distribution networks and their chronic, hard-core clientele simultaneously. The regional intelligence and information center in this distribution HIDTA also will include the electronic networking of major treatment providers, regional drug courts, and criminal justice components. The Washington D.C./Baltimore, Maryland HIDTA treatment initiatives will be monitored in order to establish a central repository of treatment data. This data will be electronically accessible by the criminal justice system and will be accessed in accordance with clients' rights to confidentiality.[12]

South Florida HIDTA

Recognizing the dilemma of coordination between federal, state, and local agencies, the 1988 legislation created within ONDCP the position of Associate Director for State and Local Coordination. The jury is still out as to how effective this office might be. However, it is extremely encouraging to note the low-key but highly proficient performance of Richard Y. Yamamoto, the director of HIDTA. In an agency much maligned, he appears to be the driving intellect and ramrod behind the strong efforts at ONDCP to build a fire under the HIDTA's, with that move, enhancing the further involvement of state and local law enforcement intelligence. While candidly admitting that there is much room for growth and professionalism in the HIDTA's, Yamamoto has had the wisdom to seize upon the South Florida HIDTA as the best example of how things should be done. Recently designated as the national HIDTA training center, the South Florida operation is a step in the right direction. Consisting of 91 federal, state, and local law enforcement agencies, the State and Local Division is run with the professionalism and innovation by John B. Wilson. One of the very few law enforcement leaders who recognized the urgent need for the intellectual and operational shift from traditional law enforcement "intelligence"—more often than not limited to case investigation activities—Wilson drove the move toward the application of a more strategic law enforcement intelligence approach. His work in creating and guiding the execution of the concept of law enforcement threat assessments must surely stand as a milestone in the evolution of law enforcement intelligence. The South Florida HIDTA Threat Assessment, reported out during September, 1995, is already taking shape as the first realistic assessment of drug trafficking activities in an area that is directly astride the cocaine highway.

The South Florida HIDTA is the place that proves that the secrets can be shared. The melding of federal, state, and local information, intelligence, and operations is a real joy to behold. Clearly head and shoulders above any other similar operation in the country, the "oneness" of the HIDTA is readily apparent.[13]

Building a Framework for Drug Intelligence

To be successfully exploited, it is important that drug intelligence must work at both the strategic and operational levels. It must be worked by, and coordinated with, agencies that operate in an international, federal, state, and local environment. As argued early on, above all else, CDI must have the capacity to share the secrets. Regardless of the capacity of the drug Intelligence Community to collect, analyze, and produce a CDI product, the entire effort is lost if that product cannot be shared and made available for action. Information and intelligence exchanges between most federal agencies requires a memorandum of understanding. This is the case, for example, even between the FBI and DEA. While several avenues do exist for information sharing, i.e., the Regional Information Sharing System , the South West Border Governors Coalition (California, Arizona, New Mexico, and Texas), and the HIDTA's, the degree to which this is taking place is still not satisfactory.

We need to move beyond what is passes for law enforcement intelligence. Traditional law enforcement intelligence does not contain the "soul" of the Intelligence process—interpretation and forecasting. What is needed is the capability to make use of the information "left-over" from traditional investigative case building. This "residue" contains information that enables a law enforcement intelligence analyst to

1. make assessments and interpretations;
2. forecast events and trends; and
3. draw conclusions and suggest options and alternatives for law enforcement policy and operations.

It should be clear at this point, that my argument moves the concept of law enforcement and drug intelligence—at each tier—into the strategic realm. The reason for this is simple and is the foundation upon which I build the argument for the ascendancy of state and local intelligence drug intelligence. If 83% of drug related arrests are made by Local and State law enforcement agencies, then intelligence is directed at those levels.[14] While the role of federal law enforcement is not to be diminished, it must be redirected to include the support of state and local law enforcement intelligence efforts. Consequently, the definition of strategic intelligence in this setting requires explanation. The scope of strategic intelligence for law enforcement should cover those physical areas that impact the law enforcement jurisdiction. Thus, it is important for state and local law enforcement to understand what happens as drugs, bound for their area, enter the country. Moreover, within each law enforcement jurisdiction, the use of the term "strategic intelligence" should further mean an understanding of the overall implications of drug trafficking activities therein and the impact of drug trafficking areas in immediately adjacent jurisdictions.

What is being proposed here is not revolutionary. In 1985, the International Association of Chiefs of Police suggested the following descriptors of strategic intelligence for law enforcement:

1. The identification of criminal principals and their associates, including current and emerging criminal leaders;
2. Descriptions of criminals and their activities within a specific jurisdiction;
3. An assessment of the extent to which organized crime has developed;
4. An assessment of organized crime capabilities;
5. The identification of business enterprises and public officials which are directly influenced by criminal elements;
6. The identification of the economic, social, and governmental problems created by organized crime and suggestions of policy and operational options and alternatives.

The question then becomes: how can this evolutionary process be accelerated?

National Drug Intelligence Center (NDIC)

The single most important service that intelligence can provide in the war on drugs is a definitive picture of the drug trafficking threat. At the federal level, it is the National Drug Intelligence Center that can best produce strategic threat intelligence products.

Commissioned in 1988, the NDIC came on line in 1993, in Johnstown, Pennsylvania. The mission of the NDIC is to craft multisource strategic organizational intelligence products for use by state and local law enforcement, the Intelligence Community, and national decision makers against drug trafficking organizations. NDIC has been the target of much criticism; it has been called a pork barrel operation designed to provide jobs in a badly depressed area.

Three years after coming on line the status of the NDIC is still in doubt. At a hearing of the House Appropriations Judiciary Subcommittee on March 9, 1995, one could see NDIC as a political hot potato that neither the FBI nor the Drug Enforcement Administration really wanted to deal with. In response to a question by Congressman Rodgers: "Where are we on the National Drug Intelligence Center?," Thomas Constantine, DEA Administrator responded:

Well, we had a study group together over the last month or so. As you know, that was apparently my history of talking to people formulated out of two agencies that didn't talk to each other was then the reason to force them to talk to one another. Well, that is probably no longer needed right now. But, the institution, the staffing and the technology is very valuable, and it was formulated under a concept of strategic planning, long-term dealing with major groups. I don't think in my review of the data that has come out of there, that has reached those goals very well. I think the Director shared that. We formed a group of DEA officials and FBI officials. They have been conducting a study for the last month to find out some way where we can take that same amount of resources, that same amount of technology and ability, and be able to help us out and perhaps help local enforcement out with the types of things that I talked to you about before.

I talked about a pointer index that I would love to see developed, starting from the states on up. There will have to be some coordinating point for that, that has a staff and some limited resources. I have read most of the reports coming out of there. They are not the types of things that I would like to see coming out of NDIC.

Congressman Rodgers then asked FBI Director Louis Freeh for comments.

Yes, I would agree with that. We want from that center strategic intelligence to tell us what the organization is, where it is, who its heads are, where are its money, and then soldiers out in the field can go out and get them. We have not been getting that product, which is why I have stopped the hiring that has gone on out there. They had proposed to hire additional dozens of people. We have stopped that; we have sent out people out to look at it. We have a report to review with the Deputy Attorney General, but we think the potential of strategic intelligence certainly can be surpassed by the product that we have seen coming out of there. Moving beyond traditional case study work, the NDIC produces intelligence products that define the many strategic aspects, and implications of the drug trafficking organizations.[15]

The struggle to make the NDIC the center for the production of strategic drug intelligence has been marked by the efforts of a few people who had the vision, leadership, and fortitude to go the distance. Those efforts are best personified by former NDIC director Douglas Ball who resigned from the NDIC and the FBI in early 1995, went to the wall trying to get NDIC out of the cross-fire. Ball sought to "reaffirm that the mission of the NDIC is primarily to produce multisource organizational analyses of illicit drug trafficking organizations."[16] Adroitly cutting to the chase, Ball argued that "multi-source, of course, means, as a minimum, DEA and FBI case file information"—something that both agencies initially refused to provide to the NDIC and only do so now, under great duress.[17]

In spite of the efforts of the Federal Bureau of Investigation and the Drug Enforcement Administration to sack the Johnstown operation, the NDIC has again managed to duck the axe. The Department of Justice recently argued that the NDIC should remain "neutral" and continue to march with its present mission of strategic intelligence production. The importance of the NDIC cannot be stressed enough. It is the only place within the entire drug intelligence community that has the mission of producing discrete, definitive, strategic drug intelligence products that delve into the functioning of drug trafficking organizations. Its forecasts to date have been based on solid, professional analysis and assessments. With a reprieve and support from the Department of Justice, the NDIC has the opportunity to continue its work and reach down to state and local law enforcement with needed, timely intelligence products.[18]

The Role of Technology

The determination of sources from which to collect information for the creation of intelligence, and the methods of collection have been and will continue to be areas of discussion and argument. The National Drug Control Strategy places great emphasis on the use of technology as a "force multiplier."[19] However, the field results drawn from the use of technical means of intelligence collection at the national level are subject to question. Experience strongly suggests that information gained from national intelligence assets (primarily signals intercepts of drug traffickers) are notoriously difficult to disseminate in a manner that would allow for their use by many federal agencies and certainly not all at the state and local level.[20] The report went on to state that EPIC was so slow that those agencies that require urgent tactical intelligence circumvent the center entirely. While it is unclear where the fault lies, one suspects, given the dismal performance of EPIC, that assets are not the issue; rather it is a case of a lack of leadership.

Even if such information could be processed quickly, the protection of sources and methods has yet to be solved. The majority of state and local law enforcement intelligence agencies do not hold Department of Defense clearances. Protection of that information in court proceedings has further hindered the use of technically gathered information. And, as mentioned previously, the means of transmission of that intelligence to many intelligence consumers is still questionable at best.

The use of national technical assets has been directed primarily toward tactical requirements and applications. That has been a misuse of those assets. With policy and programs driven by law enforcement, the tasking of national technical assets has been driven by that mindset. National systems can be extremely useful in providing strategic drug intelligence to policymakers. Because information in this form is not normally time-sensitive, or widely disseminated, the foregoing tactical limitations do not hold. In fact, national systems are ideal for obtaining strategic drug intelligence. With judicious use, intelligence can be gained, for example, about the effects of US programs in producer countries or their commitment to drug control. This intelligence could be vital in aiding policy decisions, which must now be made as a result of the 1988 Drug Act, about whether or not to certify drug producing countries for foreign aid. From my own experience, for example, I question the total reliance upon national technical assets (in this case overhead sensor platforms) for coca crop verification. My experience suggests that cloud cover in the production zone effectively shields crops, airstrips, and drug laboratories from the type of extended coverage that would provide accurate information.

There are several areas that hold promise in terms of providing supporting tools to drug intelligence. These include a mobile x-ray inspection device that can be used at ports of entry to "see" into trucks and cargo containers and the fiberscope, which enables nondestructive inspection of inaccessible areas. The device which holds the greatest potential is LIDAR (Light Detection and Ranging). LIDAR is a laser system that operates on the same principle as radar. Linking a laser, telescope, and computer, the LIDAR system can scan for miles over an area, identifying hydrocarbon sources in real time. Thus, the LIDAR could be used to scan an area-over land, sea, or air space, for signs of the presence or previous passage of combustion engine powered vehicles. Once "read," the LIDAR is capable of identifying the type of fuel that produced the hydrocarbons as well as the type of engine that it fueled. The potential here is little short of incredible. Law enforcement agencies could scan suspect areas and begin to build a geographic trend analysis to confirm or deny the use of that area as a drug trafficking route or drop site.

Databases

Counter drug intelligence databases are a matter of great controversy. Expectations of their value have not yet been met and it is doubtful that they will. Many within the CDI community argue that as a database grows in size, so does its utility decrease in proportion.[21] The issue is deeper. In fact, there appears to be an obsession with database building, not so much for the intelligence that it might produce, but rather because the CDI database has status value. The issue of database compatibility has been carried to levels of absurdity. Concern for CD database compatibility and "Tempest" level security (elaborate measures to shield a room from electronic emanations or electronic eavesdropping) has been carried to extremes. Almost without exception, databases have been overcome by events, thanks to the adaptability of the target of the databases—the drug traffickers.

There is one other roadblock for databases today. Speaking at the October 1989 meeting of Armed Forces Communications and Electronic Association, Mary C. Lawton, counsel for intelligence policy, noted that the Privacy Act requires that any new database system that contains mention of US persons must be announced in the *Federal Register*. Continuing, she noted that whenever intelligence data dealing with a US person is shared with any law enforcement agency, the person in question has the right to any government information that might exculpate him. The person named has the right to canvass all government agencies for the existence of wiretaps involving his conversations. In addition, the Supreme Court has ruled that 4th Amendment rights also apply to foreign citizens with respect to evidence gathering by US agencies.[22]

Conclusion

The status of a common ground for counter drug intelligence is still in doubt today. The assessment done by the Office of Technology Assessment in 1987 still rings true, perhaps more so today, in 1996:

- "The Nation's drug interdiction efforts suffer from a clear lack of direction;"
- the "responsibilities of the Federal drug interdiction agencies are fragmented and overlapping;"
- "data on drug smuggling, the trafficking system and interdiction activities are inadequate for effective planning and management;"

- "there is no clear correlation between the level of expenditures or effort devoted to interdiction and the long term availability of illegally imported drugs in the domestic market."[23]

To date, attempts at creating counter drug intelligence have been directed primarily toward interdiction applications. The reasoning behind this approach is that these types of efforts will allow more effective targeting.[24] There are strong arguments against linking intelligence with interdiction in the manner in which it is done now. The primary argument here is that interdiction is viewed as a law enforcement function, with the "buy/bust" syndrome foremost. The longer-term, high value of interdiction being an opportunity that leads to delivering a crushing blow to drug trafficking organizations has yet to be seized upon. The real issue here is not that intelligence and interdiction together doesn't work, but rather that the manner in which intelligence has been applied to the equation is faulty.

Chapter 3

The National Drug Control Strategy: The Intelligence Agenda

"I promised the American people that we'd do something about this problem," the President observed crossly. "And we haven't accomplished shit."

Sir, you cannot deal with threats to national security through police agencies. Either our national security is threatened or it is not.

—Tom Clancy
A Clear and Present Danger

As one traces the evolution of US drug policy from the turn of the century until the declaration of the National Drug Control Strategy of 1985 and beyond to today, a number of issues keep recurring, including these:

1. Continued attempts to stop drugs at their source;
2. A series of declarations of "war on drugs;"
3. Drug policy written and implemented primarily from a law enforcement viewpoint;
4. Attempts to link drugs with crime;
5. Attempts to link drugs with national security;
6. No central direction of counter drug programs;
7. A constant demand for "better" information and intelligence about drugs.

The results been a continuing series of policy failures, marked by a number of unanticipated events that must be regarded as strategic surprises.

BACKGROUND

In his seminal work, *The American Disease: Origins of Narcotics Control*, David Musto recounts the continuing cycle of drug addiction, a national awakening to it, and then a period of intense public debate and agitation with pronounced social, political, and legal overtones. In the 1980's the major drug was cocaine, in the 1960's it was marijuana and hallucinogens, and as we approach the end of the 1990's, heroin is returning in force. Initially, medical proof of the danger of such substances is not available, and public acceptance and widespread use follow. Then, at a later point in time, the medical, human, and social costs are revealed. The public starts to listen to the dangers and harmful effects and the pendulum swings in the opposite direction. With that swing follows the demand for legislation, treatment, and law enforcement. Inextricably intertwined in these cycles are the demands for information and intelligence which will tell the extent of the problem, pinpoint the wrongdoers, and suggest methods to quell the flow of drugs. And, in another repeating cycle, law enforcement and intelligence agencies are caught in a no-win sequence of events, thanks to political agendas that seek "victory" when in reality only something much short of that is possible.

Formally instituted drug intelligence agencies did not come into being until after World War II. The State Department must be regarded as the first drug intelligence organization because of its efforts to identify and deal with worldwide trade in opium, an effort that predates the work of other agencies by almost 20 years. Driven by the vocal efforts of Charles Henry Brent, first Episcopal bishop of the Philippines, a man close to the ear of President William Howard Taft, legislation outlawing opium sales in the newly acquired islands was soon enacted. Brent urged the calling of an international forum to cope with this problem. Taft appointed Dr. Hamilton Wright, a prominent Washington physician, to head such a commission. Wright worked closely with Secretary of State Elihu Root who felt that without national legislation dealing with drug abuse, the United States would be in a weak position to moralize internationally. Both men sought to create the basis for legislation.

In attempting to do so, Wright launched a national survey to collect data about opium use and control from prisons, police departments, boards of health, and morphine manufacturers. In so doing, Wright set an unfortunate precedent, one familiar in subsequent efforts to address drug problems: He exaggerated addiction figures.

A federal statute was soon passed that outlawed the import of opium for smoking. The Shanghai Conference on Narcotic Drugs, in 1909, led to the signing of an International Opium Convention in 1912. The result of both international meetings was to create and maintain an interest at home for drug legislation.

In 1914, the Harrison Narcotic Act was passed. It regulated all traffic in opiates, cocaine, cannabis, and other drugs and required physicians and druggists to keep detailed records. A side effect of the legislation was that the cost of heroin rose from $6.50 to $100 per ounce.[1]

In 1919, the Treasury Department issued a report entitled Traffic in Narcotic Drugs which placed the number of addicts in the United States between 750,000 and 1.5 million. Shortly after the report was published, two of the report's authors acknowledged that the figures were based upon unsubstantiated research and undocumented figures and could not possibly be true.

Throughout the late 1920's, following the passage of Prohibition legislation, anti-drug sentiment and groups continued to expound upon the dangers of such substances to the nation. By the early 1930's, the Treasury Department's law enforcement unit was reconstituted as a separate agency and renamed the Federal Bureau of Narcotics (FBN). Harry J. Anslinger was appointed director. Remaining in office until 1962, Anslinger, like J. Edgar Hoover, would cast a large shadow on US drug policy.

By 1930, officials in Washington admitted that control at the source would be a long time in coming but should remain the ultimate objective of narcotic foreign policy. Given earlier experience, this was quite a concession. The failure of the opium conferences at The Hague (1911–1914) to do more than recommend stringent control measures led the Americans to a hard-line position during the 1920's at the meetings of the Opium Advisory Committee (OAC) of the League of Nations. American delegations refused to discuss any proposal other than immediate restrictions on production and walked out of a major opium conference in 1925. When other nations, notably those in Latin America, refused to adopt US policy as their own, the failure of Washington's drug control strategy was complete. At that time, bilateral diplomacy proved no more productive than inflexibility at Geneva. Ironically, disenchantment with the international anti-narcotic movement before 1930 reflected a failure of American political will in that there was no central direction to the nation's drug policy. Independently, individual members of Congress, State Department officials, and even private citizens tried to chart a course for narcotic foreign policy. The creation of the FBN with Harry Anslinger as commissioner solved the problem for three decades.[2]

Two decisions by the FBN would have far-reaching impact. First, a conscious decision was made to exaggerate both the numbers and effect of drugs. Second, all efforts at drug education were brought to a halt. The latter ensured that the message of drugs would be lost on generations to come, thus opening them to the next wave of illegal substances. The former firmly seated the precedent set by Wright. Henceforth, government estimates and figures concerning narcotics would be ever subject to doubt. Both elements would play a major role in the last decades of the century, as new waves of drugs entered the nation.

Not until 1950 was the first government drug agent assigned overseas. Four years earlier, the State Department's Protocol section had transferred drug control functions to the United Nations' Commission on Narcotic Drugs.

The attempt at enlisting other nations into the fray, stalled by World War II, was another effort in the continuing quest by the United States to control drugs at the source. These efforts are no more effective now than they were in 1912. It was not until the late 1940's that Peru acknowledged that Peruvian cocaine might cause harm abroad. Bolivia virtually ignored all appeals to control coca leaf growth, claiming that its coca was primarily consumed domestically and did not represent an international problem. The issues of drugs in Mexico, and Mexico's role as an entry point for drugs into the United States, were long denied. In the Far East, opium and heroin were of the greatest concerns.

The point here is that it was the State Department that appears to have been the primary collector and evaluator of information related to illegal substances—in effect a de facto intelligence agency. William Walker suggests that over time it was

State Department drug experts and internationally minded police chiefs—a "gentlemen's club" of sorts—that came to dominate the scene. It was to their credit that limited attempts to maintain statistics about legitimate narcotic requirements were the bright light of early efforts at drug intelligence efforts.[3]

The United States has long attempted to compensate for the challenges posed by far-flung drug-related activities in a several ways. The FBN often used employees of other agencies, sent agents abroad, or paid foreigners to conduct intelligence operations. These steps were often undertaken without the knowledge or permission of the countries involved. During the 1930's, Treasury Department personnel in Mexico and China regularly reported on conditions there. Drug-related information reached Washington from Japan well into 1941. World War II brought a significant reduction in illegal traffic, but military intelligence kept Washington informed about conditions as needed. In the immediate postwar decade, the FBN commissioner sent personnel from the former Office of Strategic Services on missions around the world to chronicle the trail of opium and other drugs. As Douglas Clark Kinder has shown, Anslinger was doing all he could to make his bureau an integral part of the intelligence community.[4] By 1962, twelve agents had been assigned to Rome, where their work was primarily directed toward organized crime figure Lucky Luciano. Not until ten years later would drug agents be sent to South America.

THE INSTITUTIONALIZATION OF FAILURE, 1969–1973

To understand why the drug war has failed, we need to look at the crucial four-year time frame between 1969 and 1973, when the basis for current US drug strategy was established and failure institutionalized. Then, as now, conventional law enforcement agencies were judged incapable of handling the anti-drug effort; then, as now, the White House organized (and reorganized) the anti-drug effort; then, as now, "better intelligence" was demanded from the Central Intelligence Agency (CIA); then, as now, investigations into the drug trade were launched by Congress and resisted by the executive branch. Most important, between 1969 and 1973 drug enforcement became a matter of US "national security." The perverse effects of linking drug enforcement and US security quickly became apparent, if not entirely understood. The same aides to President Nixon who were in charge of the war on drugs were also in charge of the Watergate fiasco in 1972. Their dual roles as drug warriors and "Plumbers" belied an underlying congruence of interests between "drug enforcement" and "national security" as defined by all the president's men. Individual skullduggery aside, the early days of the drug war saw the White House take over the anti-drug effort, the CIA formalize its narcotics intelligence collection, and the Drug Enforcement Administration (DEA) brought into existence. Egil Krogh, the number-one drug warrior and Plumber in the Nixon White House, described the bureaucratic challenge at a 1971 meeting: "Ways [must] be found to make our narcotics suppression effort consistent with the requirements of national security."[5]

As Edward Jay Epstein notes in *Agency of Fear,* it was Krogh who first linked drugs with crime (not a novel idea), a key plank in Nixon's reelection campaign.[6]

Borrowing the theory that drug abuse leads to crime, Krogh suggested in early 1970 that attacking the former was the way to crack the latter. Thus was the drug war established as a high priority in the White House. Krogh was quickly frustrated both by the stonewalling of suspicious bureaucrats and the inability of the drug agencies to cooperate with each other. For example, when Krogh couldn't convince the Treasury Department to share information about an IRS program to seize the assets of suspected drug traffickers, Krogh turned to two willing colleagues, Myles Ambrose of Customs and G. Gordon Liddy, then an aide at the Treasury Department, who gave him the information he wanted. Krogh and his boss, John Ehrlichman, soon concluded that the answer to the drug problem lay in gaining White House control over the drug enforcement and drug intelligence agencies.

An unexpected event added urgency to the White House's campaign to centralize drug enforcement intelligence. In June 1971, during the administration's well-orchestrated media blitzes on the drug war, the *New York Times* stole the headlines by publishing the Pentagon Papers. Krogh was already developing an intelligence/enforcement weapon for White House use in the drug war. His new assignment, to head something called the Special Investigations Unit, was quite similar. Ehrlichman assigned a National Security Council staffer to the group. Rounding out the principal actors in the new unit were Krogh's old spy from the Treasury, Gordon Liddy, and a pal of Liddy's, former CIA agent E. Howard Hunt. The drug warriors had become the "Plumbers." The CIA had proved helpful. Liddy had received CIA security clearances for his anti-drug efforts in December 1969. In 1971, Erlichman told Robert Cushman, CIA deputy director, that Hunt had carte blanche from the White House; Cushman provided logistical help for Hunt.

The drug warriors and Plumbers soon went to work on a series of ventures that blurred the distinction between the rule of law and national security. One of Hunt's first acts was to break into the office of Daniel Ellsberg's psychiatrist, using a plan drawn up by Krogh. Soon afterward Hunt got a job for an old friend, former CIA agent Lt. Col. Lucien John Conein, as head of strategic intelligence for the Bureau of Narcotics and Dangerous Drugs. Conein later admitted his purpose was to oversee a unit that could be used to assassinate drug traffickers. Hunt apparently did not limit himself to spying. While working for the Plumbers, he also reportedly recruited Cubans for hit squads aimed at Latin American drug dealers. Several news journals reported that Hunt traveled to Mexico with one such team just before a plot to kill Panama's Omar Torrijos was aborted. The establishment of the Plumbers unit represented a perverse grafting of drug enforcement and national security. Although the target of each sphere of activity was different—drug traffickers and abusers versus Nixon's "enemies"—both shared the ultimate goal of establishing White House authority over an investigative and enforcement apparatus that could be used for any national security purpose White House aides chose.

In September 1971, Krogh was named by Nixon to be executive director of the Cabinet Committee on International Narcotics Control (CCINC), which was set up to coordinate the "global war" on drugs. Nominally chaired by Secretary of State William Rogers and with Richard Helms among its members, the group was left to the daily charge of Krogh. The creation of the CCINC was followed in January 1972 by

he Office of Drug Abuse Law Enforcement, the brainchild of none
on Liddy. In August 1972, the Office of National Narcotics Intelli-
ished by the White House; the original idea for this office was credited
e ran a domestic spying operation using agents detailed from the CIA
.... Krogh drew up plans for yet another anti-drug agency. This agency was
to be called the Drug Enforcement Administration. When a prominent physician told
Krogh he opposed the idea, Krogh retorted, "Anyone who opposes us, we'll destroy.
As a matter of fact, anyone who doesn't support us, we'll destroy."[7]

Krogh never quite fulfilled the quest of his superiors for a "super agency" that
would serve their political ends under the guise of fighting the drug war. Myles
Ambrose, the Customs commissioner, was slated to become the first head of the
DEA. But in May 1973, the new agency received credible reports from a reliable
undercover agent about a $300,000 heroin deal financed by Robert Vesco. This
financier and con man employed two relatives of President Nixon and had contrib-
uted $200,000 to the Nixon campaign fund. The DEA immediately shut down its
investigation of the case and withdrew the undercover agent. The agent went public with his story in November 1973. On November 27, the *New York Times* reported that the Senate was investigating the charges. That same day, Nixon attended a CCINC meeting and emphasized that he wanted to "continue his personal
involvement in drug control as appropriate." By that time, however, the Watergate
scandal was engulfing the Nixon White House and control of the DEA was slip-
ping away. The Senate investigation of the Vesco cover-up eventually led to a
broader investigation of the DEA, which concluded that the agency's "environment was conducive to corrupt and irregular practices."[8]

In Search of a Drug Control Strategy

By 1975, drug problems were increasing again in America. In April of that year,
President Ford directed that a review of national drug policy be conducted by his
Domestic Council to identify solutions to the problem. Their response was the 1975
White Paper on Drug Abuse, the base document for the 1976 Federal Drug Strategy
and a seminal document for US government policy ever since.[9] The White Paper
continued the conception of drug trafficking as a law enforcement and public health
problem. While international aspects of drug control were not ignored, the effects of
drug trafficking on foreign countries and on regional security in drug producing and
transit areas received virtually no attention.[10] Further, the White Paper established
three tests for determining drug priority: the adverse consequences of the drug for
the individual and society; the likelihood of physical or psychological dependence
upon a drug; and the size of the abusing group.[11] The need for improved intelligence
support in drug control efforts was also addressed in the White Paper. It cited a
counterproductive competition within and among the law enforcement agencies and
a lack of intelligence analytical capabilities as the main problems.[12]

The present-day National Drug Control Strategy bears an uncanny resemblance
to the 1975 White Paper on Drug Abuse. The former is clearly a recycled version
of the latter.

DRUGS AND NATIONAL SECURITY

On October 14, 1982, following a decade of increasing political pressure for a firmer stance on illegal drugs, President Reagan declared a "War on Drugs" and pledged an unshakable" commitment to do what is necessary to end the drug menace in America.[13]

In 1986, the president signed a National Security Decision Directive that called drug trafficking a "threat to the national security" of the United States and directed all federal agencies with a role in drug enforcement, including the Department of Defense, to pursue counter narcotics efforts more actively. At approximately the same time, the Congress authorized and funded a national drug control office. By 1989, it was accepted policy that the scourge of drugs was a "clear and present danger" to the nation. It is not surprising then that the military components of the 1990 National Security Strategy included reference to a counter narcotics role and the increasing importance of intelligence:

Counternarcotics will involve security assistance to source countries, the use of military forces to detect and monitor the movement of drugs to our border; intelligence coordination on an international scale is the key to this problem.

Intelligence Programs must remain cognizant of developments in the communist world, and develop their capabilities against areas threatening regional instability. International terrorism and narcotics trafficking will take a high priority; counterintelligence may take on importance as barriers to contact are reduced.[14]

NATIONAL DRUG CONTROL STRATEGY

Bound in a vibrant red cover, the *National Drug Control Strategy* (NDCS) was presented to the nation on September 5,1989, under the requirements of the Anti-Drug Abuse Act of 1988 (21 USC 1504, section 1005). In his cover letter addressed to the Speaker of the House of Representatives, President Bush stated:

This report is the product of an unprecedented national effort over many months. America's fight against epidemic illegal drug use cannot be won on a single front alone; it must be waged everywhere. Accordingly we have conducted a thorough, intensive, and unflinching review of Federal anti-drug efforts to date. And we have solicited advice and recommendations. The result is a comprehensive blueprint for new direction and effort—and for success in the near- and long-term future.[15]

The timing and tenor of the NDCS were in harmony with the mood of the nation. A Gallup Poll inquiring into the impact of drugs on the nation, conducted shortly after the announcement of the NDCS, registered the greatest concern ever expressed by the American public on any domestic issue. Sixty-seven percent of those polled were willing to pay additional taxes to help fund efforts to fight the drug epidemic. While enlisting the full complement of governmental agencies to fight the drug war, the president was about to press the military to join the war. No other domestic program had ever had a defense establishment presence.

The NDCS directed national attention toward five policy areas that were thought to be critical to overall drug control policy and program success:

1. The generation and linkage of intelligence, information, and systems;
2. The coordination of effort at federal, state, and local governments;
3. Model legislation enacted on a nationwide basis;
4. Strategic drug control planning and policy that integrates education, prevention, treatment, environment, prosecution, and corrections in a system wide approach;
5. Technological and operational advancements.

THE INTELLIGENCE AGENDA

The drafters of the NDCS determined that intelligence would be a key factor in the war against drugs. The opening line in the NDCS Intelligence Agenda stated emphatically that "The war against drugs cannot be fought—much less won—without good intelligence."

We must begin by ensuring that all appropriate Federal, State, and local information on the drug production and trafficking problem is appropriately shared. Taking care to protect sources and methods of collection, and to ensure confidentiality for certain data with special legal sensitivity, we can devise means to share information acquired in investigations and intelligence operations, in timely fashion, among all agencies with responsibilities in the drug war. Particular care must be taken to protect information on criminal investigations or enforcement operations planned or underway, and information collected from sensitive human and technical sources. Appropriate safeguards must be taken to ensure that such information is not disclosed outside of official channels.[16]

The first iteration of the NDCS emphasized that intelligence was to be addressed in enforcement terms: "intelligence frequently means information needed to build a strong case against a particular individual or group of violators."[17] While it was quite clear that intelligence was a keystone, it was equally unclear how the counter drug intelligence strategy would be created, how it would work, and how it would support policy and strategy. The NDCS spoke to the full range and scope of federal agencies that have intelligence charters. However, what was missing was an explanation as to how to get all the players on the drug battlefield working together.

The NDCS was designed to fit the framework of the New Federalism Model, i.e., federal planning and direction with implementation at the national, state, and local levels. This included plans for "increased federal funding to States and localities for street-level drug law enforcement."[18] In addition, quantified two- and ten-year objectives were drafted and published. Standing out in stark omission were any measures of effectiveness for counter drug intelligence.

The 1990 *National Drug Control Strategy* addressed general intelligence requirements, but without an implementation plan. This posed an immediate dilemma. Although the *National Drug Control Strategy* had been built on the belief that drugs were a threat to national security, one critical element had been left out of the equation—the military. Tasked to defend the country against enemies foreign and domestic, the Department of Defense was conspicuous in its absence.

Chapter 4

The Threat

What say the augurers?
They would not have you to stir forth to-day.
Plucking the entrails of an offering forth,
They could not find a heart within the beast.

Julius Caesar
act ii, sc.ii

DEFINING THE DRUG TRAFFICKING THREAT

The single most important service that intelligence can provide in the wars on drugs is a definitive picture of the drug trafficking threat. Threat definition is a traditional more often than not primary mission for national and military intelligence agencies. In military parlance, the creation of the threat estimate is a logical and orderly examination of all the factors which when combined give shape to the threat.[1] Now, as in the formative years of American intelligence, an understanding of what is truly a threat to national security is imperative so as to ensure that the interests of the United States "will not suffer nor its undertakings fail because its statesmen and soldiers plan and act in ignorance."[2]

In spite of the long-term requirement to craft threat definition, this requirement is one that has long haunted the US Intelligence Community. Shortly after the creation of the Central Intelligence Agency and the passage of the Central Intelligence Agency Act of 1949, the Board of National Estimates (BNE) and the National Intelligence Estimate were created to formally address threats to national security. In 1962, partially in response to growing concerns about the accuracy of Soviet threat estimates, the Defense Intelligence Agency (DIA) was created.

The issue of threat estimates, this time of the number of North Vietnamese and Viet Cong soldiers, came to a head again in 1967. The result was a major split within the US intelligence community, the results of which would affect it for the next twenty-five years. The schism within the Intelligence Community reached out to include parts of the policy and operations communities, further adding to difficulties.

The present lack of knowledge about drug trafficking was brought about by three factors that stretch back almost 20 years into the development of contemporary American drug policy. First is the overemphasis on a law enforcement approach to drug trafficking. Second is a faulty understanding of the complexity of the drug trafficking industry. Third is the lack of understanding on the part of the US policy makers of the impact of drug trafficking on producing and transit countries. The production and transit countries have neither the capability, nor is it in their best national interest, to oppose drug trafficking.[3]

Present-day American drug policy and threat perceptions grew out of decisions made during the Nixon administration in response to what was then considered a heroin epidemic in the United States. The policy produced an impressive success in a fairly short period of time, but the long-term effects were to cause problems for many years to come. For one thing, heroin had been firmly identified as the main threat to the United States, followed by "dangerous drugs" (a catch-all including amphetamines and barbiturates). Cocaine was seen as only a minor threat and marijuana, despite its wide usage, was considered the least threatening of the drug types. Federal investigative efforts had been concentrated on heroin, and it was in heroin cases that law enforcement careers had been made. International cooperation against opium farming and heroin production had been secured and had brought considerable success, especially in Turkey. As a result of this combination of major efforts and international cooperation, there was a sharp drop in the amount of heroin reaching the United States. This relatively quick and easy victory appeared to justify the basic policy, but that policy concentrated only on the effects of drug trafficking in the United States, with little detailed understanding of overseas aspects. It was seen as primarily a domestic, criminal justice, and public health problem, a viewpoint made clear during the 1973 establishment of the Drug Enforcement Administration (DEA).[4]

It is instructive here to review how the cocaine industry got started. In the early 1970's, the world tin market collapsed, sending the Bolivian economy into a tailspin. Bankrolled by dollars from the Alliance for Progress, Bolivians began planting cotton. Shortly thereafter, the cotton market soured, causing more financial consternation. Facing apparent financial ruin, a group of Bolivian businessmen decided to plant coca on a large scale. The rest is history. Within five years, key military and government members were deeply involved in the budding cocaine industry. Bolivian Air Force airplanes were pressed into service to move the crop, and under the tutelage of General Garcia Meza, other elements of the government entered into a thriving partnership.

Ironically, also in 1973, as the DEA was brought on line, a coup in Chile brought the Pinochet government to power. Upon assuming power, General Augusto Pinochet had the traffickers arrested. Chilean traffickers had been buying coca leaf from Peru and Bolivia, processing it, and shipping it north. The crackdown enabled Colombians to seize control of approximately 80% of cocaine processing, thus filling the void and providing a setting for the real cocaine boom.

In the next eight years, cocaine trafficking moved from a relatively small criminal activity to an international criminal industry. The amount of cocaine went from an estimated 14 to 19 metric tons in 1976, to 71 to 137 metric tons in 1984.[5] Despite the creation in 1979 of the National Narcotics Intelligence Consumers Committee report (NNICC) and its yearly publication thereafter, it was not until 1984 that the use of the term "cocaine industry" even began to gain acceptance in US government circles.[6]

While US government documents of this period acknowledged the likelihood that enormous sums of money were flowing into the hands of Colombian trafficking organizations, they reflected little understanding of the significance of this activity.

The failure to understand the inability of the production and transit countries to oppose the threat of drug trafficking resulted in a continuing series of surprises. By 1980 Bolivia had become the first narcocracy under General Garcia Meza. Bolivia provides an excellent case study, the elements of which serve as a template that is valuable today when one looks into the growth and development of cocaine trafficking in any country in Central and South America.

SEARCHING FOR THE "HEART OF THE BEAST"

In addressing the need for improved intelligence support in drug control, the 1975 White Paper on Drug Abuse noted counterproductive competition within and among the law enforcement agencies and a lack of intelligence analytical capabilities as the primary problems.[7] Competition between agencies was the result of the expansion of the drug mission, once exclusively held by the Customs Service to include the newly created Drug Enforcement Agency. Significant institutional shortcomings with DEA's intelligence analytical capabilities can be traced to its Bureau of Narcotics and Dangerous Drugs heritage. Intelligence at DEA was oriented largely to specific investigations, i.e., "buy/bust," while broader, strategic and operational intelligence efforts received little attention.[8]

Those conditions led to two critical failures in strategic drug intelligence analysis in the period 1976 to 1984. These were the failure to understand that cocaine trafficking had actually become an industry and that the industry had created a powerful, new constituency within Colombia.[9]

On September 24, 1979, at the headquarters of the Drug Enforcement Administration in Washington, D.C., a young intelligence analyst named Miguel Walsh completed a paper that described a startling growth in cocaine trafficking both within and throughout Colombia. Since the paper was intended for internal purposes, the sources available to him were extensive: the DEA's own voluminous files on Colombian police reports from Bogota and Medellin and nitty-gritty reports from confidential informants—"CI's" in the jargon—who trade information for immunity and are sometimes permitted to remain in the trade. Walsh's paper was part history, part analysis, and was intended to be "the most extensive consolidation of available data" on Colombian cocaine trafficking ever assembled. Above all else, it was a prescient warning of the danger Colombian traffickers posed. Cocaine trafficking, Walsh wrote, had achieved "quasi-industrial status." It employed thousands of people and had a "substantial spillover effect in many other sectors of Colombian life." Disciplined groups were operating as underground multinational corporations, vertically integrated with components ranging from clandestine laboratories in Colombia to tightly controlled distribution networks in the United States. Walsh warned of "the critical importance of the venality of government officials, police, judges, lawyers and politicians" who used their power and influence to support the traffickers. Their growing affluence allowed them to employ more and more sophisticated "talent," and "they thus incur increments of power both real and perceived. This is the principal aspect of the current state of narcotics trafficking in Colombia which many individuals find especially disconcerting. The cumulative effect of this problem is such that, in some regions of Colombia, narcotics traffickers command more power and respect than the central government in Bogota." Money, of course, was the root of it—sums of money so vast as to be almost meaningless, even to Walsh's sophisticated readers, unless reduced to an equation.

Employing a hypothetical model developed by other federal government analysts in 1977, Walsh attempted to estimate how much cocaine was flooding into the United States. The coca plant is the basic ingredient of cocaine and since most of the world's coca is grown in Bolivia and Peru, Walsh began by estimating the amount of land those two countries dedicated to coca cultivation. Multiplying by a factor of 1,000 per 2.4 acres gave the amount (in kilos) of coca leaf produced annually. Simple subtraction of the amounts of leaf used for more or less legitimate purposes-medical use, Coca-Cola, coca tea, and coca chewing-gave the amount "unaccounted for" and therefore available for cocaine production. That amount, according to Walsh's calculations, was some 31 million kilos of coca leaf.[10] Continuing his calculations, he determined that approximately 200 kilos of coca leaves are needed to produce one kilo of coca paste. To produce one kilo of cocaine base required 2.5 kilos of coca paste. Lastly, one kilo of base produced the final one kilo of finished cocaine hydrochloride. He then estimated that the production of coca leaf amounted to approximately 14 metric tons.

Moving to the final element of analysis, Walsh devised his own financial model, the results of which showed that coca leaves that cost fifty cents per kilo in Bolivia and Peru translated into a $37,000 single kilo in the United States. What started as $625 worth of coca leaves would bring $560,000 on the streets in the United States. The final figures produced by the model showed that for an outlay of $8 million, the return on investment was an incredible $7,784,000,000. Seen in that context, cocaine had to be the most valuable commodity on earth. The warnings contained in Walsh's paper created no great stir in Washington, though they should have. Perhaps the careful language of his paper served to disguise too well the truly alarming message it contained, which in essence was this: in just three years, the amount of land in Bolivia given over to the cultivation of coca had more than trebled.[11]

TRANQUILANDIA

During late 1982 and into 1983, hundreds of manual laborers were recruited in Bogota and Medellin and flown to Caqueta province in southern Colombia. There, on an island in the middle of the Yari River, they helped construct three separate camps and a landing strip capable of accommodating large aircraft, as well as six smaller airstrips. The camps were named Tranquilandia, Coquilandia, and Villa Coca. Guarded by the Communist Revolutionary Armed Forces of Colombia (FARC), the complex became operational in late 1983 and was soon producing four tons of cocaine per week, twenty tons a month. Obviously any operation this large would soon attract attention. Learning of the complex, newly appointed Minister of Justice Rodrigo Lara Bonilla was determined to destroy the operation with American help. With electronic transmitters secreted in 55-gallon drums of precursor chemicals bound for the island, the DEA and Colombian forces were able to track the route of the chemicals. Plans were drawn up for an assault on the island on March 10, 1984.

The raid was not entirely successful—there had been a leak within the Colombian government, a continuing occurrence even today. Nonetheless, the raiders seized and destroyed approximately 2,500 kilos of cocaine, 3,500 kilos of cocaine base, airplanes, helicopters, and a massive collection of vehicles and processing equipment. The street value of the cocaine was estimated at $1.2 billion. When the cocaine was dumped into the Yari, the river turned white. Seven weeks after the raid, as Lara Bonilla was returning home, a red Yamaha motorcycle driven by sicarios (drug mafia assassins) pulled alongside his Mercedes. Machine-gun fire from the assassins killed the minister of justice.

Prior to the assassination, US Intelligence Community efforts had been limited, largely as a result of concerns over legal restrictions on member agencies where investigations might involve US citizens. The Intelligence Community generally conceded drug intelligence responsibilities to DEA, following the lead agency concept. DEA had briefly been a member of the Intelligence Community in the Carter administration. However, because it was believed that national security information could not be safely and effectively used in an open-court environment, the DEA did not remain a community member. The lead agency for drug intelligence, DEA tended to conduct its operations without predictive threat estimates or much serious intelligence support.[12] Intelligence of the scope that would ensure that the nation's drug policy and strategy would not fail because its statesmen had planned and acted in ignorance, simply did not exist.

Richard Betts argues, there have been no "bolts from the blue" in terms of strategic surprise in the 20th century. Roberta Wohlsetter noted in her classic work on strategic surprise at Pearl Harbor that the "signals" that should have been the basis for an alert were lost in the "noise" of the surroundings. Such was the case in the 1984 assassination. As with the assassination of Archduke Franz Ferdinand of Austria by a Serbian terrorist in August 1914, the Lara Bonilla attack set into motion events that would be felt worldwide. In both cases, there were indicators and warnings that should have provided an alert. In the case of the Lara Bonilla assassination, the surprise lay in the discoveries of the scope of the power which cocaine traffickers had acquired in Colombia; their willingness to exercise that power; the complicity of members of the Colombian government; and finally the inability of the Colombian government to respond to their challenge.[13]

Whereas in the past countries were ravaged by the onslaught of armies destroying their landscape with a blitzkrieg of tanks, planes, and artillery, causing capitulation by force of arms; the cocaine attack accomplished the same results by the force of economic power through the application of money, the quantities of which were never before seen. The thrust of the economic sword, which in turn undermined states through corruption, was cemented for the long term by the selective application of violence. To the naked eye the landscape remained unscathed. Beneath the surface, however, the impact of this "soft-war" had permeated the very soul of most if not all Latin American states and had become well entrenched in the United States and was spreading to Europe.

With the requirement to perform a threat assessment, intelligence has the responsibility to issue an alert, or warning, when selected indicators suggest that danger is imminent. Prior to the Lara Bonilla attack there were indicators that should have provided an alert. In 1973 the *New York Times* carried more stories about cocaine than it did about heroin, and in response to the growing alarm, Congress passed tough new laws threatening drug traffickers with the possibility of life imprisonment. A year later the National Household Survey reported at least 5.4 million Americans had tried cocaine at least once.

Within the counter drug community before 1984 the belief had been that the real problem was identifying and seizing traffickers' bank accounts. Like related efforts to seize the drugs themselves, efforts to seize traffickers' bank accounts did not inflict disabling damage on the traffickers. By 1984 the US government was pressuring the government of Colombia to enter into joint operations to be launched directly against cocaine producing facilities, the eradication of marijuana, and the extradition of major drug traffickers. There were threats of reprisals by drug traffickers and doubts about the likelihood that the operations could be carried out successfully, but those doubts were swept away by the triumphant Tranquilandia raid. It was believed that this would be the turning point and that the US government had demonstrated that the traffickers could be defeated on their own ground.[14] The stakes remained high and violent resistance from the traffickers was expected. What no one expected was that within a month the minister of justice would be killed and a new turning point, would be reached.

THE ANATOMY OF DRUG TRAFFICKING:
COLOMBIAN COCAINE

In the Intelligence Agenda of the National Drug Control Strategy the primary mission of intelligence is to "concentrate on the infrastructure of trafficking organizations."[15] Contrary to what the press calls them, the term "cartels" is a misnomer. In fact, they are not cartels, since they cannot control the price of their product. The Colombian cocaine industry may not be a cartel, but it fulfills every other superlative people have used about it. It is the Third World's first truly successful multinational. It is the most profitable business in the world.[16] The Colombians use the term "mafia," a classification which more accurately describes the familial business aspect of such organizations.

Drug trafficking organizations should be thought of as a grouping of coalitions or consortiums that come together to coordinate mutual business enterprises—La Empresa Coordinadora (the Coordinating Enterprise).[17] An early example of the concept and practice of La Empresa took place in 1981 following the kidnapping of trafficker Jorge Ochoa's sister, Marta Nieves, by the leftist guerrilla group M-19. The heads of the La Empresa met and formed a death squad, Muerte a Los Secuestradores (Death to Kidnappers), which methodically killed the guerrillas and their families until Nieves was released.

Rather than having a well-structured corporate bureaucratic configuration, like the La Cosa Nostra (LCN) in the United States, La Empresa is a loose associative or confederate model rooted in familial and patron-client relationships, as in fact are many operating units in Italian and LCN organized crime. There is role specification, status hierarchies, and division of labor as in any organization, but the overall shape of La Empresa Coordinadora is closer organizationally to an Amway distributorship or fast food franchising service organization than some vertically and horizontally integrated privately held business (see Figure 4.1).[18]

In Colombia, as in many western countries-with the exception of the United States, La Empresa Coordinadora has been recognized de facto, if not de jure, as a *gremio* (a major interest group which the nation-state must take into account in the development and implementation of public policies). Like FEDCAFE, the coffee *gremio,* La Empresa has over the last decade become an important force in Colombian politics. In fact, there are at least 100 separate drug trafficking organizations

Figure 4.1
La Empresa Coordinadora: Structure

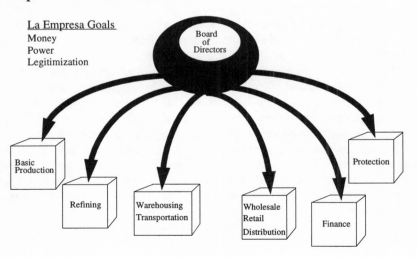

in Colombia. This is a fluid number, especially in 1995 when many *hormigas* (ants), i.e., little entrepreneurs with anywhere from 1 kilo to 20, are trying to cross a border to make a profit and perhaps earn and learn enough to become real narcotraficantes, are counted. The 100 separate groups in Colombia tend to associate with like-minded individuals and organizations in their region. Because of Colombia's topography, regional separation and identification are deep historical and cultural characteristics. Thus, groups link-up as necessary in their areas. There are five major organizations in Colombia. The top four are; the Cali family, the North Coast or Atlantico family, the Bogota/Pereira family, and the Amazonas (Leticia) organization. As is true of La Cosa Nostra families in New York City today, not all groups are equally powerful or fully autonomous. The smaller groups often work for or with the more powerful organizations like Cali or Medellin, as the situation calls for.[19]

Colombia's traffickers come from two sources: There are the old smugglers, who expanded from cigarettes and electronic goods into cocaine. Among them was Fabio Restrepo, whose nephew, Jorge Luis Ochoa, now 40, soon became one of the biggest in the business. And there are the young toughs, who tend to be more violent. Pablo Escobar, the richest criminal in the world prior to his death, was a small-time hoodlum from Envigado, a Medellin suburb, who started his career selling gravestones after sand-blasting off the inscriptions and reselling them. In 1976, Escobar was arrested for carrying 39 pounds of cocaine in the spare tire of his car. It was the largest cocaine bust in Medellin that year; the cops who arrested him and two of the judges on the case were later shot to death, their assailants never to be found. Escobar was never arrested again. Escobar and Ochoa were two of hundreds of small-time traffickers. What brought these Colombians to the top of the business was their link with Carlos Lehder. A German-Colombian who had come to the United States in 1973, when he was 15, Lehder was arrested for smuggling marijuana. In prison he met other smugglers who offered distribution outlets for a more profitable business: cocaine. Out of prison, Lehder bought a place on Norman's Cay in the Bahamas and turned the Bahamas into a transshipment point- almost single-handedly corrupting an entire country. Lehder was the first to create a system for transporting and distributing large shipments of cocaine in the United States.[20]

From an intelligence viewpoint, the La Empresa infrastructure should be thought of as a chain composed of "snap-links," much like those used by mountain climbers. Each link may stand alone, but they also have the capability of being linked together. A number are simply independent actors who only occasionally link to other members of the group as needs dictate. The groups are familial and associational-trust organizations, frequently linked by marriages of convenience to other groups. At times, some of these arrangements involve cooperation with potentially strange bedfellows like guerrilla and insurgent organizations, the police, military, intelligence agencies, and governments who are more frequently potential La Empresa opponents.[21]

To work toward mutual goals, the major families have a central council made up of members who have proved themselves via their organizational success and achievements. This body provides a coordinating mechanism, as well as a clearing house for new ideas and directions and a mediation and dispute settlement group. At the same time, however, even this key leadership is independent if it chooses, in terms of action and activities. Each member controls at least one separate link or a series of links. At times, five or six leaders may choose to associate their organizations, or independently become partners in one or more enterprises that require larger sums of capital, or involve such economies of scale that a limited partnership is warranted. This was the case in establishing the laboratories at Tranquilandia and Villa Coca. The 1984 raids on those sites also showed the dangers and costs that can come to La Empresa from having too many eggs in a single basket. This lesson has not been lost today.

To further underscore this critical point of association, confederation, and alliance within the context of individual enterprise independence, one can look at the career and actions of "El Mexicano," Jose Gonzalo Rodriquez Gacha. A central figure in the Medellin group's council, he was war minister and also in charge of security. He was also a partner in the Villa coca production facility and for a time had close relations with the FARC guerrillas. When the guerrillas threatened his interests with their taxes and demands for arms and ultimately forced him to move one of his laboratories into Brazil, he decided to go to war against them. The Union Patriotica, the political arm of FARC leadership, was decimated by Gacha and this brought the political right further in sympathy with trafficking organizations. Gacha used this to further his holdings and influence with the right wing in the banana growing regions of Uraba around Turbo and finally in fighting off the government's assaults on trafficking interests after the murder of Luis Carlos Galan, the liberals' presidential candidate.

Politicians, police, generals and presidents are on the drug trafficking payroll. Prime Minister Pindling in the Bahamas, General Garcia Meza in Bolivia, and Manual Noriega in Panama were all part of the extended drug trafficking business. Dozens of legitimate businessmen who, because of Colombia's capital-export financial restrictions, need large-scale capital to build hotels, improve their plant capacity, or upgrade their transportation fleet, come to the traffickers because of their capital fluidity.

Because of the cash flow needs of the trafficking organizations, the families of La Empresa soon made their way into banking. One of the least subtle forms of money laundering is the *Ventanilla Siniestra*, or left-handed window, of the Banco de Republica, created during the marijuana boom in the 1960's. There, it is not uncommon to see young men with numerous envelopes stuffed with large-denomination currency, passing them to the teller. The police are not called and the bank's exchange rate is better than on the street. As the government reaches out for drug money, so do its politicians. Campaigns are expensive in Colombia, and there are no burdensome government regulations about who finances them. Every recent presidential campaign was heavily financed by drug money, and the Congress is widely considered to rival the National Police as the most corrupt institution in the country.[22]

The selected application of violence is used to correct intraorganizational errors and inefficiencies. If someone cheats, lies, is disloyal, or makes unacceptable or unexplainable errors of judgment that result in product loss, violent death is meted out. *Plata o plomo* (silver or lead) is a way of life. It is understood that patrons are responsible for their clients. Therefore, if someone sponsors a relative or friend for a position in the organization, they will face the consequences should that individual err. Similarly, wives, children, and other relatives may receive extreme punishments as circumstances warrant. Families are exchanged, relocated and placed in intermarriage or hostage situations in order to maintain organizational stability as needed. It is widely believed that Carlos Lehder was offered up to US and Colombian authorities for extradition by La Empresa, because of the high profile and public exposure that he brought to the families. The case of Pablo Escobar is similiar. A combination of government forces and Cali-family members finally ran Escobar to ground and killed him.

Chapter 5

The Militarization of the War on Drugs

For nearly forty years the Fulda Gap provided the military with a safe, comfortable mission. The plan was for the United States and Russia to meet at the Fulda Gap and hold World War III. Strategic and tactical books and manuals were written, exercises held, computer war games conducted and billions of dollars spent perpetuating the myth. George Orwell would have been proud. No American officer or senior NCO, deep in their heart, could take this seriously. But none could admit it was a charade because it was an important part of the Cold War economy. Some of the same officers trained to fight at the Fulda Gap, who, in fact, stood guard there, are now directing the "War on Drugs." They are at Southern Command. They are probably at every other command which has a CD mission. They are dedicated officers who work long hours and do their best. And, they are failing miserably.

—Major James Nicholson
Chief, Analytical Support Team, J-2 US Southern Command
After Action Report, May 1992

UNWILLING WARRIORS: HELL NO, WE WON'T GO

The entrance of the military into the war on drugs was the most dramatic and controversial event in an already drug packed decade that culminated with the 1989 publication of the *National Drug Control Strategy*. (A timeline showing events of the 1980's and early 1990's is given in Figure 5.1) In *The Profession of Arms*, Sir John Hackett wrote:

It is the function of police to exercise force, or to threaten it, in execution of the state's purpose, internally and under normal conditions. It is the function of armed forces to exercise force, or the threat of it, externally in normal times and internally only in times that are abnormal. The degree of force which the state is prepared to apply in the execution of its purpose is as

Figure 5.1
The Military and the War on Drugs, 1981–1992

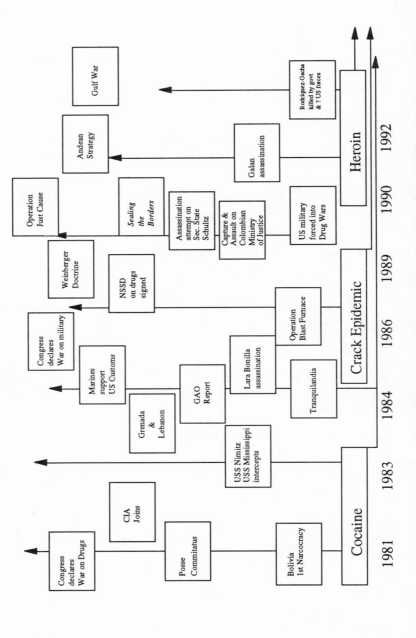

much as the government of the day considers it necessary or expedient to use to avoid a breakdown in its function and a surrender of its responsibilities.[1]

If, as some observers of the political scene have argued, it is the function of the profession of arms to bring an ordered application of force to a social problem in a democratic society, then the critical question to be answered is how does one determine what the focused application of that force might be. The thought of infantry on line sealing our South West Border, of civilian arrest powers being granted to the military, of the military patrolling the streets alongside the police, is foreign to our thinking. But the urgent cries from politicians at the local, state, and national levels to "loose the dogs of war" in an attempt to destroy the enemy further raise the question of just how the military might be used in the war against drugs.

That the times were abnormal is highlighted by the 1981 legislation that amended the Posse Comitatus Act, the keystone in civil/military affairs that closely regulated and restricted the domestic use of the military and which had been law for almost 100 years. From the earliest days of the Republic, the prohibition against the use of the military in domestic issues has been clear-cut. The uneasy legacy of the Quartering Act is still found in the body politic. The domestic use of the military for anything short of defending the borders against invaders was anathema. Responding to the perceived failure of federal law enforcement to cope with the onslaught of drugs, the Congress changed the rules.

Public Law 97-86 eased the restrictions of the act by authorizing indirect military involvement in law enforcement functions by loaning equipment, sharing intelligence, providing support personnel and training assistance, and sharing information and intelligence gained incidental to normal military missions. The reasons for such a dramatic change were clear. The Congress, frustrated after repeated appropriations to and promises from the law enforcement community and certain elements of the intelligence establishment, declared war against both communities. The primary intent of the 1981 legislation was to tip the scales in favor of the criminal justice system by making the resources of the DoD available to "assist civilian law enforcement authorities in their efforts to halt and stem the influx of illegal drugs into and across the borders of the United States."[2]

From the time of the amendment of the Posse Comitatus Act in 1981 until late 1989, the US military establishment fought entry into the wars on drugs. Their focus was on real warfighting, with the fine points of air-land battle of far greater interest than the seemingly impossible task of coping with an enemy that moved with almost complete impunity in and out of the United States. The curriculum at the Army War College said it all; only 6 hours were devoted to the study of the Vietnam War. The lessons of that debacle which would have turned the military mind towards unconventional warfare—which was precisely what was needed in the war on drugs—were purposely ignored.

The intensity of the struggle between the Congress and the military establishment was brought home in early 1991. Congressman Jack Davis (R-IL) articulated the mood of many of his colleagues: "When you have a war, who do you call in? You call in the military." A war on drugs with real troops? Frank Carlucci III, the secretary of defense, was being baited on June, 15 1991, for refusing to join Congress in a war on drug smugglers, and he did not like it, as anyone could see. Toward the end of a long morning, in a joint hearing run by the House and Senate Armed Services Committees, Representative Jack Davis (R-IL) pulled out a white handkerchief. Carlucci looked stonily across the room and clenched his jaw. "I brought this along," said Davis, with a flourish, "because it sounds like we're going to surrender." He blasted Carlucci and other Defense officials for being "bureaucratized," rigid and timid, and exploded in summation: "If I sound angry, it's because I am." Carlucci did not respond.[3]

For a number of reasons, the military wasn't interested in fighting a war against drugs in 1981. First and foremost, the state of world affairs for the previous ten years suggested that the Soviet Union was well upon its way toward a position of world dominance. The election of President Ronald Reagan was viewed by the defense establishment with all the joy of the surviving members of a wagon train surrounded by Indians as John Wayne rides into view. Now the army and the Defense Department could get on with the real business of the military—battlefield Europa.

The seeds of the war on drugs, however, were planted at the same time as the coffers of the weapons industry were liberally salted with requests for tanks, missiles, and submarines to beef up defenses against the "evil empire." Money, both for guns and measures to counter drugs, had been appropriated and action was expected. The military chose to seize upon the former and ignore the latter, just as it ignored at the same time—with studied determination—a presidential order to rebuild the nation's special operations forces. Any deviations from Clausewitzian military-style operations were dismissed out of hand.

In 1982, the Department of Defense was blissfully focused upon the Fulda Gap the narrow German valley that has been the historic invasion point into western Europe for eastern armies for 800 years. Early that same year, the Reagan White House issued an executive order bringing the CIA formally into the wars on drugs. Later in the year, the Tax Reform Act was amended to facilitate disclosure of IRS file information to other enforcement agencies. As the President announced the formation of the South Florida Task Force on Crime—to fulfill the federal government's "special responsibility" to control "massive immigration and epidemic drug smuggling"—the IRS was intensifying its Special Enforcement Program aimed at drug offenders. The National Institute on Drug Abuse household survey reported that 11.9 million Americans had used cocaine within the past year and 21.6 million Americans had used it at least once.

As the attorney general ordered the Director of the FBI to assume authority over the Drug Enforcement Administration, *On War: The Vietnam War in Context* was published. While it would reopen the agony of Vietnam for the military, of the utmost importance was its ability to initiate a soul-searching by the military for a strategy and tactics for dealing with events short of high-intensity warfare. Drug trafficking issues would soon fall under that heading.

Plans for the annual REFORGER (Reinforce Germany) exercises were well under way at the Pentagon, and at North American Aerospace Defense (NORAD) Headquarters deep inside Cheyenne Mountain, Colorado, radar screens were focused north, on the Arctic Circle, in vigilant watch for Soviet aircraft. Along the southern borders of the United States, countless drug-laden aircraft overflew the international boundary, landing with impunity to unload cargoes of marijuana and cocaine. During November 1982, the carrier *Nimitz* and cruiser *Mississippi* intercepted a tug laden with 30 tons of marijuana. Early the next year a contingent of ten Marines arrived in south Florida to fly and maintain aircraft in support of the Customs Service. In July 1983, the guided missile destroyer *U.S.S. Kidd* chased and fired upon a cargo ship laden with marijuana, the first such military/civilian encounter in history. Reacting to growing public concern, the Congress directed that all possible resources to combat narcotics trafficking should be carried out. In a June 1983 report entitled *Federal Drug Interdiction Efforts Need Strong Central Oversight*, the General Accounting Office (GAO) noted that "Perhaps the greatest untapped resource," for the mission was, "the Department of Defense."[4] On September 27,1984, a White House press release summarized the accomplishments of the War on Drugs to date. The report noted that seizures of cocaine during the first seven months of 1984 were 216% percent greater than cocaine seizures during all of 1981. Heroin seizures were 67% greater for the same period, and marijuana confiscated was up 8%. What the report failed to mention was that the overall amount of cocaine to reach the US was approximately 74 to 90 metric tons.

In October, US forces, with virtually no intelligence support stormed Grenada to successfully drive out Cuban-supported Marxist forces of the New Jewel Movement. To what degree the presence of US forces in the Leeward Island chain slowed down the steady stream of drugs and drug aircraft destined for the US mainland is unclear.[5]

Operation Hat-Trick I and II, a joint Navy-Coast Guard interdiction effort were conducted in 1984. By November, 108 tons of marijuana had been seized, the same amount as the previous year. Because of the lack of strategic intelligence, the efforts of law enforcement and the Coast Guard in the Caribbean caused the cocaine pipeline to shift west into and through the Gulf of Mexico. Those states on the gulf, and the border states soon became part of the conduit for South American cocaine.

On November 28, 1984, Secretary of Defense Caspar W. Weinberger gave a speech to the National Press Club. Those comments were directed toward an attempt to define the political/military parameters that should be considered prior to committing US military forces to combat overseas. What has since come to be called the Weinberger Doctrine listed six conditions that should be met before US troops are deployed:

1. The United States should not commit forces to combat unless our vital interests are at stake. Our interests, of course, include the vital interests of our allies,
2. Should the United States decide that it is necessary to commit its forces to combat, we must commit them in sufficient numbers and with sufficient support to win. If we are unwilling to commit the forces or resources necessary to achieve our objectives, or if the objective is not important enough so that we must achieve it, we should not commit our forces,
3. If we decide to commit forces to combat, we must have clearly defined political and military objectives. Unless we know precisely what we intend to achieve by fighting,

and how our forces can accomplish those clearly defined objectives, we cannot formulate or determine the size of forces properly, and therefore we should not commit our forces at all,

4. The relationship between our objectives and the size, composition, and disposition of our forces must be continually reassessed and adjusted as necessary. In the course of a conflict, conditions and objectives inevitably change. When they do, so must our combat requirements,

5. Before the United States commits combat forces abroad, the US government should have some reasonable assurance of the support of the American people and their elected representatives in the Congress. Of course, this does not mean we should wait upon a public opinion poll. The public elects a president as a leader, not a follower. He takes an oath to protect and defend the Constitution. The people also expect a Congress sworn to the same principles and duties. To that end the president and the leadership of the Congress must build the public consensus necessary to protect our vital interests. Sustainability of public support cannot be achieved unless the government is candid in making clear why our vital interests are threatened and how by the use and only by the use of American military forces, we can achieve a clear, worthy goal. US troops cannot be asked to fight a battle with the Congress at home while attempting to win a war overseas. Nor will the American people sit by and watch US troops committed as expendable pawns on some grand diplomatic chessboard,

6. The commitment of US forces to combat should be a last resort-only after diplomatic, political, economic, and other efforts have been made to protect our vital interests.[6]

In attempting to prevent another Vietnam, the Weinberger Doctrine sought to firmly set military force in the relative security of the Clausewitzian concept of Trinitarian warfare, i.e., the government, the people, and the military. The fatal flaw of that doctrine was its failure to understand that warfare had radically changed. The impact of a world coming together and falling apart at the same time-the chaos of a postcolonial, multitribal world, had already savaged the concept of Trinitarian warfare. What the Weinberger Doctrine failed to recognize was the radical change in the nature of the threat to US national. As such, any new strategic thinking as to tactics for this new world of disorder would not come to pass. Two weeks later, in remarks entitled the "Ethics of Power," Secretary of State George P. Schultz argued that there is never any guarantee of public support for the use of force except to use it in a moral way in keeping with the highest principles of the United States. The ensuing national debate was seized upon by the press, which ensured its continuation but no resolution.[7]

The Army War College made the Weinberger Doctrine a part of its curriculum, placing the issue squarely in front of students who were soon to move on to senior level staff and command positions. With more hours devoted to the doctrine and its potential application within a European scenario, inclusion of the Weinberger Doctrine strengthened the case of those within the Department of Defense/military establishment who opposed a counter drug mission.

In 1986, President Reagan signed a national security decision directive that equated the impact of drug trafficking with a "threat to the national security of the United States" and directed all federal agencies with a role in drug enforcement, including DoD, to pursue counter drug efforts more actively. At this point, the handwriting was on the wall. With the directive signed, the question of whether drug trafficking was a matter of national security or not was settled. With the pen now mightier than the sword, the military could not hold out much longer.

The RAND Study

In early 1987, the office of the under secretary of defense for policy, anticipating that the military services would be tasked to assume a substantial share of the war on drugs, requested that RAND "carry out an analysis of the consequences of further increases in the military involvement in drug interdiction efforts, focusing particularly on how this involvement might influence the consumption of cocaine and marijuana."[8]

Written a year and a half before the military was forced into the war on drugs, *Sealing the Borders: The Effects of Increased Military Participation in Drug Interdiction* was to have a profound impact on the role that the military would play in the war on drugs. The authors of the study argued that the critical issue was "whether the military could significantly increase the effectiveness of interdiction at the Mexican border." It is unclear why the study cast the military solely in a domestic border-interdiction role, rather than reflecting the charter under which it was commissioned to write: "the consequences of further increases in the military involvement in drug interdiction efforts." In light of the fact that US law enforcement agencies alone had civilian arrest powers, it is also curious why an implied law enforcement role was even considered.

Moreover, it is curious why the military would be forced to limit its efforts to a border defense role in light of the strategic and tactical options that existed in Central and South America, particularly in light of the fact that the US military was already there. Part of the shortcoming may be found in the fact that the study was primarily built around an econometric model, with the military aspects being secondary. Casting the military role in a traditional economic framework when so much was known at that time about the non-traditional nature of the drug trafficking industry suggests that a study was sought to confirm preconceived notions and to buy more time to keep the military out of the fray.

The primary task should have been to explore the full range of military strengths and limitations as they would impact the drug trafficking threat both domestic and foreign and to address the costs—fiscal and political—of such actions. Such an approach would have addressed the roles that each of the services might play and, more specifically the roles of the various branches within each service. These roles could have then been overlaid against the various levels of play and geographical locations where it might be practical to consider such moves. Within each of the phases of drug trafficking-production, transit, and border entry-there are a number of strategic areas where interdiction activities might have an impact, by either drug law enforcement agencies or the military.

Failure to take such an approach must be considered a glaring, fundamental omission. Further, the study failed to consider the effects of a role in which the military might become the primary interdiction agency rather than continuing in a support role. This should have been obvious, since the Congress, resigned to the failure of the federal drug law enforcement agencies, had been fighting for almost six years to move the military into a lead position. In the least, the study should have addressed the range of roles the military might assume, to include its strengths and weaknesses in interdiction and in detection and monitoring, both of which would soon become the DoD mission.

Sealing the Borders gave the role of intelligence short shrift—either by commission or omission. In commenting that "little is known about the organization of the drug smuggling business," the authors set the stage for a half-hearted attempt to address the role of intelligence, something the military continues to ignore today.[9] It is important to note again that at the point in time when the study was drafted, a great deal was known about the drug trafficking business. While there was no central repository of information-nor is there today-detailed information was available-if one wanted to look for it.

In addressing the varieties of intelligence, the study noted that "human intelligence cannot be augmented by military involvement, although its utilization might be improved."[10] This is an assertion that is unfounded. There are in fact a number of ways to support the human intelligence process, i.e., providing the full range of support to other intelligence disciplines.

In another erroneous assumption, the authors of the study state that "intelligence is of very slight importance for the interdiction of air smugglers." They note that "the small role of intelligence appears to be not so much the result of weaknesses in the intelligence process as of the short duration of vulnerability of air smugglers."[11] Such a statement denotes a total lack of understanding by the authors of the uses of intelligence. Whether it is the use of national intelligence assets that detect and monitor drug-laden aircraft leaving the Guajira Peninsula in northern Colombia, bound for Mexico, or communications intelligence combined with radar tracking of aircraft leaving Mexico to fly into the United States, it is intelligence—the type that can only be provided by the military—that can make a difference.

The authors of *Sealing the Borders* go on to state:

Our assessment, admittedly subjective, is that the drug smuggling process is not one for which intelligence is likely to play a very large role. There are simply too many places, routes, and times of entry available to smuggling organizations and, at least for air interdiction, too short a time in which to make use of intelligence. The equipment needs are also not highly specific, so suspect equipment lists (a principal component of the intelligence process) provide little assistance to interdictors. Highly specific human intelligence, notoriously hard to generate in large quantities, appears to be the only kind of intelligence that could significantly improve the performance of the system.[12]

The RAND study was a reflection of the prevailing military mindset of the day, a belief that the drug problem was primarily a domestic law enforcement issue. It is not clear if the study was commissioned with a prescribed set of findings already in mind. Nonetheless, the end result was an erroneous picture of the role that the military might play in the wars on drugs. It is an interesting commentary that to date, no one has questioned the underlying assumptions of the RAND study. Still accepted as dogma by many senior officers today, *Sealing the Borders* stands as a serious impediment to understanding the role the military could and should play.

THE TURN OF THE TIDE: THE MILITARY JOINS
THE WARS ON DRUGS

Reflecting a European set-piece-war frame of mind, the military announced that it would require a "massive shift" to begin drug interdiction.[13] Translated into force structure and equipment this meant 90 infantry battalions, 50 helicopter companies, 54,000 Army troops, 110 AWACS aircraft, 30 E2C Hawkeye surveillance planes, 90 P3 antisubmarine aircraft, 50 tethered balloons carrying radar gear, more than 1,000 fighter aircraft, and 160 cruisers and destroyers. To reach that plateau, the Joint Chiefs of Staff announced that it would cost an additional $6.2 billion a year to operate those ships and aircraft, and another $14 billion to purchase another 66 AWACS. With great anguish, numerous senior Pentagon civilian and military officials decried the fact that the drug wars would detract from traditional military missions. A typical response was: "don't believe for a moment that I can execute that kind of drug role as an enhancement to my readiness of my traditional military role."[14]

Clearly, the failure, and in some cases refusal, to recognize the "gray" non-traditional nature of drug trafficking, reflected the long standing military aversion to anything beyond traditional roles. Still smarting from the congressional injection of the Goldwater-Nichols Bill, which forced the military to accept special operations into the military establishment, the DoD dug its heals in even further. The mood of the Congress during the military hold-out was reflected in some of the bizarre attempts to legislate the military into action and the tremendous public pressure to "do something." Chairman Les Aspin (D-Wis) of the House Armed Services Committee said he shared some of the military's concerns but added, "The train is moving and cannot be stopped. The pressure on us to do something about drugs is coming from outside the Beltway so we have to do something about it."[15]

Senator John W. Warner of Virginia, ranking Republican of the Senate Armed Services Committee, and Chairman Sam Nunn had worked to defeat numerous "extreme" anti-drug proposals during 1988, including ones that would have given most of the military the task of sealing the US border with Mexico and given every soldier de facto power of arrest over civilians. On May 18, 1989, an attempt by Senator Pete Wilson to create a special joint-service command to direct military drug interdiction missions also died in committee. The bill would have boosted the status of drug-interdiction missions by making a senior officer accountable for complying with congressional direction and giving him the authority to command troops.

With the wagons circled as tightly as possible, Secretary Cheney pointed to "additional factors," that "have to be considered." Cheney stated that "society should not expect the Department of Defense to resolve every problem that comes down the pike just because we're big and have a lot of resources."[16]

However, on September 18, 1989, the DoD finally threw in the towel. Secretary Cheney issued a directive which abruptly caused the military to do an about face. The secretary identified the DoD counter drug effort as one of his highest priorities, a signal which was not missed inside the department. In short order, the secretary of defense guidance directed that the military would "attack drugs at the source-provide increased training and operational support for host nations; attack drugs in transit-combat the flow of drugs across the Caribbean and US borders; attack drugs in the US—assist drug law enforcement agencies and the National Guard."[17]

Cautious Engagement

After nearly a decade of refusing to join the fray, the military entered the wars on drugs. In spite of its acceptance of the counter drug mission, there were, and there continue to be, strong institutional hang-ups that the military establishment harbors as it is bent to the oars of the drug wars. While never publicly articulated by senior commanders, there has been, a continuing fear of drugs contaminating US forces. The memories of the late 1960's and early 1970's, with the attendant drug use that saw the military eaten from within, remain alive today. The specter of drug-induced corruption and compromise has already been realized. Drug smuggling from Panama to the United States by military personnel and attempts to buy Coast Guard patrol schedules are but the first attempts to buy out the US military.

Until recently, with events driven by the "revolution of 1989," there was a mindset in the officer corps, particularly field and flag officers, against a military role in the drug wars. Theirs is a sense that whatever one must do to fight a drug war, it is not what "real soldiers" should be doing. Dealing with the drug war is seen as demeaning, certainly not as important as leading a battalion, and definitely not career enhancing. The sense of a "fair fight," with its Clausewitzian principals of war, is seen to be missing in what is considered to be a dirty, often brutal struggle against an ignoble enemy in which the rules of engagement are more conducive to a back-alley mugging. To a certain extent, this disdain is disappearing, for it is now the accepted wisdom that "it's the only war in town." In addition, several sources suggest that the military has skirted monetary restrictions in many cases to use drug dollars to "get well."[18]

It is the combat arms officers who are assigned to the operations billets at commands with drug war missions. The result to date has been that what little has been devised in the way of strategy is primarily attempts at adaptation of mid to high intensity war strategies and tactics that are clearly ill-suited to fight a business. One of the early, continuing, and devastating failures of the military has been to approach the war on drugs from a conventional, Clausewitzian dogma-driven viewpoint.

The issue of maintaining combat readiness has been the primary argument against committing troops to the drug war. It is the combat arms branches who raise this cry the loudest. How, they ask, does one maintain an appropriate level of training for an artilleryman, tanker or infantryman, or sailor in the unorthodox world of the drug war environment? In addition, the fear of losing personnel from training when they might be required to testify in a court of law has also been a point of concern.

It is interesting to note that the "combat readiness" argument is still alive and well. Gathered together in San Antonio in early 1992, the general and flag officers responsible for the primary "drug fighting" commands, appeared not to understand that the drug mission assigned to them is a primary mission.[19] It is one of the many new missions they will be required to undertake to support US foreign policy in the new world disorder.

The result, short of those far-fetched ideas such as massing artillery units along the South west border to fire illumination shells at night to restrict the movement of traffickers, is to simply shy away from doing anything. The bottom line is the fear of becoming the scapegoat in a hopeless war.

The National Defense Authorization Act of 1989

The National Defense Authorization Act of 1989 laid out three counter drug missions for the military:

1. Act as lead agency for detection and monitoring of aerial and maritime transit of illegal drugs into the United States;
2. Integrate command, control, communications and technical intelligence assets dedicated to drug interdiction into an effective network;
3. Approve and fund governors' plans for expanded use of the National Guard in support of state interdiction and enforcement operations.[20]

The DoD's primary mission is "to serve as the single lead agency for the federal government for the Detection and Monitoring (D&M) of aerial and maritime transit of illegal drugs into the United States." This mission has since been amended to include land activities. Clearly, this is first and foremost an intelligence mission, written in large script.

The DoD has specific statutory authority to support certain activities of civilian law enforcement agencies, both in a domestic and international application. The DoD also has the authority to support the State Department's International Narcotics Control Program and to support other federal, state, and local agencies which have a counternarcotic role, even though the agencies are not civil law enforcement agencies (CLEA's).

Under the statutory limitations of US Code 10, sec. 371–374, the DoD may provide information gained during normal military training or operations; and *shall* "to the maximum extent practicable" consider the information needs of CLEAs when planning normal training or military operations; and *shall* "to the extent consistent with national security," share intelligence with CLEA's.

However, in spite of having the full backing of the law, the military has yet to fully exploit the opportunities that would enable it to fully enter the fray.

IN SEARCH OF A NEW INTELLIGENCE

With the collapse of the Iron Curtain the threat of monolithic world communism suddenly ended. The dog that had chased the car all those years had suddenly caught it. The new world disorder demanded new strategy and tactics, the likes of which would have to be buttressed and underwritten by an intelligence community that was in tune with the new world. The National Defense Authorization Act for Fiscal Year 1991 directed the Secretary of Defense, together with the Director of Central Intelligence, to conduct a joint review of intelligence and intelligence related activities.

Additionally, the act also mandated an overall 25% manpower reduction in the National Foreign Intelligence Program and the Tactical Intelligence and Related Activities (TIARA) programs from 1992 through 1996. This act spurred the DoD to review its intelligence activities. The result was a plan for the implementation of defense intelligence restructuring. One of the driving factors in this plan was the recognition that warfare would in all probability fall into the low to middle range of intensity. This realization opened a Pandora's box for intelligence. The fog-shrouded battlefields of the war on drugs were indicative of the shifting, elusive nature of intelligence in the new world disorder.

Pressured by congressional mandates because of the failure of the federal law enforcement community to make a dent in the war on drugs on the one hand, and caught astride the horns of an internal doctrinal, strategic, and tactical fight on the other, military intelligence was hard pressed to regroup. Nowhere was this dilemma more apparent than within the United States Army. Army intelligence today is in the throes of an attempt to cast off the mantle of Combat Electronic Warfare and Intelligence (CEWI). The primary argument against CEWI is that it "confused the distribution of intelligence resources with intelligence support."[21] Driven by support directed to the corps and division level, intelligence never found its way down to the user.

CEWI was birthed in the pivotal year of 1975 as the Army was attempting to articulate its fighting doctrine in a new field manual (FM-100-5). It was an attempt to expunge the bitter Vietnam War experience and was designed to change the Army's focus from dismounted infantry operations to armored operations. CEWI provided for organic intelligence assets at the tactical level, the result of the deep distrust of intelligence by the combat arms in Vietnam.

From World War II until Vietnam, the style of Army intelligence can best be characterized by the ULTRA secret mentality, otherwise known as the "Green Door" (green was the color of the vault door behind which the intelligence sections worked).[22] This was an era where in order to protect sources, the best and most sensitive intelligence (compartmented intelligence) was not shared with the combat commander except at the highest level. It was the case in Vietnam (in all services) that in order to protect sources and methods intelligence was frequently and deliberately withheld from those who might make the most use of it. The results of such short-sighted policies were paid for in blood. The legacy of the war was an active attempt to decentralize intelligence; the continued inability of the centralized intelligence system to deliver its product in a timely manner; and, a lasting distrust (often bordering upon open internal warfare) between intelligence and the combat arms.

The depth of this distrust was such that in 1974 the chief of staff of the army directed that a study on intelligence organization and stationing be initiated to review the organization of Army intelligence. Under the direction of Major General James J. Ursano, the study recommended that intelligence be channeled down to the battalion level. The result was the belief that the only way to get intelligence was to "own" it. Thus, CEWI drove a "stove-piping" of intelligence and with it the pervasive misconception that widened distribution of intelligence was akin to greater intelligence support.[23] By the early 1980's, officers who had been denied intelligence assets as company and battalion commanders, had achieved enough rank to effect change at the Army level. The advent of CEWI brought with it a large, relatively immobile, delicate, high-technology system that consumed large personnel assets at its multiple levels (corps, divisions, and major army commands). The result was a highly structured, equipment-heavy intelligence system that lacked flexibility and failed to address anything but a "Red versus Blue" enemy.

MILITARY SUPPORT TO THE WAR ON DRUGS

Defense Intelligence Agency (DIA)

The DIA is responsible for the provision of foreign military intelligence information. Prior to joining the war on drugs, some intelligence activities had been focused on low intensity conflict, (LIC) with the result that information had been collected on illegal narcotics activities in foreign countries.

Following the September 1989 directive, by Secretary Cheney, it was determined that DIA would concentrate on developing the necessary data bases, automation, communications, and collection management necessary to improve the foreign intelligence contribution. With the intent of developing pre-movement tactical information, support of the DoD detection and monitoring mission was emphasized early by identifying the overall structure that led to the movement of narcotics. DIA intelligence support would be provided, as required, to any of the participating law enforcement agencies (LEA's). (Initially this was interpreted to mean federal LEA's. Only of late have state and local LEAs been considered, and then with a decided lack of enthusiasm.)

Further DIA participation was given focus when the Assistant Secretary of Defense for Command, Control, Communication, and Intelligence (C_3I) directed the agency to develop a collection strategy, organize a production plan, establish coordination with the law enforcement community, and identify resource shortfalls.

One of the most difficult and continuing problems was the lack of a data base to support the analysis effort. Initially, it was thought that the necessary information was held in law enforcement community files. Early examination revealed that the data contained material on US citizens, which made receiving and storing it in the DIA an illegal act. The quickest way to overcome this was to contact the LEA's holding the needed information and ask them to share it. Further investigation showed that the LEA's operated in a predominantly paper environment and automation was not available. Thus, they could not rapidly separate US citizenship data from foreign intelligence data.

The mirror image of this was experienced by some elements of the law enforcement community. They believed that the answers to their numerous problems were held inside the foreign intelligence community-classified and inaccessible. Recurring attempts were (and continue to be) made to remind originating elements to classify their information at the lowest possible level. Nevertheless, when the prospect of courtroom disclosure was addressed, some data was too "caveated" to be of use to the law enforcement officials. When attempts were made to get some data released, the protection of sources and methods seemed to justify the LEAs' reluctance to release their information.

To alleviate the burden on the Drug Enforcement Administration because of a landslide of requests for information, DIA established the Counter Drug Coordinating Office (CDCO). This resulted in the requirement that all DoD requests for DEA information had to be submitted to CDCO for review and validation before DEA would be tasked for a response. In turn, DEA invited DoD to create a unit to be stationed at DEA headquarters to exploit DEA intelligence files. The Defense Reporting Element, staffed by analysts from DIA and DoD, reviews both case files and raw field reports.[24]

DIA's EMERALD intelligence system has received poor reviews to date. With the first iteration outdated before it ever reached the field, the value of EMERALD II is unclear. As it presently makes its way to some commands, analysts and operators still express great skepticism as to its timeliness, flexibility, and richness of data. The EMERALD system raises the issue of the value of a centralized database for the entire military CD establishment. The primary issue is the sharing of data for and through a common database. This is something that will be very difficult to overcome, thanks to the very nature of intelligence and drug trafficking.

Anti-Drug Network (ADNET)

In an attempt to build a secure, interoperable communications network, ADNET was designed to connect multiple DoD and law enforcement agency sites. ADNET links the Joint Tasks Forces (JTF's) and the C_3I centers. ADNET consists of Joint Visually Integrated Display System (JVIDS) terminals connected via the Defense Secure Network 1 portion of the Defense Data Network. JVIDS evolved from the Joint Operations Tactical System (JOTS, a command and control system that displays worldwide force-locating data).

High-resolution graphics enhancements were made to JOTS with the Visually Integrated Display System to produce the JVIDS terminal. JVIDS can display color maps depicting geographic features, tracking overlays, targets and political boundaries. JVIDS allows an operator to receive a contact and then electronically transfer it to other JVIDS operators who can simultaneously view its location and movements. Currently, over 40 sites are connected via ADNET, with eventual plans calling for a network of over 120 locations.

As noted in Chapter 3, the Drug Control Communications Network has not met expectations to date, nor is there reason to expect that it will. The concept is new, it is being implemented by the military for both military and non-military users, and its potential users are not all security cleared. There is much to be done before even rudimentary results are forthcoming.

United States Atlantic Command (USACOM)

USACOM, until recently Commander in Chief Atlantic (CINCLANT), established Joint Interagency Task Force East as its primary agent for counter drug operations. Detection and monitoring operations take place within the Atlantic area of operations-Caribbean Sea and waters adjacent to the coasts of Columbia, Central America, and Mexico. Located at Key West, JITF East's mission is to provide early detection of drug traffickers and early notification to appropriate law enforcement and other DoD activities by concentrating operations within departure and transit zones.

Within its Joint Operations Control Center, JITF East has attempted to pull together command, control, communications, and intelligence functions. Here, operations and intelligence personnel work side by side. Once detected, targets are monitored in transit until a positive hand-off or other disposition is coordinated with C_3I East or the US Customs Service.

In early 1992, in a move that greatly disturbed US Southern Command, CINCLANT established a small intelligence production effort in the US Embassy in Bogota, Colombia, well ashore and seemingly outside of the maritime element. There is reason to believe that the information/intelligence provided to the embassy was of such value that the State Department pretended not to hear the SOUTHCOM protest.

United States Pacific Command (PACOM)

The United States Pacific Command is the largest of the military's unified commands. Covering 105 million square miles, an area that hosts 62% of the world's population, it deals with the threat of heroin.

There are no choke points on the approaches to the United States. The Pacific Ocean area off the Central and South American coastlines is not PACOM "territory." When operating in those waters, PACOM "chops" to US Atlantic Command. The Commander in Chief, Pacific established Joint Interagency Task Force West at Alameda, California. Initially, 2 to 4 ships, supported by P-3 maritime patrol flights, were tasked to conduct random patrols of perceived narcotrafficking lanes and high probability areas. It was soon determined that without intelligence queuing such patrol activity was a waste of resources, and in June 1990 random patrols ceased and attention was directed toward developing intelligence driven operations. The Commanding General, US Army Pacific, became the focal point for support to law enforcement agencies on land.

Today, primary emphasis is on the development of "actionable" intelligence" on illicit drug transshipments. Unfortunately, intelligence databases—both substantively and technically—were found to have withered since the Vietnam War. Consequently, CINCPAC is looking to technological exploitation C_3I to enable them to better perform the mission. One of the major problems to be faced is that of maritime tracking. While national intelligence systems have proven themselves to be capable of tracking vessels, the amount of commercial traffic is enormous-approximately 5,000 ships at sea on any given day.

Plans for the creation of a joint intelligence center, similar to those found in the Caribbean are being finalized. At the request of US Customs, CINCPAC is automating a manual reporting network of customs organizations from some 29 US territories, possessions, commonwealths, and sovereign nations across the Pacific. Operation Cook, as it is called, once required weeks, if not months, to get ship movements reports to US Customs, often by mail. The expectation is that this can be accomplished in minutes. Plans are being made to expand Cook to Southeast Asia.

JITF West claims as to the large quantities of cocaine being carried aboard maritime conveyances, particularly through the Eastern Pacific route, have been met with the argument that the Alameda based command is attempting to sing their own praises. Independent research strongly suggests that their claims are indeed correct. CINCPAC and JITF West arguments that their theater demands more resources thanks to the cocaine traffic and the heroin traffic have fallen on deaf ears to date. It is interesting to note that there is not a commonly accepted and used CD maritime methodology at this time. The first attempt to build a methodology was to have been attempted at the El Paso Intelligence Center in early April 1993. That such an effort has not been attempted prior to this further suggests the lack of centralized command and decentralized, area-specific strategies.

North American Aerospace Defense Command (NORAD)

NORAD has the primary responsibility for the detection and monitoring of all aircraft suspected of transporting illegal drugs in the United States. NORAD established the NORAD Tactical Intelligence Center (NORTIC) in 1990 to conduct counter drug operations. The NORTIC receives air tracks from a number of sources, compares them with other data and attempts to produce a comprehensive air picture that is available to both DoD organizations and law enforcement agencies. The NORTIC also claims to have the intelligence analysis capability to develop long-term trends and patterns in aerial drug trafficking.

More concerned with "getting better" through the use of drug money, NORAD appears to be obsessed with acquiring the Over the Horizon Back Scatter Radar (OTHB). This radar supposedly has the capability to look from the ionosphere to the surface of the earth, creating an electronic screen which finds any and all intruders. NORAD believes that this would enable them to find and intercept all inbound drug aircraft. In light of events to date, i.e., the shortcomings in C_3I West, C_3I East, the cost and failure of the chain of aerostats, and AWACS, and ground radars, such expectations appear to be far-fetched. Air Force sensibilities as to total control of all military air assets, an obsession that started during the Korean War and continued to the Gulf War with poor results in each conflict, continues to hinder NORAD thinking.

NORAD claims of success in closing down the South West Border are subject to considerable doubt. According to a NORAD spokesman, "North American air space has been leak-free for the past year, with only a few cases of successful penetration since the command was assigned primary authority for antidrug surveillance under the 1989 National Defense Authorization Act."[25] Drug laden aircraft cross the South West Border with virtual impunity. As described at length in Chapter 6, the "dead-space" of both aerostat-borne radars and ground radars at C_3I West allowed drug aircraft to fly under the radar "screen." The NORAD system was originally designed to identify and track Soviet bloc bombers and fighter aircraft. Today, drug carrying aircraft still cross the South West Border without much chance of being apprehended.[26]

The Tip of Spear: United States Southern Command (SOUTHCOM)

The first major command to become involved with the drug war, and the only "warfighting command," SOUTHCOM, by virtue of its area of operations directly in the forefront of cocaine production and transshipment, is at the "tip of the CD spear." Its detection and monitoring mission which sets the stage for the entire drug "pipeline," is driven by five distinct elements: its history, the Linear Strategy; the Andean Strategy, the personalismo of General George Joulwan, the CINC from 1991 to 1993, and the vagaries of US drug policy.

Headquartered atop Quarry Heights overlooking Panama City, SOUTHCOM is the center of the US military's presence in Latin America. Reacting to rising tensions in Central and South America, US Southern Command came into being in 1963. With approximately 10,000 personnel, predominantly Army, but with the required mix of Air Force, Navy, and Marine Corps, SOUTHCOM has been traditionally led by an army general officer. The primary mission of the command has always been the defense of the Panama Canal. Overtime, however, a significant mission developed to help install pro-US leaders in Latin American militaries through training and weapon sales. The command runs approximately sixteen security assistance organizations throughout the region, whose primary functions are to maintain ties with local militaries and with the US ambassador in that country.

Within a year, of SOUTHCOM's founding, internal troubles in Panama boiled over. US troops fired upon Panamanian demonstrators, killing twenty-eight and wounding more than three hundred. SOUTHCOM sources suggested that the Guardia Nacional had encouraged the rioters. With the Guardia developing its own agenda, one different from the ruling elite, more trouble was just around the corner in the form of Colonel Omar Torrijos and a young intelligence officer, Captain Manuel Noriega. In 1968, a successful coup placed Torrijos in power. As the new president consolidated his power, Noriega, Torrijos' staff intelligence officer, developed close ties with SOUTHCOM. Following the death of Torrijos in a mysterious aircraft crash in 1981, Noriega moved to consolidate his own personal power just prior to the presidential elections in May 1984, he had promoted himself to brigadier general and consolidated his power behind candidate Nicholas Barletta. As election results began to come in, it became clear that Barletta was headed for defeat. The Panamanian Defense Force (PDF) suspended the vote count and rigged the election which resulted in Barletta's "victory." While the situation in Panama was distasteful to SOUTHCOM and Washington, the Reagan administration accepted the situation overlooking Noriega's activities—particularly drug trafficking— while counting upon him to hold Panama stable and remain the linch-pin in its anti-communist strategy in Central America.

In May 1987, General Frederick F. Woerner, Jr. assumed command at Quarry Heights. During the change of command ceremony, General Woerner directed his remarks to Noriega. Commenting that never in US history had there been a "man on horseback," Woerner stated that the "ingredient of legitimacy is a fundamental un-derpinning of a professional military."[27] A month later, following the suspension of several articles from the Panamanian constitution, the US Senate passed a resolution deploring the action and urging the restoration of those constitutional rights. Noriega responded with a PDF- sponsored attack on the US Embassy. At that point, the Reagan government directed that ties with Noriega be severed. He was now the enemy.

Harassment of US service personnel escalated, while at the State Department, the decision was made that Noriega would have to be removed. For General Woerner and SOUTHCOM, pressure to depose Noriega raised the possibility of fighting the forces it had trained and equipped. Contingency planning began as General Woerner was faced with two options: a commando-type strike or a large scale intervention. Contingency planning continued under the code name Prayer Book with provisions for actual fighting given the code-name Blue Spoon and another annex called Post Time.[28]

For General Woerner, attacks were coming from two sides: Noriega and Wash-ington. The stepped-up attacks by the PDF caused much concern within SOUTHCOM. Woerner's efforts to develop a Panamanian solution, versus a Wash-ington solution, soon led his own officers and men as well as the Pentagon to refer to him as "WIMPCOM."[29]

Following a visit by Senator McCain and Representative Murtha, the "WIMPCOM" story was given a sharper bite when General Woerner told the two that he had information that if they observed the up-coming elections, they would be arrested and incarcerated. The general warned that he could not ensure their safety. Returning to Washington, Senator McCain told President Bush, "that man is no damned good."[30] McCain's comments were the final straw. Caught between Washington, where his own recent criticism of the Bush administration had further isolated him; Noriega's increasing belligerence, and his own command, which railed against his seeming unwillingness or inability to stand up to the daily PDF harassment, Woerner's days were numbered. When General Carl Vuono offered Woerner the option of resigning or being sacked, the man reviled as "WIMPCOM" opted for the former.[31]

General "Mad Max" Thurman, a hard-driving workaholic who expected his staff to be ready on a moment's notice, was selected as the new CINCSOUTH. Thurman's arrival signaled the imminent move to topple Noriega. As planning continued for what would become Operation Just Cause, it became clear that SOUTHCOM intelligence had but a sketchy picture of Noriega. This was the case in spite of the fact that SOUTHCOM headquarters looked directly into Noriega's headquarters. The problem was that SOUTHCOM intelligence was targeted against American strategic interests, primarily in South America. Then, as today, SOUTHCOM intelligence was never fully focused.[32]

Since the beginning of the "Panama Crisis" in June 1987, intelligence units at SOUTHCOM, Quarry Heights; US Army South, Fort Clayton; and the 470ᵗʰ MI Brigade, Corozal, had been engaged in low-level collection and analysis against the PDF and Noriega. But there was no real focal point, mission objective, or even coordination. In September, 1989, military intelligence in Panama was forced by an exasperated Washington to assume a more aggressive role. SOUTHCOM opted to play its weakest cards.

In September 1989, the National Security Council, through the Joint Chiefs, directed SOUTHCOM to begin military surveillance of General Noriega. The surveillance tasker went to the SOUTHCOM J2 and was passed to US Army South. Brigadier General Marc A. Cisneros ordered that two surveillance plans be drafted, one a low-profile effort, and the second high profile. The planning was assigned to Major James Nicholson, who would form the Analytical Support Team (AST), J2, three years later. Nicholson took it upon himself to draft a third plan, C.

Plan A called for three static surveillance sites, all on US controlled property, which commanded a view of the Commandancia, the PDF offices and barracks at Fort Amador and the PDG airfield adjacent to Albrook Air Force Station.

Plan B was to be a series of static surveillance sites with discreet mobile surveillance teams which would scramble whenever "Target One" moved.

Plan C provided for full-blown coverage, static sites, "lock-bumper" mobile teams and air coverage.[33]

Maintaining its "WIMPCOM"—We don't want any problems"—mentality, CINCSOUTH selected Plan A, which was then code named Operation Phantom Rider. A month into the round-the-clock surveillance, which soaked up the resources of the 470ᵗʰ to the tune of more than 100 personnel, Nicholson advised the chief of staff that unless surveillance went to at least a semi-mobile status, Noriega could never be tracked more than an average of three days out of seven. As expected, light coverage was selected, thus setting the stage for Operation Just Cause, which ensured that Noriega would not be found in a timely manner.

Operation Just Cause must be regarded as the only real "battle" in the war on drugs. Commencing with a Ranger assault on Tocumen airfield in the early morning hours of December 20, 1989, the operation was a success from a military standpoint. However, its overall legacy to the drug war is unclear. Initially, argue the authors of *Operation Just Cause*, "US troops encountered the drug problem firsthand, only to find that their hands were tied. The closer that US troops got to Colombia, the closer they got to drugs, confronting them with a mission even murkier than rebuilding a country. Their responsibility in the drug war was undefined. Drugs, once at the forefront of US policy toward Panama, had become a secondary issue in the post-invasion sweep."[34]

Colonel Linwood Burney, commander of the 2nd Brigade, 7th Infantry Division, had the mission of dealing with the PDF outside the Canal Zone. One of his areas of concern was the Darien, the thick jungle area south of the canal which abutted Colombia. Officially the US mission was to make a presence in an area in which the PDF was still acting like a military force. Burney, however, was also "concerned about reducing the long-term threat of drugs to the stability of the new

Panamanian government. His soldiers repeatedly stumbled across evidence of drug trafficking, particularly of cocaine. The province was a known thoroughfare for drug shipments from Colombia to North America. But the soldiers had no authority to pursue drugs at their source, i.e., the processing laboratories. They received a briefing from DEA officials in the former PDF garrison at Panama Viejo on what cocaine-processing laboratories might look like, but with the understanding that the DEA would act on any information gathered."[35]

Burney sent soldiers to watch areas of suspected drug activity. At one point the mission was threatened with cancellation by the Joint Task Force, after it received word of his activities. Burney never knew what became of the intelligence that his troops gathered. The brigade turned over its intelligence to the Joint Task Force, which in turn had the responsibility of turning it over to the DEA. It was one of the most frustrating aspects of Just Cause that the brigade was unable to act on its leads, Burney says. "I think we could have pursued some of the leads and produced hard results. But we were forbidden to even be looking for those kind of things. The drug thing kept coming out, again and again and again, to the point where we just couldn't ignore it. But we couldn't go after it."[36]

Operation Just Cause raised important questions about US drug policy and the role of SOUTHCOM in the implementation of that policy, specifically the ability and willingness of Southern Command to act in a supporting role to drug law enforcement agencies. Today, 6 years after the invasion, a number of issues remain unanswered, in particular the incident that triggered the operation. That "trigger" was driven by a unit that from that time until March 1994 played a pivotal role in CD activities.

The death of Marine Lieutenant Robert Paz at the hands of the PD, on December 16, 1989, was the spark that ignited Operation Just Cause. According to the Pentagon, Paz and three other officers had become lost while driving to dinner in Panama City. Taking a wrong turn they ended up at a PDF checkpoint near Noriega's Commandancia. When the guards attempted to force them from the vehicle, the officers sped off and shots were fired. Paz was fatally wounded and the driver, Marine Captain Richard Haddad, was slightly wounded.

Following what it considered to be an "extensive inquiry," the *Armed Forces Journal International* claimed to have "uncovered new details about the incident which seriously challenge the Pentagon's version of events surrounding the young officer's death." They also called into question whether senior Pentagon officials had access to key information about Paz's murder and had time to relay those details to the President before he gave the go-ahead for the invasion."[37] AFJI argued that it is "virtually certain that President Bush ordered the invasion of Panama based upon a sketchy, preliminary report of the incident-long before he, or his senior defense advisors, had time to delve into the glaring inconsistencies."[38]

The facts, as AFJI saw them are as follows:

1. "Three of the four US officers in the Paz vehicle were assigned to a small counternarcotics cell operated by the US Southern Command."

2. "Haddad—of Lebanese descent—told investigators that one of the persons who approached his car at the checkpoint "was Middle Eastern definitely not Panamanian. Israelis, among others, have conducted paramilitary training for Colombian drug traffickers."
3. "Paz was raised and educated in Cali, Colombia, where his family still resides. After his death, a US military officer told his mother that Paz had been awaiting a temporary reassignment to the US Embassy in Bogota, where, apparently, his unique qualifications would continue to be used in US counternarcotic activities."
4. "The area surrounding the Commandancia had long been a well-publicized off-limits area for US servicemen."[39]

The AFJI, intent on determining if the four officers were on a counternarcotics mission, questioned General Maxwell Thurman. The general responded in the following manner:

"I'm not saying they were on one or were not on one—I can't attest to that because I didn't have any cognizance at that instant over what they were doing. There are others who may provide clarifying testimony about that. If they had been sent on a mission, I'm not disputing it."[40]

The Paz affair highlights the tremendous impact of the Southern Command J3-DDD (Deputy Director for Drugs, Operations) on all counter drug operations. Created early on as a counter drug element, albeit a "small counter narcotics cell," the DDD (which took on an almost autonomous life of its own) grew like Topsy. Soon evolved into a section, from the time of Operation Just Cause onward, the DDD—for better or worse—would be the driving factor in SOUTHCOM CD activities. DDD, forged in the shadow of "WIMPCOM," created a new ethos for SOUTHCOM. Led by Colonel Keith Nightengale, former Ranger battalion commander and key planner in the Desert One debacle, DDD with its new "Strike Command" mentality, came to dominate SOUTHCOM CD operations. Staffed with officers with special operations backgrounds, Nightengale became a favorite of General George Joulwan. The end result was that between November 1991 and March 1994, the DDD was perceived as "calling the shots" in Panama and throughout Latin America. Nominally a part of the operations division, DDD demanded and got 20 analysts from the J-2, in order to create its "own" intelligence section. This virtually stripped the J2 of all its CD analysts. The DDD appears to have dominated whatever little CD planning took place. Shortly thereafter, what came to be called "surge" operations became the order of the day. Demanding that intelligence be made to fit the operation, the DDD drove a series of much-touted surge operations. The DDD was alleged to have provided the forces that killed Rodriquez Gacha, and was also the controlling agency of the C-130 that was shot-up after becoming "lost" over Peru. The presence of Nightengale's "spooks" was felt near and far. In short order, it became clear to the other staff sections that DDD was "the" force to be reckoned with. However, amongst the DDD analysts the word "surge" produced constant laughter because of the ineffectiveness of the concept. Even with the 20 pirated analysts, it is unclear just how much analysis and intelligence production really took place. The SOUTHCOM J-5 (Directorate of Policy, Plans, and Strategy, Wargaming Division) noted that, "the amount of intelligence data received at SCJ5-DDD exceeds its capability to analyze it efficiently. Local analysis is manual. It relies on memory and intuition." And while DDD uses JVIDS, like so many other "hi-tech" counter drug items that the military purchased, the utility of JVIDS is questionable. Tasked with trying to "automate" the counter drug intelligence process, the J-5 noted that JVIDS "is not a robust data analysis tool;" rather, its "primary purpose is data transfer."[41]

Because of the dominance of the DDD, the J5 was tasked with providing automated intelligence support to SOUTHCOM's "rogue elephant," instead of to the J2.[42] Although it is one of the first commands in the counter drug business, SOUTHCOM had only begun to look into some type of counter drug intelligence in June of 1992. Why the J5 was assigned the task of upgrading SOUTHCOM intelligence capabilities remains a mystery. Nonetheless, it was the J5 that sent its people back to the US to look at and capitalize upon whatever methods and equipment the intelligence community might have that would enable SOUTHCOM/DDD to get into the intelligence business. Turning to NORAD, with its Air Target Board, and to the 12th Air Force, Director for Operations, Narcotics Intelligence (DONI) with its Low Intensity Conflict Enemy Situation Threat Advisor software, the J5 argued that a "prompt implementation of analysis tools at SCJ3-DDD will give SOUTHCOM a jump start into intelligence data exploitation"—this at the eleventh hour. Further, the J5, noted that "right now, most drug traffic data to seed our databases can be obtained from DONI and NORAD. In addition, to support provided by the 12th Air Force, SCJ3-DDD will have self sufficiency and therefore, faster response and focus on SOUTHCOM's decision maker's priorities."[43] One can only wonder how much more "self-sufficiency" DDD wanted, or needed.

It is interesting to note that the DDD/SOUTHCOM focus was directed against narcotraficante air movements in the Andean Ridge production countries, not D&M support as the SOUTHCOM mission charter clearly delineates. In spite of more than convincing evidence that there are many more lucrative targets with the SOUTHCOM area, the obsession with the Andean Ridge continued unabated.

Commander in Chief, South (CINCSOUTH)

A former Corps commander in Europe, with no Latin American experience, George Joulwan took command in November 1991 with great gusto and much fanfare. A hard-driving tank officer, he blended his "spearhead" approach with the charisma of a newly minted politician.

Never properly briefed that the raison d'être of the Latin American military is one in which they consider themselves to be the final arbitrator of what is best for their country—regardless of constitutional considerations, General Joulwan attempted to implement the Andean Strategy. It appears that he never learned that the military in Latin America is a strange breed of cat, entirely different from the military establishments that he was so familiar with in Europe.

Unaware, thanks to the domination of the DDD and the failure of the primary staff sections to provide him with a solid grounding on the nuances of the game,

General Joulwan did not recognize the growing movement throughout Latin America that sought to hold the military in check in hopes of preempting new "men on horseback." The end result was Joulwan's overtures to the Colombian, Bolivian, and Peruvian military for their direct support in counter drug operations, much to the irritation of the civil governments. This was dramatically underscored when SOUTHCOM committed to Operation "Support Sovereignity." This was to be a coordinated drug interdiction operation (the term "surge" had fallen from favor) by the CD forces of Honduras, Guatemala, and Belize. The United States would provide equipment and intelligence support. Only after the operation kicked off was the South Command Operations Center jarred by the discovery that these were not NATO forces which could be ordered by a US four-star general to march forward in lock-step. Hours after the operation began, the command center in Honduras reported back to SOUTHCOM that Guatemalan commanders refused to put their soldiers in the command center under even the nominal control of Honduran officers. At the same time, Belize, hardly informed that an operation was underway, initially refused to allow overflights of its territory. A hapless drug runner accidentally stumbled into the operation and was snared. Within a short period of time, SOUTHCOM announced the "seizure," declared the operation a success, terminated it, and returned to Panama.[44]

"Andean Squares" and Counter Drug War Games

In September 1990, the Army Chief of Staff authorized Southern Command to use the US Army Decision Systems Management Agency to design, acquire, integrate, and implement a Command Management System to support the SOUTHCOM counternarcotic efforts. Designed to be built in phases, the first increment was to establish a baseline capability to support selected embassies in Central and South America, SOUTHCOM headquarters in Panama, and selected agencies in the Washington, D.C. area. The system was designed to support transmission and receipt of large volumes of sensitive, integrated image-voice-text data files and display such data in an integrated manner.

It was the hope of General George Joulwan that a network resembling the television game show "Hollywood Squares" could be constructed. With such a system in place, it was argued, virtual "eyeball to eyeball" communications (via interactive telecommunications) would be greatly enhanced, enabling the SOUTHCOM-directed "One Team, One Fight" initiative to function more smoothly, from Washington to Bogota. Fortunately, the cost of such a venture and the dubious results that might be accrued from it kept "Andean Squares" from ever coming on line.

What occurred instead, was the design and creation of the SOUTHCOM Counter Drug "War Games." Under the aegis of the J5, the first game—a developmental exercise—was conducted in December 1991. In spite of advice and warning to the contrary that the games must be viewed as the SOUTHCOM team aligned against a business—La Empresa Coordinadora—the game was basically a Cold War "Red vs. Blue" exercise. Game focus was on the "counterdrug operational and strategic levels, looking at a basic change in operational direction vis-à-vis the narcotrafficking and insurgency problem in Peru."[45] Emphasis was on the operational level, with interagency strategic considerations as a major factor. As it quickly became clear that the threat was a business, not the Soviet army, the follow-on games were restructured around a more realistic set of scenarios that portrayed the real world of drug trafficking.

SOUTHCOM CD "war games" must be regarded as a political success, albeit by default. While the conduct of each of the following games left much to be desired, the games had resulted in two important results. First, the concept of the "threat" as a business entity began to take hold. Second, and of the utmost importance, was the bringing together of all counter drug agency players in a central forum. There, the reality of the drug wars was brought home. Agencies came slowly, and more often than not begrudgingly, to understand what the real "game" was all about. By the time of the June 1993 game, all agencies were at least represented. The most interesting event at each of the games was to watch both the attitude and performance of the Washington Interagency Group. Their lack of knowledge, naiveté, and arrogance of the realities of drug trafficking was something to behold. Used to operating at "echelons above reality," the "nitty-gritty" of the real world came as a total shock. Driven by a professional "Red Team" that operated as narcotraficantes, each of the games proved time and again the conceptual failure of the Andean Strategy and continuing attempts by SOUTHCOM to make the impossible work. Building from a historical precedent and using current-time OSINT derived "ground-truth," the Red Team stymied the SOUTHCOM and country team players on every move. Red Team successes, structured on current narcotraficante business operations, appeared to mystify the Washington Interagency players. In several cases, this led to verbal fist-fights and the promise of physical mayhem. Interagency group comments to the effect that Red Team play was "a distraction worse than useless," as opposed to the majority of comments which indicated the value and realism of Red Team play, were in fact a testimony of their own lack of knowledge of the drug wars.[46]

Analytical Support Team

The one bright spot in Southern Command counter drug intelligence was the Analytical Support Team (AST). Beginning operations in January 1992, the AST was created because SOUTHCOM had a need for predictive, actionable intelligence—something the entire command could not or would not come to grips with. The idea of taking a small group of analysts, giving them information, not tying their hands with red tape, and encouraging them to think and produce predictive, actionable intelligence was given free rein. The AST was made up exclusively of reservists who did tours of duty for up to six months in Panama. For security reasons, they did not wear uniforms, nor was their workplace highly guarded. Tasked to provide direct support to DEA, the AST was involved in 8 major intelligence driven operations. They were responsible for breaking the code of a major drug trafficking organization, which in turn allowed them to "roll-up" the trafficking organization. In support of another operation they produced 35 flow charts of trafficking organizations in Guatemala and Intelligence/Geographic binders for field use by DEA agents. The AST was the only SOUTHCOM organization that was able to provide long-term support to the DEA.[47]

Major James Nicholson, commander of the AST, developed a close working relationship with the DEA in the person of Special Agent John McFarland, who envisioned a DoD-DEA partnership that could "stove-pipe" intelligence from the AST to agents in the field. It is much to the credit of Brigadier General Trent Thomas, the SOUTHCOM J-2, who gave Nicholson a blank check, and more importantly, protection from other SOUTHCOM intelligence fiefdoms. With Thomas's blessing, the AST named its own missions (read "Opening the Book to the Right Page") and operated without interference from the DDD or any other J2 elements. As a matter of course, the AST made end runs around the SOUTHCOM bureaucracy and turf wars to forge direct links with DEA field operatives throughout the theater. The DEA would place an "order" and the AST would respond to it, shipping out a product often within hours. The AST let the "customer's" needs determine the shape and size of the product. Timely and effective, the AST production system bordered on a market driven/intelligence enterprise. It was also viewed as a den of heretics.

In April 1992, Thomas came under intense pressure from the General George Joulwan to produce "tangible" intelligence products that would drive Operation "Support Sovereignty." Time was running out and no J2 element had taken the reins or produced any real products. Thomas had one shot and he turned to the AST. Within 20 days, the AST, drawing "ground truth" from the three host nations involved in the operation (including a collection team sent to Honduras) and using all-source collection, produced 113 target folders—in English, and in Spanish—for the operation.[48]

In early May 1993, the AST was disbanded by the SOUTHCOM J2. The successful production of timely, actionable intelligence products had sounded the death knell for the AST. Protection from on high was not enough. Professional jealousy on the part of a number of field grade officers brought an end to the AST.

The National Guard

The National Guard remains the unsung heroes of the war on drugs. Operating under Title 10 authority, they have provided support to law enforcement agencies around the country. This support is primarily logistical, with emphasis placed on sustaining law enforcement operations. With the exception of several Mohawk aircraft units that are equipped with electronic intelligence collection devices, the Guard has no intelligence units. Nonetheless, their contribution has far and away overshadowed anything that the regular military establishment has done to date. The key to success is that the National Guard understood its mission, supported it both in spirit and action, and came to stay for the long term. In reality, the only real effective use of military units in the war on drugs was done by the National Guard. Counter drug operations and programs conducted in particular by the California, New Mexico and Texas National Guard serve as a blueprint for the future. These troops do the foot-slogging grunge work of inspecting containers on docks, manning border crossing checkpoints, and manning ground surveillance radars along the border.[49]

United States Coast Guard

The Coast Guard deserves special attention because of its unique status and the fact that it could well serve as a prototype for a new model of federal law enforcement counter drug intelligence.

In 1984, the Coast Guard Intelligence Coordination Center was established in Washington, D.C. The center is a 24-hour substantive facility that provides current intelligence, all-source analysis and production, and indication and warning services for the entire Coast Guard. Most significantly, it functions as a focal point for access to the Intelligence Community and to the intelligence arms of the federal law enforcement agencies. It also ensures that CG intelligence reporting is quickly disseminated to the national intelligence community and in turn selects and sanitizes intelligence community reporting using established procedures for dissemination to CG units.

The CG is in the unique position of being both a federal law enforcement agency and a military service, so it works in both types of intelligence. However, since the primary operations to be supported are basically concerned with interdiction, the decision was made to model the overall intelligence organization and operations after the other military services. This was also more reasonable since the CG is an armed service, already fielding secure communications systems that are interoperable with DoD, and all but the smallest units of the Coast Guard are able to process classified material.

The CG also uses the same Intelligence Information Report format as the other services. Because of this military-oriented structure, the Coast Guard is the only law enforcement agency with a centralized collection management mechanism able to task field units and track intelligence requirements. This minimizes independent, unilateral field operations and maximizes intelligence collection and reporting to all levels inside and outside the Coast Guard.

Unlike other law enforcement agencies, the Coast Guard uses classified methods and sources when available and applicable. While most of the other law enforcement agencies attempt to keep classified material to a minimum so as to not complicate trial procedures, the Coast Guard uses classified information for interdiction operations. Intelligence sources and methods are protected in court by using procedures contained in the Classified Information Protection Act to prevent disclosure. In those rare cases where the judge has ruled that the information must be revealed, the Coast Guard has dropped the case rather than risk compromise. This has only occurred twice in the last twelve years.[50]

Intelligence, the Military, Strategy, and the Drug War

Carl von Clausewitz disdained intelligence. His remarks about it are mostly pejorative, and he limited his thoughts to three short paragraphs.[51] He defined intelligence as being among the least important factors of military activity. He relegated it to a secondary role in all aspects of war. In the war on drugs today, the US military exhibits the same attitude. In spite of testimonials to the contrary, the military establishment has not embraced intelligence as the primary tool that it brings to the war on drugs. The entry of the military and its role in the war on drugs has been both confused and unproductive to date. Operating for the first time as a support agency, the military establishment is uncomfortably feeling its way into the game. Focused in the past on a war in the European theater, the concept of attacking a business operation is totally foreign. Without a vision of the enemy as a business, something that may never come about thanks to the inability or refusal of military leadership to see intelligence as driving operations to support law enforcement, there are real doubts as to what value the armed services might be. By the time the US Army begrudgingly entered the drug war, Army intelligence—one of the key elements that could have made an impact in the wars on drugs—was in a state of disarray. Caught up in a major doctrinal dispute, distrusted by the rest of the army, and haunted by domestic intelligence abuses spanning the 1950's to the early 70's, Army intelligence today is at a crossroads. Whether or not those who wear the rose and the sword insignia can rise to the opportunity and the challenge presented by counterdrug intelligence will be driven by one factor: Army Intelligence seize the initiative and fix a place for themselves. Operations-driven drug operations simply don't work.

The GAO report, *Impact of DoD's Detection and Monitoring on Cocaine Flow* noted that the military had significantly expanded but not fully integrated national capabilities for detecting and monitoring cocaine. The GAO report suggested that the authorization act of 1989 did not define the DoD's "lead agency" role for detection and monitoring and conveyed no clear authority to allow DoD to control the resources or direct the operations of civilian agencies. The DoD has concluded that it has only "the authority to require consultation" and therefore can integrate detection and monitoring operations only with the voluntary cooperation of other agencies. At the time of a GAO team's visit in March 1991, DoD officials in the Caribbean had "largely settled for separate military and civilian planning, coordinated only to the extent necessary to avoid conflicting operations."[52] Not until July 1991 did DoD officials at the headquarters level report progress during the previous few months in achieving better integrated operations. In reality what this meant was that the DoD and federal law enforcement agencies had finally come to an agreement on the definition of the cocaine threat.

The Andean Strategy, an ill-conceived plan directed to solve the complex problem of drug trafficking has been a stumbling block since its inception. Set in stone in 1989, the strategy was the result of faulty planning, an approach by which the United States Government would work with Andean Region governments to disrupt and destroy the growing, processing, and transportation of coca and coca products within the primary source and processing countries. In September 1989, the president's National Drug Control Strategy directed that a five-year $2.2 billion counter narcotics effort begin in fiscal year 1990 to augment law enforcement, military, and economic resources in Colombia, Bolivia, and Peru. The Andean Strategy has met with poor response, both in the host nations, in the United States, and also among SOUTHCOM officers. As noted in Chapter 3, it is not in the best interests, nor within the power, of drug producing countries to stamp out illegal drugs. The revenue derived, between one-third and one-half of the gross national product of the production countries, more often than not dooms any plan that attempts to destroy drugs at the source. While the US State Department argues that implementation of the Andean Strategy has resulted in "notable achievements in many areas," the reality of the situation is total policy and strategy failure.[53] In retrospect, the Andean Strategy, much like the National Drug Control Strategy, was strong on hope but lacking in realistic purpose and totally devoid of "ground truth"—the critical information that would ensure successful policy and strategy construction and implementation.

Chapter 6

The South West Border: La Frontera

Despite its eminence as a drug conduit, there is a critical lack of usable intelligence information to support interdiction along the Southwest Border. Much of what is known resides in the files of myriad federal, state, and local law enforcement offices and is not accessible to the IC. A coordinated DoD, Law enforcement, and IC effort is required to centralize domestic drug intelligence, integrate foreign intelligence data, and provide actionable all-source intelligence for law enforcement interdiction operations on the border. The sharing and dissemination of both law enforcement and IC-derived intelligence data is critical to the development of predictive actionable intelligence. The IC must work with the newly-created JTF-6, and Operation Alliance representatives to establish a framework-with EPIC as the focal point-for the creation of an intelligence structure responsive to the needs of the border interdiction agencies. This framework must attempt to reduce redundancy and duplication to the maximum extent.

—Central Intelligence Agency, 1990

Written in Washington, DC, the opening quote is well intended but out of touch with the reality of the South West Border (SWB). The US-Mexican border is the place where policy, strategy, and tactics meet face to face with the day-to-day reality of the drug war. It is here along La Frontera that the mettle of the National Drug Control Strategy and the Intelligence Agenda is challenged on a daily basis. It is the place where the failure of the National Drug Control Strategy is clearly apparent.

BACKGROUND

On Sunday, September 21, 1969, the US government embarked upon Operation Intercept to deter and detect the illegal importation of marijuana across the

US-Mexican border. Heralded by US Customs officials as an "unprecedented historic effort" that "proved for the first time we could effectively interdict the flow of marijuana into the US," this new public policy was widely acknowledged to be the most extensive attempt in US history to curb the importation of illegal drugs.[1]

Operation Intercept was the highly visible implementation of a pledge made by President Richard M. Nixon to the American people that he would adopt strong policies in order to combat the drug abuse problem in the country.

This concentrated attack, waged along 2,500 miles of the US-Mexican border, represented a great investment of manpower hours as well as financial and material resources. According to the *New York Times*, "Operation Intercept is being waged by nearly 2000 agents of the Bureau of Customs and the Immigration and Naturalization Service. Working around the clock from the Pacific to the Gulf they stopped 2,384,079 citizens of the United States and Mexico at 31 border crossings in the drive's first week." This policy totally altered previous border inspection practices. As stated by the *New York Times* four days after Operation Intercept went into effect at 2:30 p.m. Sunday, in the past "inspectors took less than a minute to process a vehicle and its passengers. Only one car in twenty was given the present three-minute treatment, including thorough scrutiny of the trunk and engine areas, under seats, and behind cushions and door panels." This new policy "calls for a 100 percent inspection of all persons and vehicles crossing into the United States, and there are no exceptions."[2]

Operation Intercept was also being implemented by other means in the attempt to detect and deter all persons involved in the illegal drug market. As noted in *The Nation* on September 30, 1969: "It involves the veritable mobilization of federal agencies and the use of aircraft (both fixed wing and helicopter), patrol boats, radar, esoteric instruments such as people-sniffers and marijuana-sniffers and, above all, the full weight of the government's publicity apparatus." Further, as reported by *Newsweek*," A new system of keener radar will go into operation later this month (September 1969), and just two weeks ago the FAA issued stiff new rules requiring US-bound pilots to file flight plans before taking off from Mexican airports." The new policy was also aimed at destroying the supply at its source. According to *Newsweek*, "The task force suggested that the US supply Mexico with recently developed aerial sensor devices capable of detecting marijuana or opium poppy fields from the sky and also with benzyldiethyl amino benzoate, a deadly marijuana defoliant. Thus equipped, Mexican planes could fan out on search-and-destroy missions across the offending countryside."[3]

Under pressure from the Mexican government as well as Mexican and American businessmen, Operation Intercept was officially concluded on October 2, 1969. It was immediately followed by a new policy, called Operation Cooperation, which was publicly presented by John Ingersoll, former director of the Bureau of Narcotics and Dangerous Drugs, as follows:

Presently, a less economically severe plan called Operation Cooperation has replaced Operation Intercept. While this is also an intensive surveillance effort involving the cooperation of numerous Federal agencies and the Government of Mexico, it is less burdensome economically to those persons who are engaged in lawful commerce between the United States and Mexico.[4]

On March 11, 1970, more than five months after Operation Intercept was abandoned, a comprehensive agreement incorporating the goals of both Operation Intercept and Operation Cooperation was reached by the US and Mexican law enforcement officials. Noting that smuggling had steadily increased from the time Operation Intercept ended, a news release stated:

The recent easing of Operation Intercept, after pressure from the Mexican government, was only a shift in emphasis, Hundreds of extra customs agents are still stationed along the border, but they are intent now on the big time professional smugglers instead of tourists. At the same time the US, in an attempt to stop drug traffic at its source, has made available to Mexico an undisclosed amount of equipment along with American advisory personnel.

A Justice Department press release dated October 23, 1969, underlined the government's long-term projections:

The long term effectiveness of the program—now called Operation Cooperation—is expected to substantially increase in the near future because the Mexican government is cooperating in a concentrated, intense and joint effort to stop smuggling, to destroy the sources of these drugs in Mexico and to crack down on the large scale distribution systems.

Both news releases underscore the failure of policy makers and the Intelligence Community. The latter has never realistically portrayed the crucial role of Mexico in the drug trafficking scheme of things. The former, then and now, continue to seek a quick fix. As history has recorded, the aims and goals as well as many of the strategies and tactics employed during the days of Operation Intercept were incorporated into succeeding policies. They are still in effect today.[5]

LA FRONTERA

Stretching from Brownsville, Texas, on the Gulf Coast to San Diego on the Pacific Coast, the US/Mexican border is a study in contrasts. The reality of the border is little understood by Washington bureaucrats and policymakers. Rather than an arbitrary line separating two countries, La Frontera is a state of mind that stretches for fifty to one hundred miles on either side of the border. Its magnitude is awesome in scope and often impossible to comprehend in operational terms. It is an area in which the law on both sides has been the traditional enemy. Vast and deceptively open, it has been the place of smugglers and contrabandistas for two centuries. Contrary to popular belief, the southern border of the United States is little more than a three-strand fence that rambles from the Gulf of Mexico to the California coast. With the exception of heavy fencing near El Paso, Texas, and San Ysidro, California, the border is easily crossed by anyone. It is not a question of if it can be crossed, but where.

Representative of the contrast of La Frontera is the border between New Mexico and Mexico. Sitting on an outpost atop Guzman Mountain near the "boot heel" of New Mexico, one is struck by the almost ocean-like vastness of the rugged terrain. As far as the eye can see, the sparse vegetation of the high desert stretches to the horizon. To the west, toward Deming, New Mexico, with its tethered aerostat, is the country of Geronimo and General Crook. There, in the late 1870's and 1880's, US cavalry chased the elusive Apache into the Sierra Madres. Starting a campaign in the spring of 1873, the troopers returned to Fort Wingate some nine months later with their uniforms worn to rags, their boots replaced by makeshift moccasins, and most of the troopers wearing only long underwear. The terrain today is equally unforgiving and porous as it was then. At night, to the east, in distinct contrast to what appears to be the barrenness of the high desert, one can just discern the lights of El Paso del Norte. Today, El Paso, Texas, is a modern, bustling border city situated across the Rio Grande from Cuidad Juarez. It is also El Paso de Las Drogas. Here, as is the case with all other South West Border crossings, the El Paso port of entry is a primary entry point for vehicular drug traffic from Mexico.

THE THREAT

In Chapter 4, "The Threat," I constructed a picture of the drug trafficking threat in the cocaine production and source countries. What follows is a picture of drug trafficking along La Frontera, drawn from a Drug Enforcement Administration report entitled, *The Pablo Acosta Organization:*

Acosta's organization is very fluid and many of the members know only the person with whom they deal directly. Because of this, Acosta is very well insulated. Being a blood relation or having a long-time family or business relationship is the exclusive qualification for membership. The organization is extremely difficult to penetrate because of this criteria for membership.

The Acosta organization accomplishes its smuggling operations mostly by land and sometimes by private aircraft. Acosta's heroin is noted for its high purity, known to be as high as 93 percent, which is known as black tar due to its appearance. His marijuana has improved, with most of the recent seizures traced to the organization being of high quality.

This organization is also responsible for approximately 70 percent of all 4X4 and pickup thefts reported in the Texas Panhandle, West Texas, and eastern New Mexico areas. Thefts usually involve new and used Ford Broncos, GMC Jimmies, Chevrolet Suburbans, Blazers, four-wheel drive vehicles, etc. These vehicles are then driven directly to Mexico and traded for drugs. The Acosta organization is also a reported major receiver of stolen weapons traded for drugs. There are over 500 known members of the Acosta organization.

He pays a high level protection for this freedom from the federal to the local level of Mexican government and spends close to $100,000 per month for this protection.

Acosta directs his organization from Ojinaga with an iron fist and does not tolerate rebellion overt or covert. If a leak is suspected or if a member or associate fails to act as expected, they are removed quickly and permanently. He has a strict enforcement policy, which is killing the delinquent customer. Acosta takes a personal and active interest in any bad business practices or talking by his enemies or competitors. His killings are very flamboyant and are done in a distinctive manner as an example to others. He is a vicious and extremely dangerous person who has little regard for human life if it stands in the way of his operation. Although he is small in stature, he does not hesitate to become involved in a gun battle with his peers or with law enforcement personnel. Acosta has put out several contracts on competitors and has been implicated in two Hobbs, New Mexico murders and four in Mexico. His organization has been linked to at least twenty murders since 1982, and the total may even be double that number.[6]

This description of the Pablo Acosta organization provides a brief but comprehensive glimpse of a border drug trafficking organization. Its structure, however, reflects the basic nature of all drug trafficking organizations that use Mexico as their jumping-off point for the entry of drugs into the United States.

Today, there are approximately 150 to 200 Mexico-based groups involved in smuggling drugs into the United States. Established for generations, these groups are primarily built around close-knit family units.

In addition, the presence of Colombians has been established to the point where it is clear that the "Colombianization" of drug activities on the border has taken place. It is not surprising to learn that Pablo Acosta had allowed Colombians to warehouse cocaine in Ojinaga in the early 1980's.[7] This trend appears to be a repeat of a similar takeover of drug activities in Florida in the early 1980's by Colombian organizations. Additionally, growing reports of Peruvians, Bolivians, Salvadorans and citizens of other Latin American countries along the border suggests that the "mercado de drogas" or "la plaza" along La Frontera is expansive enough to accommodate all who can pay.

Under the concept of "la plaza," the drug trafficker buys his "license" or "franchise" from the local "jefes"—the police commandante, the mayor, the local military commander—or, in some situations, after negotiations with the local patron, mine owner, large landowner, rancher, or a major businessman. These same individuals also provide intelligence on competing drug groups and US law enforcement activities. Normally, these individuals not only represent the power of money and the "personalismo" that in Mexico goes with it; they also represent the Institutional Revolutionary Party (PRI), which has dominated Mexican politics since the 1920's. Large-scale corruption in Mexico is channeled and often flows through the variegated familial and elite associational patterns to Mexico City via the PRI.[8]

Writing in *Drug Lords and Narco-Corruption*, Peter Lupsha argues convincingly that even with the major personnel changes that took place in the Mexican judicial and police agencies during the early days of the Salinas administration, the new cast of players were as deeply involved as their predecessors.[9] This holds true in the Zedillo administration.

Corruption is such a persistent fact of Mexican political life that the US handbook on Mexico includes it under "The Rules of Political Competition." It is "both the glue that holds the Mexican system together and the oil that makes it work."[10] There are two major forms of corruption; *la mordida*, the bribe paid to low-level officials, and, large-scale corruption "such as kickbacks from contracts, insider financial deals and the like."[11]

The narcotraficantes who operate along La Frontera have the best equipment that money can buy—secure communications, radio monitoring capabilities, night vision devices, and automatic weapons—thanks to virtually unlimited budgets. Of equal importance, those dollars also enable them to buy information on both sides of the border. The result is an increasingly sophisticated intelligence and counter-intelligence system that identifies upcoming operations, undercover activities, and intelligence initiatives and works to thwart their effectiveness.[12]

It is believed that as early as the mid-1980's the El Paso Intelligence Center (EPIC) was targeted by narcotraficantes. This effort was aimed toward learning the names, telephone numbers, home addresses, and automobile license plates of EPIC personnel. In addition, rudimentary but effective communications traffic analysis was directed against EPIC by individuals-both in El Paso and Ciudad Juarez-with ties to drug trafficking groups.[13]

The discovery of a tunnel running from Agua Prieta, Sonora, to Douglas, Arizona, confirmed the ingenuity, financial capability, and technical application capabilities of trafficking organizations. Five feet high and four feet wide with a hydraulically controlled floor platform for entrance, the tunnel ran between warehouses on either side of the border. It had been in operation for approximately eight months. It is of some interest to note that many border law enforcement agencies suspect that there are numerous tunnels under the border that are much more sophisticated than the Agua Prieta/Douglas discovery, some of which are thought to be large enough to accommodate vehicles.[14] One or more tunnels is believed to run from Juarez, Mexico, under the border to El Paso, Texas.

THE SOUTH WEST BORDER DRUG CONTROL STRATEGY

The National Drug Control Strategy (NDCS) of February 1991 noted that the success of interdiction forces in the southeastern United States and the Caribbean islands and sea had caused drug smugglers to shift their focus toward Mexico as a primary transfer point into the United States. Interdiction of drugs along the 2,000 mile border between the United States and Mexico poses a unique problem to law enforcement agencies, in part because drug shipments are all but lost in the large volume of legitimate commerce between the two neighbors, and in part because of the border's sheer length and terrain. Since the Southwest Border continues to be the principal corridor for moving drugs (especially marijuana and cocaine) into the United States, the area retains its designation as a High Intensity Drug Trafficking Area (HIDTA). Recent intelligence reports and threat assessments-which indicate a stockpiling of narcotics along the border and an increasing control of Mexican trafficking organizations by Colombian cartels-support a continued strategic focus on South West Border trafficking. Today, there is a consensus within the drug intelligence community that at least 70% of all cocaine entering the United States, is brought across the South West Border.

To interdict drugs shipped across the Mexican border, the US government continues to stress law enforcement efforts in this area, deploys sophisticated technology to monitor the enormous volume of relevant traffic, and cooperates, to an extent with the Mexican government in coordinating mutual efforts. These efforts are undertaken in accordance with the Southwest Border Drug Control Strategy, developed under the auspices of Operation Alliance.[15]

Published in July of 1990, the *South West Border Drug Control Strategy (SBDCS)* mirrors the national drug strategy and is intended to complement and implement national drug policy. The strategy stresses interdiction of drugs along the border and includes an expanded Department of Defense role to support this effort.

In light of the emphasis in the NDCS on cooperation and coordination of the efforts of law enforcement agencies at all levels, the SWBDCS was drafted by Operation Alliance after all concerned border agencies were invited to provide input to the plan. Operation Alliance came into being in 1986 with the mission to "foster and support coordinated drug law enforcement efforts in the southwestern border states, with emphasis on interdiction."[16]

With increasing pressure for tighter border control, driven by the lack of any measurable degree of successful operations along the SWB, the Office of National Drug Control Policy (ONDCP) sought to put some "teeth" into strengthening counter drug activities along La Frontera. Designed in 1994, with implementation planned during 1995, the National Drug Control Strategy's: 12 Month Action Plan for Reducing Crime, Violence, and Drug Availability, directed efforts and assets to the South West Border. The third target of the plan, an expansion of border control efforts, consists of the following initiatives:

1. ONDCP will attempt to coordinate and oversee a review of current drug enforcement efforts along the SWB and determine the steps law enforcement should take to effect a measurable reduction in the amount of illegal drugs smuggled across the border and a measurable reduction in violence along the border. The underlying factor here is that there have been no measures of effectiveness. With no one really in charge of policy, strategy, and results on La Frontera, efforts to see what is being done right, and wrong, fall through the cracks.

2. The US Customs Service has been directed to devote increased resources to seizing illegal drugs, arresting smugglers, and also to reduce violence along the border. In addition, Customs has been tasked with testing cargo inspection technology. The statement that Customs will "launch a reinvigorated effort" to fully identify and dismantle organizations involved in drug smuggling suggests that many in Washington are not happy with the Customs Service. Tasked with the impossible mission of trying to stop everything at the border, Customs is again placed in a no-win situation. With the specter of Operation Intercept in mind it should be clear to even the most benighted bureaucrat that the ports of entry are not the place where law enforcement is going to make major apprehensions. Rather, using a "tip system" driven by human intelligence (something that would provide insider information on drug loads before they reach the POE), coupled with a series of offensive efforts just north of the border, might well prove more productive.

The Valley Project which was announced in January 1995, is structured like Operation Alliance. This operation coordinates the efforts of 17 federal, state, and local law enforcement agencies, as well as military support, to deter the flow of drugs into and through California's Imperial Valley. The investigative efforts are supported by a Combined Intelligence Center. The Valley Project is supported by the California Regional Border Alliance Group. This organization consists of the following:

•   US Attorney's Office for the Southern District of California, is responsible for strategy, guidance, and prosecutoral support;
•   US Border Patrol and the Imperial County Sheriff's Office, is responsible for tactical control of the operation;

- The DEA and San Diego/Imperial County Regional Narcotics Intelligence Network, are to be the lead agencies for intelligence gathering;
- The California National Guard and JTF-6, are responsible for infrared scopes and sensors and border aircraft flights;
- The Immigration and Naturalization Service and US Customs Service, are responsible for surveillance and inspections at the POE's;
- California Highway Patrol, is tasked to provide enhanced patrol response in the area.

The FBI, San Diego County Sheriff's Department, Bureau of Land Management, California Bureau of Narcotics Enforcement, Imperial County District Attorney's Office, Arizona Alliance Planning Committee, and the Naval Criminal Investigative Service; each of which are tasked to provide support to the overall operation.[17]

As with Operation Alliance, the real question here is who really runs the show? Coordinating committees and alliances are no match for the stream-lined operations of the drug traffickers.

Operation Alliance

A September 1988 report by the General Accounting Office, entitled *Border Control: Drug Interdiction and Related Activities Along the Southwestern US Border* notes that:

As discussed with the Subcommittee, we could not clearly distinguish Operation Alliance activities from other existing law enforcement activities along the Southwest border. Participating federal agencies support Operation Alliance through their normal operating budgets, which do not specifically identify personnel, equipment, or expenditures associated with Operation Alliance. Similarly, drug seizures also cannot be separately attributed to Operation Alliance.[18]

The management of Operation Alliance rotates between US Customs and the Border Patrol, each agency assuming command for six months. Operations take place primarily within 150 miles of the US/Mexican border and in the coastal waters adjacent to the Texas and California borders with Mexico. Housed in a nondescript commercial business mall in El Paso, Operation Alliance has no command and control authority or budgetary authority. Membership is voluntary, with actual participation in activities and operations driven by the whim of its members. As a coordinating agency, it can only request that it be informed of member-planned and executed operations. Hence, it is not uncommon to find one agency tripping over another. In fact, it is the rule of thumb.

There is no common system for determining locations on the ground. Each agency uses a different method. The result is an operational nightmare. Fortunately, these near misses have not resulted in any friendly casualties. While coordination is slowly increasing for the better, there are numerous feuds such as the running controversy between Alliance and NORAD over notification and control of air operations.

The dispute between the Bureau of Land Management—the "landlord" for all public lands along the border—and other border agencies over notification of the bureau concerning all operations to be conducted on public lands will continue for some time to come. The number of near misses between the agencies operating along the border raises the question of future provisions for adequate command and control. In addition, there are no common communications networks, and of the existing networks, few allow secure communications.

Operational security (OPSEC) is a serious problem within Operation Alliance. There are strong indications that the majority of Alliance counter drug operations are compromised due to poor or nonexistent security.[19]

Corruption aside, the lack of OPSEC, when combined with a business as usual attitude, compromises counter drug operations at no cost to the narcotraficantes.

Over the past five years, an alarming increase in the number of allegations of corruption in law enforcement agencies at all levels along the SWB has been documented. This is but the tip of the iceberg.[20] It is not clear if Operation Alliance has taken this factor into account and addressed it through the implementation of a personnel security clearance system similar to that used by the Western States Intelligence Network.

SHARING THE SECRETS ON THE SOUTH WEST BORDER

The most important service that Operation Alliance has performed is a study conducted to determine if SWB law enforcement agencies would share intelligence. At the July 1990 Operation Alliance Joint Command Group meeting, it was suggested that a feasibility study should be conducted to determine what intelligence exchange and management might be supported by member agencies might support. In April 1991 the study was published.

A survey questionnaire was distributed to 1,741 state law enforcement agencies, as well as 15 federal agencies. The purpose was to analyze current computer capability and the extent of information/intelligence exchange. For the purpose of the survey, information was defined as "written or verbal reports, formal or informal, long or short, which describe an event, activity, person, vehicle, etc." Intelligence was defined as "processed information that has been evaluated, collated, analyzed, and reported."

The response was as follows:

Texas	17% (1,106 mailed, 183 returned)
New Mexico	17% (89 mailed, 15 returned)
Arizona	28% (116 mailed, 33 returned)
California	23% (430 mailed, 98 returned)
Federal agencies	60% (15 mailed, 7 returned)

The report noted that the overall survey response of 29%, was, "less than spectacular." This was interpreted to mean that, "Findings resulting from the responses especially opinions and attitudes, are fairly representative of the total, and, if a majority of the law enforcement agencies who received the survey had responded, the findings would not have been much different."

Of those surveyed, 90% indicated a willingness to integrate data from all concerned agencies into a single source for the South West Border. "Disturbingly," however, while 81% of the respondents indicated they would want access to the data of other agencies, only 67% would allow access to their data. In looking further into this question, it became clear that almost all respondents would only allow indirect access to their data. This question had an extremely low response, as for example, in California. Of 68 respondents with computers, only 46, or 68%, would allow outside access, 12 would not allow outside access, 4 might, and 6 did not respond to the question. Of the 7 (out of 15) federal agencies who responded, all indicated some type of access, mostly indirect. Of the 169 respondents, 128 (75%) indicated some sort of restriction on data sharing. One hundred and ten (65%) indicated the "existence of internal policies such as right/need to know, law enforcement or criminal justice personnel for law enforcement purposes, release upon approval on a case by case basis, use of passwords or codes for access or audit trails, formal memorandums of understanding, third agency rule, etc. (The third agency rule involves the passing of one agency's information by another agency to a third agency.)" Of the 353 respondents, only 169, or 47%, responded to the question concerning their capability to receive information from outside agencies via computer linkup. Thirty-five percent that they could receive information electronically. Most of the respondents noted that they could "only input information through manual means." Only 15 respondents indicated that some type of input could be accomplished electronically. Of critical importance is the fact that those respondents with computers indicated that their systems were primarily used for analysis in an "investigative, case specific nature." Nowhere in survey responses was any mention made of data manipulation for the purpose of creating predictive, actionable CD intelligence.[21]

Following the logic used by the Operation Alliance Study Group—that the survey is reflective of the entire law enforcement community across the four border states—then it appears that *less than 50%* of law enforcement agencies have computers, and, the majority that do, do not have the wherewithal for electronic data entry or connectivity. In terms of the latter case, 16 different operating systems were found to be in use of the 169 computer owning respondents.

The majority of survey respondents were not satisfied with the present situation, characterizing information/intelligence exchange as being "hit or miss," with actual "intelligence business" being conducted by personal contact and investigator meetings-in short, on a case by case basis. They cited "limited connectivity between existing and planned networks" and "limited integration of federal efforts with those of state and local."

The survey notes that with the "advent of asset forfeiture seizures and the lure of big cash returns, intelligence sharing has declined. Some investigators query systems but are reluctant to provide information to input. Fears of 'claim jumping' lucrative cases have prompted previously cooperative agencies to act much more cautiously." Additionally, "guarding drug intelligence and concealing major enforcement activities have created dangerous officer safety and resource misallocation problems."

One survey finding—the significance of which appears to have been totally overlooked by the Alliance Study group—suggests that "it has become increasingly apparent that the availability of public and commercial information is a necessity in identifying traffickers and organizations and their activities."[22] Similar findings were confirmed during the conduct of the Counter Drug Technology Assessment Survey conducted by Los Alamos National Laboratory during the summer of 1991. Initial results of that survey were even more pessimistic, for it showed that the majority of local law enforcement agencies do not even own a computer.[23]

To date, the use of open source materials has not been addressed. It is not yet clear if the South West Border Governor's Coalition will use open sources and OSINT as they gear up for the information sharing system.

JOINT TASK FORCE 6 (JTF-6)

On September 15, 1989, ten days after the president presented his National Drug Control Strategy, the Joint Chiefs of Staff established Joint Task Force 6. The secretary of defense announced shortly thereafter that the mission of JTF-6 was to serve as a planning and coordination headquarters to provide DoD support to federal, state, and local drug law enforcement agencies along the South West Border. Working to enhance the effectiveness of South West Border law enforcement agencies, JTF-6 handles all requests for DoD support. The immediate goal of the task force was to "significantly increase the pressure against all modes of narcotics smuggling along the border." This is to be accomplished through

- an effective command and control system;
- a system of planning to provide timely, flexible response;
- integration of all border intelligence systems;
- the ability to "contribute to the resolution of legal constraints.

The long-term goals is to "significantly reduce the supply of illegal narcotics across the border." This goal is to be accomplished by

- sustaining a close rapport with drug law enforcement agencies,
- sustainment and expansion of military operations,
- providing budgetary support for joint operations,
- the development of joint rapid response teams linked to an integrated C_3I system.

As was the case with all other military units assigned to support law enforcement there were severe growing pains. The command was unique in two aspects, it had no organic troop or equipment resources, and the personnel mix of JTF-6 appeared to be a balance between the four services rather than a balance of the appropriate skills required to do the job—a continuing legacy of the Desert One "jointness is goodness" mentality— that ensures that the lowest common denominator is the driver.

Initially, Joint Task Force 6 created "cells" which would provide support to each of the states at some point in the future. JTF-6 intelligence capabilities appeared to be predicated on the output of the Forces Command. The Operation Alliance survey noted that "the intelligence division (J2) of JTF-6 is fleshing out its EMERALD data base and eventually hopes to obtain connectivity with national level intelligence data bases." In light of my comments in Chapter 5, the role of EMERALD I, or II, is doubtful for JTF-6, or any other potential user.

Fused and analyzed intelligence products, though mentioned in JTF-6 literature, in reality were not the case. Speaking at the Southwest Border Seminar in Phoenix, May 28, 1991, Brigadier General Behrenhausen, who commanded JTF-6, told the four state audience that his command "was not in the intelligence business." He stated that his mission was to "coordinate things." He stated further that the El Paso Intelligence Center was the "JTF-6 intel center."[24] It appears that Behrenhausen's statement was primarily driven by the still vivid experience of his predecessor who had been sacked. Conversation with JTF-6 staff members suggests that the relationship with EPIC is tenuous at best. Task Force attempts to get EPIC to produce predictive actionable intelligence have been stonewalled. This situation does not appear to have improved even with the addition of analysts from the Defense Intelligence Agency to the EPIC staff. EPIC's refusal to allow military personnel into the center in uniform is indicative of the monolithic mindset and dinosaur style of management that has haunted EPIC.

With the assumption of command of JTF-6 by Brigadier General John Pickler, things began to happen. Smart, savvy, and personable, Pickler not only understood his mission but set out to carry out his "marching orders" to the best of his ability. Understanding that support of Operation Alliance—despite its checkered operational record—was an important first step, Pickler tactfully offered low-profile assistance. Aware that existing operational support reaction time was far too long for local law enforcement, he pushed to cut the turn-around time. JTF-6 intelligence products soon increased in quantity and quality. Thus, by the time that General Pickler was reassigned to Forces Command, JTF-6 was providing the type of support that law enforcement could use.

On October 1, 1995, Joint Task Force 6 assumed responsibility for all military support missions within the continental United States. Following in trace of Forces Command, which as a matter of policy had done as little as possible to support counter drug missions, it is too soon to tell what the impact of JTF-6 will be. South West Border law enforcement are not greatly enamored of JTF-6 and would prefer that they quietly faded away. Citing an aggressive approach which is personified by the vision of an 800 lb. gorilla attempting to dispense intelligence products in a military manner, JTF-6 assistance is not something many South West Border law enforcement agencies want to deal with.[25]

EL PASO INTELLIGENCE CENTER (EPIC)

Subject of controversy since its creation, EPIC was created in 1975 as an interagency clearinghouse for the analysis of acquired information and timely intelligence support to facilitate international interdiction, US border interdiction and domestic interdiction. Such a mission is impossible to execute. Chartered to perform three major missions, each of which are unique and more often than not contradictory in law, policy, and execution, EPIC has done none well.

The Department of Justice, in an internal memo, alleged that EPIC which receives, sorts, and interprets drug war intelligence data, is overwhelmed and operating on a "hit or miss basis." EPIC is operated by 12 federal agencies and is the primary clearinghouse for intelligence data on the movement of drugs and drug traffickers worldwide. According to the DOJ memo, EPIC is plagued by poor planning and major understaffing in its computer operations and is using some computer equipment which is "woefully inadequate." The report says narcotics agents often are unable to get information they need quickly enough to make decisions about suspicious planes or boats. According to EPIC officials, the center has been flooded with too much intelligence data and EPIC is "victim of its own success."[26]

The truth of the matter is that EPIC was never designed as an operational intelligence production center. Speaking to intelligence support shortcomings in collection and management at EPIC, the South West Border Drug Control Strategy states that "EPIC's current computer and communications capabilities require significant improvement to enable it to provide a more comprehensive intelligence and investigative support service. The Department of Justice should provide support for this enhancement."[27]

Additionally, the border strategy recommends the establishment of a collection management cell, with Signals Intelligence, Human Intelligence, and Imagery information sources to be carefully exploited. Regularly scheduled meetings are also recommended for the purpose of defining intelligence requirements. Strong emphasis is placed on encouraging EPIC to develop foreign intelligence.

In conclusion, the drafters of the strategy recommended that a two-way information exchange between the field and EPIC begin. This issue is the primary complaint from law enforcement agencies, who feel that EPIC is more than willing to take information but will not reciprocate. This problem was also addressed in the study on *South West Border Law Enforcement Computer Capabilities and Information/Intelligence Management Exchange* in which it was noted that:

The contention expressed by the IISS plan of the four states that existing federal centers do not service their intelligence needs is, for the most part, accurate at this time. But there is no reason to believe that this situation cannot be remedied. The fact is that state and local agencies do have access to EPIC, but indirectly through their state narcotics agencies. For whatever reason, political or otherwise, some local and county agencies choose not to utilize this method to access the EPIC source of information, or they are simply not aware of it." It is contended that such a network is necessary to fill the void in current efforts to collect, analyze and disseminate *investigative* information and intelligence required by *state and local* law enforcement agencies; and, further, that existing centers such as EPIC and FINCEN (Treasury Departments center for tracking the financial dealings of drug traffickers) focus on supporting *federal* agencies in their interdiction and financial disrupting efforts. It is contended that these federal centers were not structured, in terms of mission, staff, and hardware, to support the drug/criminal investigative needs of state and local agents.[28]

Border States Counter Drug Seminars

Some of the more useful activities from which to collect information and "feel the pulse" of counter drug activities along La Frontera are the Border States Seminars. They provide a forum at which the full range of topics relating to drug trafficking are formally discussed.

The third iteration of the Border States Seminar was held in Albuquerque, New Mexico, on January 2–4, 1991. Designed as a follow-up to a gathering held in Palm Springs in early 1990, the succeeding meetings were aimed toward discussion and resolution of problems identified by border states counter drug agencies. The January meeting was focused upon the issues of command and control, communications, intelligence, operational planning, and demand reduction/prevention.

As was expected, major interest by the participants was directed toward the first four issues. Of greater importance-and a factor that was overlooked by many-was the crucial interrelationship between those elements. While great effort was taken to identify these issues, no effort was made to pull the elements together to create the basis for a responsive, proactive system.

Soon to follow was the May 1991 South West Border Seminar, which was held in Phoenix, Arizona. There it was announced that overall drug seizures were down, street prices were holding steady, and drug production was up. In terms of actual interdiction, statistics revealed that approximately 60% of drug seizures were taking place after the drugs had crossed the border.

Following comments by Warren Reese, the coordinator of the Southwest Border High Intensity Drug Trafficking Area (HIDTA), to the effect that "we have turned the corner on drugs," there was a palpable rumble from the audience. Several law enforcement officers felt compelled to step up to the podium to question that assertion, some pointedly so. At that point, Reese felt it necessary to return to the podium to "clarify" his statements by suggesting that the corner turned was "a long one."[29]

Concrete discussion and attempts at resolution of actionable, predictive all-source CD intelligence-acknowledged throughout the conference as the key to success in the drug war, was glaringly present in its absence. The statistics mentioned early on were a reconfirmation of findings of a study commissioned by the New Mexico Department of Public Safety in 1989. In a survey entitled *Southwest Border Seizures: The New Mexico Corridor*, it is noted that:

The most noticeable statistic is the lack of cocaine seized by Customs and Border Patrol in the New Mexico Corridor. Cocaine is being brought into and transported through the state in large amounts as is indicated by other agency seizures in central New Mexico. The lack of cocaine seizures reported by federal interdiction efforts near the border raises reasonable operational questions.[30]

ON THE FRONT LINES

A review of the operational techniques of the Dona Ana County (New Mexico) Sheriff's Office (DACSO) reflects the mixed bag of border intelligence activities.

With jurisdiction from El Paso west to Columbus, New Mexico, DACSO faces the central thrust of drug trafficking activities into New Mexico.

Drugs are brought through the patrol area that DACSO is responsible for, by aircraft, four wheel drive vehicles, ATVs, commercial vehicles and by burro's— two and four legged. Drugs are crossed at ports of entry and, more often then not, by simply cutting the fence and driving or walking through.

Like the majority of local law enforcement agencies along La Frontera, DACSO is an all-source intelligence user. Information is collected on a "get-what-you-can, when-and-where-you-can" basis, from Customs, DEA, Border Patrol, Immigration and Naturalization Service, Bureau of Land Management Law Enforcement, local ranchers, Mexican federales, EPIC, JTF-6, the New Mexico National Guard-in short, from anyone who has something of value. The sheriff's office does not have a formal intelligence unit or intelligence center to work the border. A watch commander with extensive border experience is primarily responsible for intelligence activities. DACSO does not have secure communications capabilities, nor does it have special intelligence gathering equipment. The department recently received basic computers; however the information storage is centrally housed and operated by non-police personnel in an unsecure facility because of budget constraints. No one in DACSO has a security clearance. Consequently, even if the sheriff's office wanted to partake of sensitive intelligence, the wherewithal to do so is nonexistent.

With few exceptions, the hope and promise of counter drug intelligence, as envisioned in the National Drug Control Strategy and the Border Drug Control Strategy, is lost to the Dona Ana County Sheriff's office and their counterparts along the South West border.[31]

LOOKING AHEAD

In addressing intelligence analysis, the drafters of the border strategy suggested that there should be an emphasis on "predictive interdiction intelligence," as opposed to the present practice of working only with investigation information. Also recommended was the requirement to "establish a common data base format that can be understood by all participating agencies." Lastly, the drafters of the strategy argued for an "all source intelligence perspective concerning smuggling operations." That argument is valid today. In simple terms, what is needed is "local strategic intelligence," based upon evaluated information, that can be shared amongst law enforcement agencies.

The hope for automated distribution of information is far-fetched at this time, because of the lack of law enforcement computing equipment and a mindset and budgetary restraints that preclude such a thing. The hope of "sanitizing" federal intelligence and pushing it down to state and local law enforcement operations is also a will-of-the-wisp. It will not happen anytime soon. Federal agencies and the Intelligence Community simply have not given any thought to this, nor can such a thing be accomplished in reasonable time.

As was noted in the strategy:

Many of the drug law enforcement strategies require the establishment of a closer working relationship between intelligence agencies and interdiction agencies. Some strategies will require additional computers and security equipment. More importantly, it is the cooperation between intelligence personnel and their respective agencies that will have the largest impact on the overall success of the intelligence function along the SWB. Additionally, there should be an expansion and redefinition of what intelligence means to law enforcement. Intelligence should be more than just record keeping and statistical analysis. It should integrate all sources of information into a better picture of drug organizations and develop courses of action to defeat them. This is imperative if intelligence is to become a true interdiction multiplier.[32]

In spite of claims otherwise, in particular from Operation Alliance, intelligence on the South West Border is neither defined, integrated, or effective. The secrets are not being shared. It should also be clear at this time that technology is not a substitute for strategy. Unfortunately, this truth has yet to be learned along La Frontera. The chain of aerostats that are supposed to overlook the SWB are of questionable value. Frequently down for maintenance, they are operational only 50% of the time.[33] The fact that the C_3I West radars at March Air Force Base, California appears to have difficulty in "seeing" below a certain altitude causes many border law enforcement agencies to question their value in identifying potential drug laden aircraft. The situation on the SWB, much like the "McNamara Line" along the demilitarized zone during the Vietnam War, strongly suggests that attempts to rely solely upon technology, without a strategy within which technology is but a supporting element, are doomed to failure.

The situation in Mexico offers little promise of change in the future. That ensures that the situation on La Frontera will remain the same. Federal seizures of cocaine in the Southwestern states more than doubled from 1990–1992, representing one-third of the national total, according to DEA statistics.[34] Today, in January, 1996, they continue to rise. A partial reflection of the increase in drug activity is to be found in cash reserves in banks along La Frontera. During 1994, the annual cash surplus reported by the Los Angeles branch of the Federal Reserve Bank tripled to $9.3 billion from $3.4 billion in 1990. El Paso and San Antonio also are among the top five districts in the country reporting cash surpluses.[35]

The sixth year in office for the President of Mexico, El Sexteno, is known as "the year of Hidalgo." This tradition comes from the lines of a poem that states that, "This is the year of Hidalgo; he is a fool who does not steal something."[36] The reference is to the rifling of the treasury and the corruption and payoffs that have coincided with the final year of the president in previous administrations. What has become all too clear is that during the Salinas administration the curse of "el sextano"—albeit in a new manifestation, thanks to the influence of drug trafficking—has evolved into an every-day occurrence.[37]

Perhaps the closing words of Terry Poppa in his superb text *Drug Lords*, are a fitting summary of the situation along La Frontera and in Mexico today. Writing about the situation after the death of Pablo Acosta, Poppa observed that: "Things changed in Ojinaga for a while. But within a year, informants reported that the airlifting of cocaine to Ojinaga had resumed. One of the runways they were reportedly using was near the village of Tecolote, within view of the hill where Pablo Acosta is buried."[38]

Chapter 7

Getting It Right: Opening the Book to the Right Page

Intelligence is not the formulator of objectives; it is not the drafter of policy; it is not the maker of plans; it is not the carrier out of operations. Intelligence is ancillary to these; to use the dreadful cliché, it performs a service function. Its job is to see that the doers are generally well informed; its job is to stand behind them with the book opened at the right page to call their attention to the stubborn fact they may be neglecting, and—at their request—to analyze alternative courses without indicating choice.

—Sherman Kent
Strategic Intelligence for American World Policy

INTRODUCTION

What if drug war policy makers, after having their attention called to the stubborn facts they may have neglected, had the wisdom to request that open source intelligence be tasked to provide a policy review and evaluation of the war on drugs?

Sherman Kent argued that intelligence should not be an apologist for policy. Rather, intelligence has a twofold job: first, the exhaustive examination of the situation for which a policy is required; second, upon completion of the first task objective and impartial exploration of alternative solutions which the policy problem offers.[1]

The case study that follows, the master link in the chain of studies in this book is an exercise in policy and strategy evaluation guided by open source intelligence. It is the exhaustive examination that Kent argued intelligence should provide. It is also in keeping with the spirit of George S. Pettee's argument that the best way to chart a course of action that would provide guidelines for future US intelligence activities was through the application of intelligence as an evaluation tool. Writing in 1946, Pettee argued that "the study of the detailed record of our wartime intelligence is the most direct means we have to study the whole problem of how well we have learned the lessons of the war. For in intelligence problems all other problems of war and politics, from weapons and tactics to technology and economics and management, are brought to focus."[2] This is a study of the "lessons" of the war on drugs. The goal of this case study is "to provide a body of descriptive material which will enable serious public discussion to begin."[3]

A word of caution is in order. When properly crafted, open source intelligence products are significant for their breadth of depth, scope, and the accuracy of their findings and forecasts, the likes of which have caused many to argue that such products should be classified. Such a move would defeat the very purpose of OSINT. Nonetheless, such benighted thinking is still prevalent and promotes statements such as the following, from a spokesman for Lawrence Livermore National Laboratory: "The fact that classified information has appeared in print, on TV, in speeches or in open meetings does not make it unclassified."[4]

What really constitutes "classified" intelligence on the one hand, and open source intelligence on the other, will have to be resolved by the Intelligence Community. The present knee-jerk approach to the classification of intelligence is a prime hurdle to be overcome. But progress is being made. In an address entitled "Teaching the Giant to Dance: Contradiction and Opportunities within the Intelligence Community," the deputy director of the CIA, Admiral William Studeman noted that "open sources have proven to be enormously valuable to intelligence. In my view open sources should be the Community's first step to satisfy our information needs."[5] While these comments were in part "sound-bites" aimed at pacifying a particular audience, the reality of the situation is that OSINT has taken root. While the Office of the Open Source Coordinator has not moved with the speed and zeal that many hoped for, nonetheless the process of recognition and implementation has at long last begun.

DEFINING THE THREAT

The single most important service that intelligence can provide in the war on drugs is a definitive picture of the drug trafficking threat. This picture should be dynamic and ever-changing so as to make the threat definition foremost and clear.

LA EMPRESA COORDINADORA

As described in the initial threat definition in Chapter 4, the concept of La Empresa Coordinadora remains firmly entrenched today. A loose confederation of families and associates, La Empresa remains a familial collection of organizations engaged in trafficking activities. While the DEA holds that La Empresa is a vertically integrated, almost monolithic organization, extensive research strongly suggests that cocaine trafficking organizations can best be described in terms of tiers.[6]

The first tier consists of the Cali, North Coast (Atlantico), Pereira, and Leticia families. The Medellin family of Pablo Escobar has been decimated and its "market share" appears to have been seized by Cali and several new entrepreneurs, some in the Medellin area. Troubled in late 1995 by the capture or "surrender" of five of its top seven lieutenants, there is clearly a reshuffling with the Cali family and the manner in which the first tier does business. Well established, managed, and funded, these organizations appear to control approximately 70% of the cocaine industry.[7]

The second tier consists of the *Empresarios Nuevos* (new entrepreneurs). Spawned by the apprehension, arrest, maturation, or retirement of many of the leading members of the first tier, the second tier consists of Colombians, Bolivians, Peruvians, and a rapidly growing number of Mexican groups who seized upon gaps in the industry to set up their own operations. Internecine warfare in Colombia allowed newcomers to enter and establish their own operations. Thanks to the first-tier players' inability to render immediate pay for the finished cocaine product during difficult times in 1989–90, Bolivians, for example, set things in motion to expand beyond paste and base production. To a lesser extent, the same thing happened in Peru, but this trend has been somewhat balanced by the recent influx of Colombians. The second tier accounts for approximately 20% of the overall market.

The third tier, *Las Hormigas* (the ants), is a growing phenomenon characterized by individuals who traffic in small amounts of cocaine—from twenty to several hundred kilos. Having recognized the profits to be made, these individuals may be found using relatively unsophisticated means of smuggling. Collectively, this tier accounts for approximately 10% of the overall traffic, but is expected to show the most growth during the next 3 years. Like remoras around sharks, the impact of Las Hormigas will continue to grow.

It is important to note that the drug trafficking threats in South, Central, and North America have certain universal characteristics. However, depending upon the situation and terrain of each area in which they operate, narcotraficantes adapt with great skill to each new setting.

COLOMBIA

Colombia remains the home and corporate headquarters for most of the trafficking organizations. Franchising to other criminal groups—Italians, Russians, Chinese, Japanese, Corsicans; and, the further legitimization of our position here in Colombia and elsewhere are our working goals. As the supply of coca, diversification of refiners and refining nations has increased, competition has increased among some La Empresa associates, in particular rival nationalities. Demand in new market areas Europe, the Pacific Rim, as well as within Latin America, and in future Eastern Europe has blunted this. Wholesale prices have fallen within US markets due to supply, competition, and weakened demand factors, thus profit margins are much tighter than in the 1980's.[8]

To no one's surprise, with the exception of the US government, drug trafficking is not at the top of the Colombian government's agenda. Even with the death of Pablo Escobar at the hands of government forces and the incarceration of five of the top seven Cali lieutenants, the Colombian government must still focus upon a balanced approach to the real problems and opportunities that face the country. The development of the Cusiana and the Cupiagua oil fields, with an estimated 1.2

billion and 1.5 billion barrels respectively—the exploitation of which would establish Colombia as an OPEC caliber production country—is crucial to the country's
economic recovery. The protection and early development of these fields is the
bottom line for Colombia. Since the discovery of the oil reserves, the government
has begun to establish security zones around those two locations. The problem at
hand is how to project a positive security image in order to convince investors that
it is safe to finance petroleum production infrastructure.[9]

The attempt to build stability in Colombia has been dramatically thrown askew
by the constitutional crisis that griped the country in early 1996. Never able to distance himself from allegations that his campaign was being funded with narco-dollars, President Ernesto Samper Pizano appears destined to be forced from office. On
January 22, 1996, Fernando Botero Zea, former campaign manager for Mr. Samper
testified that the president accepted money from Cali narcotraficantes to fund his
election. In what the press called an "astounding exchange of correspondence" between the Cali drug mafia and President Samper's election committee, letters thought
to have been lost suddenly appeared on February 18, 1996. One was a letter to Samper
from cartel leaders Miguel and Gilberto Rodriquez Orejuela, complaining that Samper
was not living up to the "accord" he made in exchange for the millions they contrib-
uted to his 1994 campaign. The other was a small memo to Cali listing the Samper
campaign officials authorized to receive cartel money. It was signed by Fernando
Botero, Samper's campaign manager. The notes did not provide evidence that Samper
knew directly of the Cali donations. They only mentioned him as an addressee, and
the president maintains that any contacts between Cali and his campaign were carried out behind his back. Writing in *El Tiempo*, the assistant editor of the Bogota
daily stated that, "the underlying fact we now have is that drug money infiltrated the
presidential election and was very likely decisive in it."[10]

Further revelations revealed that huge amounts of money were flown to several departments (districts) of Colombia between the tight first round of the presidential race and the second round on June 19, 1994, which Samper won. In each
region where the drug money was distributed, Samper's votes increased significantly. In Cordoba, for example votes for Samper jumped by more than 50,000
between the first and second rounds. Samper won the final by only 156,000 votes,
or less than 2 percent of the total votes cast. "Where the votes went up most is
where most of the money was spent," noted *El Tiempo* assistant editor, Enrique
Santos Calderon.[11]

Samper was exonerated in December, 1995, by the "commission of accusations" in the lower house of the Colombian congress. The commission said it found
no evidence against the president. As the commission was made up of members of
the president's party, requests for a second investigation held out little hope for a
different finding. There is strong speculation that Samper has already agreed to
leave office. "The man is packing his bags," says political scientist Sergio Uribe of
the University of the Andes.[12] In light of the request of many prominent businessmen to the president to withdraw from office, it would appear that only the details
of Samper's departure remain. Safe passage to Spain and a guarantee of immunity
from prosecution have all been mentioned in the capital press.[13]

If Samper does leave office, it is unclear who would succeed him. According to the Colombian constitution it is the vice president who would assume office if the president resigns or is removed. In his charges against Samper, Botero made it clear that Vice-President Humberto de la Calle had no knowledge of the drug money. If the election was proved to be fraudulent then the issue of succession could well be in doubt and the question of the status of Mr. Pastrana who opposed Mr. Samper could come to the forefront.[14]

The present crisis overshadows substantive issues that Colombia must address, constitutional crisis aside. These include:

- developing the oil reserves
- developing a realistic counter drug policy and legislation
- continue to grow a fledgling democracy in the face of deeply entrenched narco-corruption.

By a strange twist of geography and history, the areas in which the oil was discovered are the same locales in which the Revolutionary Armed Forces of Colombia (FARC) and the Peoples Liberation Army (EPL) operate. If the oil reserves are to be developed the guerrilla forces will have to be held in check. During 1992, 1,100 attacks on the primary Colombian oil pipeline and electro/communications facilities that serve that line resulted in the suspension of oil production. Crude oil had to be imported from Ecuador. In an attempt to turn that situation around, the Gaviria government initiated a $228 million antiguerrilla campaign. The monies from this program were to be used to attempt to professionalize the military, with stability the endgame. Funding for this effort will come from a "war tax" levied against the business and industrial community. The on-again, off-again peace talks with the guerrilla front organization continue to drag; however with priorities established, it is clear that the government is prepared to apply the hammer, even with a negotiated settlement seemingly in the offing. While the state of emergency has been extended from time to time, the government has at the same time instituted a number of programs each of which is designed to lessen the effects of the violence. A program to "insure" its citizens against "terrorist" attacks has been initiated. It appears that attempts to buy-out the guerrillas is having some degree of success. In part, because of the murder of more than 115 Colombian journalists, rewards for informants have been offered.

Although Colombia and the United States in 1980 signed a Mutual Legal Assistance Treaty, Colombia has yet to ratify the treaty. It remains to be seen if the treaty really is in Colombia's best national interests. During 1993, the criminal code was modified by the legislature making it more difficult to bring mid-level and senior to justice. While it was hoped that this would be changed during 1994, such was not the case, giving further rise to speculation on the extent of narco-induced corruption in the legislative body. The Colombian Congress did not pass bills introduced by the Samper administration to counter money laundering activities and asset retention by illegal enterprises and those who participate in them.

Of the 15,000 active criminal corruption cases filed by the Attorney General against government officials, 21 of those indictments are against members of the congress.[15] Amongst those alleged linked to the Cali mafia are Eduardo Mestre Sariento, former Liberal Party leader and congressman; Norberto Morales Ballesteros, former National Congress president; Rodolfo Gonzalez Garcia, former Controller General and former presidential candidate. Fernando Tello, a relatively new member of the congress was also linked.[16] The Drug Enforcement Administration claims that 50 to 75 percent of the Colombian Congress is influenced by the drug mafia.[17] During September 1994, a bill that would have diluted the existing illicit enrichment legislation—a move that had the backing of numerous narcotraficantes was defeated by the government. However, as in 1993, there were no arrests, incarcerations or fines imposed on traffickers during 1994.[18] On March 12, 1994, after almost a year of rumors and negotiations, Cali family leader Julio Fabio Urdinola surrendered to Colombian authorities 100 days after the death of arch-rival Pablo Escobar. Urdinola arrived at the Palmira penitentiary, 18 miles outside of Cali and turned himself in. Under terms of the new penal code enacted in 1993, narcotraficantes who surrendered to the government and disclosed the nature of their operations could gain leniency.

Beginning in 1992, the government began to track suspected drug aircraft on the return leg to Colombia. To date, the apprehension and seizure rate has remained extremely low. In 1994, Colombian authorities seized 28 aircraft and destroyed 21 clandestine airstrips. Many of the seized aircraft made their way back to their owners, while most of the airstrips were repaired and in use within a short period of time. In February 1994, the government authorized a force-down policy of suspected aircraft. Under specific circumstances private aircraft failing to respond to orders to land could be shot down. In May, citing concern about liability issues, the US government halted the sharing of information on suspect flights. In addition the US stopped the sharing of law enforcement information provided by the US Justice Department because of the Colombian governments inability to protect that information.[19]

The Colombian government sought and won passage of legislation to legalize the herbicide glyphosate for use against coca cultivation. In December, 1994, a coca growers protest brought the eradication program to a virtual halt.[20] Government seizures of cocaine (62 metric tons) in 1994 were above 1993 seizures, but still below the 1991 total of 86 metric tons. There are an estimated 111,000 (45,000 hectares) of coca being cultivated in Colombia today. This reflects a 13 percent increase over 1993 figures. Should this trend continue, Colombia will be capable of producing its own raw product, thus enabling it to surpass Bolivia as the second largest source of coca after Peru. And, in spite of US provided air and herbicide assets, the amount of opium poppy eradicated was almost 50 percent less than in 1993.[21]

Unusually adept at restructuring their operations, the Cali mafia appear to always be one step ahead of the law. Colombian law enforcement believes that the Cali family has devised a new strategy of maneuvering its entire logistical apparatus towards other regions of the country and abroad in order to prevent attacks against their operations in the Valle del Cauca.[22] The Cali mafia has evolved its drug trafficking activities into a business conglomerate that has three main operating divisions. There is an armed branch which provides protection to key family members and provides an umbrella to those areas of business operations that require special attention. The financial sector operates close liaison with groups in the metropolitan area and other key cities that have ties with useful political, legal, public relations, and legislative organizations and agencies. The intelligence function deserves special mention since Cali has institutionalized their intelligence apparatus. Centered around an operational nucleus of former military intelligence officers and non commissioned officers, Cali intelligence is centered around three activities; active intelligence, communications intelligence, and counter-intelligence. Communications intercepts are of key importance to the Cali mafia. During a May 1994 raid it was discovered that the commo-intercept section was actively monitoring the Metropolitan Police, the Valle Police, the military air base, the Colombian Army's Third Brigade, and the Cali Airport. The government's 12 Immediate Action Centers were also believed to be monitored by Cali intelligence.[23] They are believed to have purchased HF radios equipped with frequency changing devices that make them very difficult to intercept. In addition the intelligence division has purchased control of a pager company. Top of the line computers capable of intercepting and storing conversations on 180 telephone lines have been confiscated by the Search Bloc Police.

The political power of the narcotraficantes which is bought by approximately $3–7 billion back into Colombia each year is rapidly growing. A study of documents captured after the death of Pablo Escobar revealed that he had compromised or bribed key politicians, judges, and military officers. The documents suggest that Escobar had reached out beyond Colombian borders to people close to former Venezuelan president Carlos Andres Perez and into Cuba all the way up to Raul Castro.[24] Search Bloc (special police) report that the Cali family had "bought" almost the entire Cali Police Department—117 officers—of which 10 officers and 7 agents were immediately dismissed. In addition, the entire Cali Airport police force was fired en masse.[25]

Members of the technical staff of the Cali prosecutor's office were found listed amongst those who were in the pay of Cali. Also noted in the records were a large number of employees from Cali banks, customs and civil aeronautic's officials, and employees of the El Valle telephone company. During June and July 1994, 18 murders were committed in El Valle de Cauca Department. Each of those killed was in some way connected to private and state agencies that handled telecommunications in the Valle. Colombian police believe that each person was involved in Cali communications and security systems intelligence gathering and communications counterintelligence. A list of 200 telephone numbers, each related to investigations being conducted by the Regional Prosecutor were discovered.[26]

The sophistication of the Cali mafia warrants close attention. Using a combination of intimidation and very selected violence, the drug mafia has taken the concept of *plata o plomo* to new heights. Their public relations efforts are personified in the use of beauty queens and soccer teams. They have infiltrated the government, army, court system, and the banking sector. It is estimated that there are 5000 mafia collaborators. They have shown brilliance in developing a positive image making strategy seeking both nationalist and pacifist support for their regime. Recently they have incorporated a new tactic of moral terrorism. The Ministry of Defense claims to have evidence that the mafia has made sizable deposits into bank accounts in Colombia and abroad in the names of honest individuals, thus enabling the family to wrongly indict government officials who refuse to cooperate with them.[27]

The network spun by Cali ranges from a fleet of taxi drivers-equipped with cellular telephones that enable them to report in from throughout the city, to close ties with the most well-known firms. Money is laundered through medicine and cosmetic distributors, poultry and agribusiness firms, construction companies, cultural organizations and the largest banks. During July 1994, 171 people employed in the construction industry met untimely deaths. Rumors circulated that these murders were committed to silence workers who had a hand in construction of tunnels and hideaways of the narcotraficantes.[28]

US government officials continue to criticize the Colombian government for what they perceive as its soft treatment of traffickers. The US State Department noted in its annual INCSR that "widespread corruption as well as intimidation by traffickers complicated the drug control effort of many Colombian institutions." Adding insult to injury, Senator John Kerry, Chairman of the Senate Foreign Relations Committee wrote in a Washington Post article in 1994 that, "recent actions and statements by Colombia's chief prosecutor threaten to bring about his nation's capitulation to the Cali cocaine cartel." The infuriated response from the Colombian government and news media was immediate and vitriolic. In a strongly worded diplomatic note, Colombian ambassador Gabriel Silva wrote that "The Colombian government vehemently rejects the affirmation that Colombia is a narco-democracy."[29]

The key to understanding the types of policy decisions that must be made by the Colombian government is to be found in its desire to minimize the violence associated with drug trafficking. Colombia is tired of the violence. From 1988 to the end of 1989, the period of the greatest violence from the drug wars, more than 40,000 people were killed. By the end of 1990, 25,000 Colombians had died in the escalating violence that attacked every segment of society.[30] When queried after the death of Pablo Escobar, 76% of Colombians stated that they would rather he had surrendered. Over half of those polled did not expect drug trafficking to decline and 34 percent stated that law and order would not be affected by Escobar's death.[31]

The demise of the Medellin mafia following the death of Pablo Escobar signaled the end of one criminal organization and its trademark violence. It does not mean that drug trafficking is over. The Medellin cartel has been dismantled, and the Ochoa brothers are in prison awaiting trial. But the drug-trafficking business continues unabated adapting to new opportunities in the international markets. After the death of more than 60,000 people in Colombia in the past five years, among them more than 1,000 policemen, 60 judges, 70 journalists, 1,500 leftist union and political leaders, an attorney general, two cabinet ministers, four presidential candidates, a governor, and several police chiefs, Colombia has finally managed to dismantle the most virulent and vicious drug cartel in the world.[32] Ironically, it was the Cali mafia that in large part helped to still the violence. "It was one thing to fight among themselves, but attacking government and civilian targets was something else. They [Cali] rejected the violent actions taken by Medellin using words that could have come right out of a movie: It's bad for business."[33]

In balance, it is important to take note of the fact that violence in Colombia has lessened. This factor coupled with time to both stabilize and afford narcotraficantes the opportunity to legitimize should provide Colombia with breathing space. The presence of a growing drug addiction problem might well prove to be the catalyst for real Colombian interest in the domestic aspect of drug production. 1995 proved to be a banner year for the apprehension of key narcotraficantes. In May the government offered a $1.5 billion peso (approximately US $1.7 million) reward for information resulting in the capture of the Rodriquez-Orejuela brothers. A month later special police arrested Gilberto Rodriquez-Orejuela in Cali. In early August, brother Miguel was also captured. In July, Jose Santacruz-Londono, believed to be the number three man in the Cali family was arrested. During this time, three high-ranking Cali lieutenants surrendered to Colombian authorities. What at first was touted as a major blow to drug trafficking was not. These arrests appear to have had no impact on the flow of drugs from Colombia. The January 1996 "walkaway" from prison by Jose Santacruz-Londono raised again the issue of capture and surrender and the deep penetration of the Colombian government by the drug mafia.

Lengthy incarceration under conditions that isolate the key traficantes from their business associates appears to be the key in attempting to stymie the drug families. Such sanctions, however, do not appear likely. In November of 1994, Ivan Urdinola Grajales was approaching the end of his four year sentence. This sentence—a mere slap on the wrist given the indictments against him—was brought about when a Colombian judge, citing Julio Fabio Urdinola's confession and his "cooperation with justice," levied the minimal decree.[34]

Always alert to market fluctuations and the need to adapt their organization to the ebb and flow of the market place, the Cali mafia are now in a transition period. Arguing that the need to launder money was their downfall, Francisco Thoumi of the University of the Andes says that "it became impossible for even a group so sophisticated as the Cali cartel to find enough legitimate investments for their cash, and they were exposed. Every illegal organization needs a base where it can bribe officials to keep out of trouble and safely launder the bulk of its income, but Colombia's ability to absorb it limited."[35]

It is for this reason that cocaine operations appear to have shifted to Mexico and why there is strong argument for Brazil as the next trafficking growth area. The growth of cartelitos (little cartels)—operated by the new entrepreneurs of the second tier—seemed destined to fill part of the vacuum created by the lessened activity of the super drug mafia's. Salomon Kalamanovitv, director of Colombia's central bank notes that "there are indications of about a $1 billion decline in Colombia's share of the wholesale cocaine market over the last eight months." He attributes this drop to the mounting cost of the illegal drug trade in Colombia after a year of increased drug seizures, stepped-up crop eradication, and dozens of high-profile and less-touted arrests of cartel operatives.[36] Always adroit, the Cali mafia can be expected to focus more on their legitimate holdings, managed with the help of the bevy of high-powered business managers they have cultivated from among the world's best business schools. Illegal drugs will still be a profitable part of the ledger, but at a reduced and less ostentatious level. From his jail cell in Bogota's Picota Prison, Gilberto Rodriquez Orejuela has baptized this the "new cartel." The "new cartel" will not be easy to attack. The Cali mafia alone is believed to own more than 100 legitimate companies in the US which are involved in everything from car sales to pharmaceuticals.[37]

On January 29, 1996, assassins killed Felipe Lopez, the former director of Colombia's federal prosecutors office, outside of his apartment in Bogota. The police had no suspects, and speculation ran the gamut from a government ordered hit to one arranged by traffickers. As regional prosecutor, Lopez was in a position to know about donations from the Cali mafia to the Samper campaign.[38]

What the future holds for Colombia remains to be seen. A new president will soon be ensconced, one with a clear mandate that narco-corruption must be overcome. No matter who dons the presidential sash it will take time for Colombia to press on through the storm, assaulted on the one hand by internal forces, and on the other, by an unrealistic drug policy that the United States continues to push. This time frame will last at least a generation, a period of time in which governmental crisis and the growing legitimitization of the narcotraficantes will run together, hand in hand.

BOLIVIA

> Luis, I want you to come and see our facilities, with your own eyes. We have landing fields big enough to accommodate a 747. In the jungles, near the Brazilian border, we have built whole cities underground. I do not exaggerate, Luis. Come see for yourself. The Colombians think they own us. They pay what they want and then overcharge the Americans. If we could find the right American customers, we could eliminate them from the middle.
> —Jorge Roman, narcotraficante, to Mike Levine
> *Deep Cover*

The election of Gonzalo "Goni" Sanchez de Lozada, on June 6, 1993, had Bolivians in La Paz dancing down the Prado chanting over and over, "the corruptos are leaving." The wide margin of victory appeared to give hope to "Goni's" campaign pledge to fight "hypercorruption." As planning minister in the mid-1980's, Sanchez de Lozada won well-deserved recognition for taming Bolivia's hyper-inflation. Bolivian democracy, barely a decade old, faces monumental challenges. As is the trend throughout Latin America, so in Bolivia has there been the hue and cry for the end of the use of public office as a platform from which to generate personal wealth. Although the Bolivian constitution requires an absolute majority Sanchez de Lozada was confirmed as the president elect with approximately 36% of the vote. Garnering only 15% of the vote, General Hugo Banzer, an early favorite, conceded the election, ensuring that the country would not have to go through weeks of haggling in the Congress. Frequently compared to Mexico's notoriously corrupt Institutional Revolutionary Party, Sanchez de Lozada's Revolutionary National Movement Party is now at center stage.

Modern Bolivia is built upon the events of the revolution of 1952. Memories of a severe beating by the police forces during the revolution still haunt the army. Today, the army makes every attempt to limit the role of police forces for CD work or any paramilitary role. In turn the government fears any expansion of missions for the army. While the government will take US CD monies, they have successfully resisted US attempts to bring the military into the picture, fearing any wider use of the army.

The government has traditionally looked down upon the campesinos on the one hand and fears them on the other, backing down to their requests while attempting not to honor them. Starting with the near riots during Operation Blast Furnace in 1985 which effectively put an end to any other similar US ventures in Bolivia, to present-day protests over eradication, the campesino is a force to be reckoned with. Cocaleros make up one-fourth of the Bolivian congress, thus ensuring that any attempt at coca eradication are always high-profile and unpopular.

Corruption, nepotism, and favoritism are widespread. Police positions are "sold" as are positions within the judicial system, and the drug traffickers have "bought" into all political parties. In addition, Bolivia has a history of regional disputes, the primary one being the removal of the capital at Sucre and its placement at La Paz. Infighting between the central government and the nine departments to determine who has control remains fierce today. Bolivia has no effective apolitical institutions. The military and police are divided by political and party loyalties. Below the top levels, jobs are given to political hacks and relatives. With a combination of highly centralized government, little government presence in the countryside, and limited funds, little happens.

While most politically aware Bolivians understand the nature of the drug problem the majority believe that coca and cocaine are important economically and that the overall issue presents few costs to the country. In a 1989 poll, drugs ranked last out of 40 issues affecting the country. Bolivia is willing to permit certain US CD activities, but only on a quid pro quo basis, i.e., sizable economic assistance. The relationship between the US and Bolivia appears more often than not to be competitive rather than cooperative. While the internal drug abuse problem is growing, most Bolivians don't see the problem. Partly because of the relative lack of violence associated with drugs, most Bolivians see the problem as a struggle between foreign consumers and foreign cocaine manufacturers.

During 1994, Bolivia was the world's second largest cultivator of coca. Coca leaf production of approximately 89,000 metric tons, is the largest tonnage yet produced in Bolovia. Most of the Bolivian-produced cocaine base is transported to Colombia for conversion to cocaine hydrochloride.[39] In an attempt to lessen the tracking of cocaine products, odorless chemicals such as nitric acid are being substituted for kerosene, acetone, sulfuric acid and sulfuric ether.[40]

On March 11, 1994, Bolivia's former dictator Luis Garcia Meza was arrested in Sao Paulo, Brazil. Garcia Meza, known as the "cocaine dictator," due to his connections to cocaine trafficking organizations had been sentenced to 30 years imprisonment in absentia. Bolivian authorities also arrested Jose Faustino Rico-Toro and Issac Chavarria, both of whom were connected to the Medellin mafia. Rico-Toro is believed to have been involved in the shipment of cocaine from Bolivia to Miami since the early 1980's. On March 31, 1995, he was extradited to the United States to face drug trafficking charges.[41] In spite of the apprehension and surrenders of narcotraficantes there is still great concern that they will escape the full measure of punishment thanks to the lenient terms of the Repentance Law. By late November 1994, two of seven narco bosses who were sentenced in 1991 were on parole with five more soon to follow.[42]

As in the case of Peru, the US government has again cited vital national security interests as the basis for recertifying Bolivia's counter drug program. Denial of certification would likely terminate much of Bolivia's multilateral development bank assistance, which would have an extremely harmful effect on the Bolivian economy. It would reduce significantly the resources available to the GOB to combat narcotics trafficking and would foster conditions in which more Bolivians would be driven to engage in illicit coca cultivation and trafficking. Because the World Bank and Inter-American Development Bank are Bolivia's largest aid doors, USG opposition to loans to Bolivia by those institutions would result in strident calls within Bolivia for the GOB to cease its counternarcotics cooperation with the USG. Economic instability could lead to a loss of confidence throughout the country and thereby serve to undermine Bolivia's still-fledging democratic institutions. Should Bolivia's current democratically-elected government be followed by an authoritarian regime, narcotraffickers might gain a strong foothold, as they did in the corrupt dictatorships of the early 1980's.[43]

The 1995 decision by the US State Department to confiscate the visa of former President Jaime Paz Zamora, who served between 1989 and 1993, because of revelations that the ruling MIR party accepted gifts and cash from drug trafficker Issac (The Bear) Chavarria, will undoubtedly cloud relations between the US and Bolivia.

PERU

In early 1995, citing vital national security interests, the US government again certified Peru for continued assistance and funding for counter drug activities. Noting that a "decrease in narcotics with the Government of Peru would result in more cocaine entering the United States," the State Department went on to enumerate the reasons for concern on the certification process:

In 1994, there was no measurable reduction in the flow of coca base from Peru to Colombia and no systematic mature coca eradication. While the amount of coca under cultivation remained the same, coca leaf production increased by six percent due to new, more productive coca plantings in expanded new areas that are superseding older areas, such as the Huallaga Valley. There was no progress toward the critical goal of reducing mature coca cultivation. There was concrete evidence of refined cocaine HCL processing and shipment from Peru to Mexico by Peruvian trafficking organizations, raising the specter of Peru as a potentially large-scale cocaine refining and shipping center, similar to Colombia.[44]

As the world's leading producer of coca leaf, coca paste, and cocaine base, Peru remains a key element in the cocaine equation. During 1994 and into 1995, coca production shifted from the Upper to the Lower Huallaga Valley the Apurimac River Valley, and the Aguaytia River Valley. In the past five years, Peru has seized but 1% of the 600 metric tons of the cocaine base that is produced in the country.[45] On January 9, 1995, Peruvian National Police raided a warehouse near the northern Pacific coast Port of Piura and seized a record 3.3 metric tons of cocaine. This was the first confirmation that Peruvian drug traffickers could process enough cocaine hydrochloride to assemble ton-quantity shipments.[46] In spite of the shoot-down or ground destruction of 30 suspected drug aircraft between January and July 1994, cocaine base is flown out of the country to Colombia by twin-engine aircraft.[47] US information sharing was suspended in May 1994 after US concerns about liability for information dealing with airborne drug traffic. This ruling was reversed in December 1994.[48]

To understand the drug trafficking situation in Peru in early 1996, one has to reflect back on events that have transpired over the previous four years. The April 1992 autogolpe (self-coup) of Peruvian President Alberto Fujimori cast a new light on drug trafficking in Peru. Responding in typical knee-jerk fashion, the US government froze all counter drug funding. The move ensured greatly lessened US observations into the country and invited Peruvian responses that were less than friendly. On April 24, 1992, three weeks after the coup, a C130-H launched from Howard Air Force Base, Panama. The aircraft, which was crammed with sensors and camera's, flew toward the Upper Huallaga Valley. Following up on suspected links between the Peruvian military and drug traffickers, the aircraft, which was part of Operation Furtive Bear was tasked to apply the full range of technical intelligence assets against the valley. Their mission was to photograph airfields and coca production areas; and, also to record suspected radio transmissions between narcotraficantes and certain government agencies. As the aircraft completed its mission and headed toward the Pacific Ocean, the Peruvian Air Force scrambled two Su-22 fighters which strafed the aircraft, killed a crew member and wounded others; and forced it to land at Talara Air Base. The US government denied any wrongdoing, claiming the plane had wandered off course. The Peruvian government argued that they thought it was a drug aircraft and that the attacking pilots could not make out any markings on the C-130, nor did the blacked-out transport respond to radio calls. The end result was a stand-off. It would be a year before the Peruvians admitted they knew it was a US aircraft. The truth of the matter was that US Southern Command had been caught spying.[49]

Allegations of military/narcotraficante ties have continued during the Fijimori administration. Early on, Lima-based journalists alleged that following the autogolpe, files information dealing with corruption were destroyed. Vladimiro Montesinos, right-hand man of President Fujimori, a former army officer turned lawyer who had defended narcotraficantes, appeared to have acquired more power, becoming the shadow behind the president. New edicts allowed security and intelligence officers to seize any information vital to the "interests of the state."[50] On December 21, 1995, in a significant shift in policy, President Fujimori announced that Peru's armed forces would no longer be involved in anti-narcotic efforts. The president acknowledged that the military's role in the fight against drugs had been tainted by corruption. The announcement came as 11 army officers stood accused of collaborating with drug traffickers.[51] Fujimori praised the armed forces' efforts during 15 years of "internal war" against leftist guerrillas and noted that while not denying some cases of corruption in the officer and enlisted ranks, they had been punished.

Seizures of pasta basica in 1995 were half of what they were in 1990. Low morale and salaries are also responsible for the fact that the army loses one officer a day to the private sector. Not surprisingly, corruption abounds. During June 1993, National Police General Director Victor Alva Plasencia admitted that Dinandro (the anti-drug division) Director General Frank Reategui San was responsible for the release of drug trafficker Luis Molqui Cardenas Guzman ("Mosquita Loca"). Interestingly, not one major trafficker was apprehended during 1992; and, of the 600 tons of cocaine produced in Peru, only 8 tons were seized. (This was the same amount seized during each of the previous five years. It appears that the Peruvians have figured out that this is the amount that will enable them to meet US imposed standards while not over stressing the fragile political balance in the country.)

During 1993, responsibility for the Upper Huallaga Valley was turned over to the military. In spite of conflicting stories as to the effect of the coca fungus, there was a production shift to the south and the west UHV by the end of the year. The Huallaga remains a focal point for coca growth. The Peruvian Air Force controls 9 of the 30 legal airfields in the valley, but only from 7 a.m. to 6 p.m. Military helicopters (Soviet made, some of which had been recently acquired from Nicaragua) are used to transport drugs at $50,000 per flight. At airfields "controlled" by the army, each 500 kilos' worth costs $5,000 in "fees." Aircraft flights, the workhorses of the valley, are still the primary mode of transport and still total approximately 700 per year.[52] Operating in the UHV it was the activities of Demetrio Chavez Pena Herrera "El Vaticano," that epitomized the fear of the "Colombianization" of Peru. Supplying approximately 5000 kilos per month to the Cali group, El Vaticano allegedly paid "protection" fees of $300,000 per month to the military to operate unhindered in the valley. To further make the issue of eradication in the Huallaga Valley more difficult, leaders representing the 200,000 coca growers continue to demand that the government reject a US-Peruvian agreement which prioritizes a military solution to the drug problem, while ignoring social and economic dimensions.

Sendero Luminoso

Any discussion of Peru and drug trafficking is not complete without a consideration of Sendero Luminoso. In the weeks before the September 12, 1993 capture of Abimael Guzman, many analysts feared a victory by the Shining Path. Poised to invest Lima, the fear of a new Pol Pot regime was not far-fetched. With Sendero Luminoso in control of most of the departments in the country, Lima had been encircled and the real possibility of tightening the noose by closing the main roadway to the heartland of the country appeared close at hand. At the eleventh hour Peruvian intelligence and security forces seized Chairman Gonzalo. Overweight and appearing nothing like the bloodthirsty leader of the ideologically driven band of zealots who were about to seize Peru, Guzman was whisked away, tried, sentenced, and placed in a maximum security prison.

Testifying before a congressional subcommittee, Gustavo Gorriti argued that Guzman's capture did not, and will not, spell the end of the organization. On the contrary, much like Hezbollah of Lebanon, Sendero Luminoso has not collapsed, though it is changing. It is the nature of that reorganization that remains to be seen. To date, there has been a long pause, and then a series of attacks and assassinations, the likes of which reflect the old days. From a drug trafficking standpoint, knowledge of the new directions that Sendero might take is critical.[53] There appear to be two primary paths that Sendero Luminoso will take in the future. One would be to continue to be driven by the unique ideology that wreaked havoc throughout the country in the past. The other is a more capitalistic approach that continues to build upon the benefits of drug trafficking. Present information indicates that at least some Shining Path members continue to operate in the coca production areas and have forced the price of "protection" for the use of drug airstrips much higher than the traffic will bear. Brigadier General Eduardo Bellido Mora, commander of the Huallaga military command, stated that Sendero Luminoso obtains more than $100 million from drug trafficking.

While the new leaders of Sendero continue to endorse the message of Chairman Gonzalo, nothing appears to indicate that they are capable of a strategic reordering. Their increased violence and brutality appears to be playing into the hands of the government as more and more people in the countryside are providing information about guerrilla movements. Concurrently, government training programs to win hearts and minds in the countryside are showing success as the number of human rights abuses and disappearances have showed a marked decline.

With Peru's economic situation rapidly improving, a further wedge could well be driven between the government and the Shining Path. Fujimori's harsh economic programs have paid off. Inflation is down 20% from the 1990 high of 7500% and should drop lower in the future. The gross domestic product grew 7% in 1993 and continues to grow today. The budget is balanced and most state enterprises have been privatized. Instead of 16 exchange rates there is now but one.[54]

The political and economic situation in Peru is remarkably like that of Colombia and the Peruvian government's attitude toward drug trafficking, although somewhat lower key, appears to be much the same. The capture of El Vaticano may have bought some breathing space from the US, but as the country that produces 60% of the world's coca, Peru will undoubtedly continue to place its economy first, and do just enough to keep the US happy. In an important turn of events, during September 1994, liquid or latex opium was seized for the first time in Peru along the Ecuadorian border.[55] Concern about the growth of opium is on the rise in Peru as the discovery of the heroin producing plants was announced in 2 of the 25 departments that make up the country. Both Colombian and Mexican traffickers have encouraged the growth of poppies in Peru. A number of cases have been documented wherein the traffickers have provided free seeds and or paid the campesinos to cultivate the plants.[56] In April 1995, reports circulated through the country that Juan Carlos Escobar was in Peru setting up a drug trafficking operation. Dinandro reported that Escobar had approximately 20 of his father's gunmen with him.[57]

As 1995 came to a close, the Peru-Ecuador border war still cast a long shadow as the Peruvian government recalled its ambassador from Washington to protest the sale of Israeli Kfir warplanes to Ecuador. Powered by engines made in the United States—thus requiring US permission for the sale—the aircraft deal has driven a wedge in already uneasy US/Peruvian relations.[58] President Fujimori's decision to leave the fight against drugs to the police, with support from the judiciary and the Attorney General's Office in close support, could well set a precedent for other Latin American governments. However, it remains to be seen if such a move is either realistic or possible. Peruvian police have not been immune from suspicion from drug-related corruption, particularly the illegal distribution of captured property from drug traffickers.[59] Nonetheless, such a move appears to be a step in the right direction, albeit, fraught with danger. Such a move could dampen criticism of the strong handed tactics of the military over the past decades—and the human rights abuses—and force the government to shore-up the police forces. This move has the possibility of further creating more balance in the Peruvian government thanks to a more clear-cut balance of power between the military, civil government, and the judicial/constabulary branch. The "tell-tale" will be how the narcotraficantes react to this change.

THE "SQUISH" COUNTRIES

As pressure has been applied to the drug trafficking organizations in the production countries, the narcotraficantes have responded by "burrowing" in deeper or moving their operations to adjacent countries. Referred to as the "squish" countries, analogous to stepping on a piece of fruit with the result that the meat of the fruit oozes in all directions, these areas have the potential to become second-tier production and finished-product departure locations.

Brazil

The "sleeping giant" of South America, Brazil is the only country in the region that has not shown positive economic growth in the past few years. With inflation running at 1,200% and a 1.5% drop in the economy in the past year, drug trafficking issues are not at the top of national concerns. While attention has only been drawn to Brazil in the past eighteen months to two years, the reality of the situation is that Brazil has been involved in drug trafficking, particularly as a finished-product pass-through location and also as a supplier of precursor chemicals, for the past decade. Brazil remains one of the primary sources of ether and acetone. These products are also sold by pharmacies. Under Brazilian law pharmacies may only sell one liter per customer. However, Brazilian newspapers have documented cases in Corumba, on the Bolivian border, where the chemicals are being sold wholesale with false receipts to show single liter sales. Of some interest is the fact that in 1988 approximately 20 pharmacies were located in Corumba. By 1991, the number had grown to more than 50, although the need for such a marked increase in pharmacies in that city was certainly not apparent. Today, that number has grown almost exponentially.

While certified by the United States in 1995, Brazil is a major transit country for cocaine from Colombia destined for the United States and Europe. Increasing cocaine and precursor chemical trafficking and money laundering contribute to Brazil's escalating narcotics problem; corruption allegations against counternarcotics officials in Brazil persist. The Brazilian government has not hired new police or provided increased funding for the federal police narcotics unit. The government has not yet enacted legislation—first proposed in 1991–to implement a national drug control strategy. Brazil has not yet proposed specialized anti-money transactions involving amounts over $10,000.[60]

Initially, rumors of corruption came primarily from the state of Rondonia, on the border with Bolivia. Within a short period of time, it became clear that the corruption stretched from border guards to members of the Brazilian congress. It is now clear that the states of Rondonia and Matto Grosso, both of which touch the Bolivian border, are sites for cocaine laboratories. During the first months of 1993, the Brazilian news media was filled with stories dealing with rampant corruption involving ties between the police and narcotraffickers. Kidnapping is at an all-time high in the country, and the murder rate has gone off the charts. The Red Command, the Brazilian version of Sendero Luminoso, has literally created an enclave in the slums of Rio de Janeiro. There, they operate with virtual impunity, trafficking in weapons and drugs. In early January 1994, 30 men armed with automatic weapons and wearing police vests stormed a jail in Rio and overpowered seven "real" police officers on duty. The officers were handcuffed, the jail's armory was stripped, and the men drove away in police vehicles. Luis Carlos Goncalves, a cocaine trafficker convicted of kidnapping and murder was among those who escaped.[61] Rio mayor Cesar Maia best describes the situation when he stated that "[W]e have one state of formal institutions, elected officials and relatively reliable services, but in the favelas (slums) there is a second state run by gangs of drug traffickers." In the past two years the armed forces have invaded the favelas twice and failed to return control to civilians.[62]

The depressed state of the Brazilian economy follows a pattern very much like other countries that were faced with the choice between trafficking enforcement and the benefit of repatriated drug dollars run through the economy. While the extent of money laundering in Brazil is unclear, the government estimates that approximately $4 billion a year are illegally processed through the country. With Rio de Janeiro established as the primary embarkation point for cocaine bound through Casablanca and on to Spain and Portugal, a recent United Nations report states that Brazil is firmly an established link in the cocaine chain.

With the announcement of the discovery of a major gambling ring, Brazilian state prosecutors have placed charges against 63 individuals including the heads of the narcotics division, the anti-kidnapping unit, and the tourist police. Two prosecutors and several state legislators were also indicted. As the government continues to search seized records, the list of names grows. Former president Fernando Collor de Mello, who was impeached in 1992, Rio State governor Nilo Batista, and Rio mayor Cesar Maia, were also named. Clearly, the situation will remain ripe for the further growth and entrenchment of narco-corruption.

Cocaine consumption increased 50% during 1994 with expectations that it would continue on a steep upward spiral in 1995.[63] The suspected link between the Cali and Italian mafias and Brazil was confirmed in July 1994 when 43 Italian mafiosi were arrested in the largest cocaine seizure in Europe—five tons hidden in a shoe shipment. The shipment which arrived in the port of Genoa, originated in São Paulo, Brazil.[64] The actual business of trafficking has become more sophisticated as Brazilians are now acting as sub-contractors to the Colombians and the Brazilian real is now accepted as payment—a dramatic change from the past when only dollars were accepted.[65]

Francisco Thoumi of the University of the Andes argues that Brazil is well on its way to becoming the next big growth area. "It's a big country, which makes laundering easier, and there are large areas with little or no government control."[66] The one drawback to Brazilian growth on a scale the size of Colombian traffickers is the fact that Brazil does not have large immigrant communities in the United States—something that enables the Colombian mafia relative ease of operation in the US. Nonetheless, with the Nigerian-Brazilian connection responsible for the outflow of at least 10 tons of cocaine each year, and increasing, Brazil will continue to play a major role in hemispheric trafficking.[67]

Ecuador

Ecuador is a bridge between the world's largest supplier of coca leaf, Peru, and the world's major processor of cocaine hydrochloride, Colombia. Traffickers use Ecuador as a transit point to ship a minimum of 30–50 metric tons of cocaine to the US and Europe, as well as to smuggle chemicals into Colombia for cocaine processing. Money launderers take advantage of Ecuador's loose banking laws and extensive offshore banking system.[68]

In 1991, it was estimated that between 66,000 and 88,000 pounds of cocaine passed through Ecuador. During June 1992, a billion-dollar drug trafficking ring was broken by the police and security forces. Like the tip of an iceberg, this takedown simply confirmed what most observers suspected, that all the elements of drug trafficking were well entrenched. In early 1992, the US embassy in Quito quoted local newspapers which stated that of the 35,000 tons of chemicals imported into the country in 1988, approximately 10,000 are believed to have been directed toward Colombia for cocaine processing.

While the extent of money laundering is unclear in Ecuador, it appears to be directed through traditional means and also through trade transactions with

Colombians. A DEA report noted that many Ecuadorians do not want to deal with the police because of the depth of corruption that is to be found there. Ecuadorian judges are subject to trafficker intimidation which has obstructed efforts to bring Cali-connected kingpin Jorge Reyes Torres to justice. Corrupt judicial practices have precluded indictments in Reyes Torres related cases, specifically the Banco De Los Andes case.[69]

Ecuador is a good example of the quirks of US drug policy. The United States provided Ecuador with drug sniffing dogs, the Ecuadorians could not find money to purchase dog food. US personnel involved in the program ended up feeding the canines themselves.

Most of the cocaine moved from Colombia to Ecuador, transits the Pan American Highway, and then moves west toward Guayaquil and other major seaports, where the volume of commercial ocean-going traffic is such that it is difficult to track drugs. While SOUTHCOM has provided personnel for a TAT, it is unclear what the TAT has been tasked to do. In light of the fact that other TAT's in the region have turned into "more bodies" for certain embassy's rather than turned to intelligence production, the jury is still out.

In spite of traditional tension between Ecuador and Peru because of disputed land on the common border, Ecuador recently agreed to participate with Peru and Colombia in US sponsored regional drug efforts. Ecuador went a step further and committed air force assets to monitor and intercept drug aircraft violating its airspace.

Insurgency continues to be a concern to the GOE. In spite of the fact that the Alfaro Vive Carajo guerrilla organization was disarming, the rise of the Sol Rojo group and the spillover of Sendero Luminoso elements is a reason for concern. The influx of arms from El Salvador, Germany, and the states of the former Soviet Union, continue to plague the government. Concerns for stability and national sovereignty are first and foremost.[70]

Venezuela

As a major drug transit country, traffickers ship an estimated 100 to 200 tons of cocaine through Venezuela each year.[71] Precursor and essential chemical trafficking and money laundering are also serious problems. In the latter case a study prepared by the Institute of Higher Studies for National Defense argues that money laundering in Venezuela accounts for at least $4.5 billion a year with other estimates ranging much higher.[72] This takes place primarily through new construction, investments in hotels and nightclubs, the purchase of precious metals and speculation in urban real estate.

The recent customs union agreement between Colombia and Venezuela has resulted in a 30% increase in trade, with goods carried primarily in trucks between the two countries. With commerce speeded up, thanks to the lessening of border checks, the flow of cocaine has increased dramatically. The mountainous terrain between the two countries is now the site of coca fields and processing laboratories for both cocaine and heroin. The states of Falcon and Tachira that abut Colombia have experienced tremendous growth in drug trafficking activities with most of the seizures being in the thousand kilo range. The port of Maracaibo is a focal point for bulk shipment of cocaine in oil tankers bound for the United States and Europe. The ingenuity in the design of devices and containers in which to secret cocaine is a distinguishing mark of the Venezuelan traffickers.

One of the telltales of drug trafficking is the increase in local drug consumption. This holds true in Venezuela where the use of basuco and the attendant rise in addiction have been noted with alarm by government officials. Of further concern is the fact that almost 30% of all chemicals legally exported by US chemical companies to Latin America go through Venezuela. In addition, large quantities of chemicals are received from Holland, Belgium, and Germany. It is no surprise that Venezuela is a primary conduit for primary cocaine production chemicals into Colombia.

Increasing evidence of corruption amongst military and police officers, and in the courts is to be found. In 1994, the Guardia Nacoinal (GN) seized 5 tones of cocaine and 15 kilograms of heroin. Recent arrests of two GN members for trafficking 250 kilos of cocaine through Maiquetia Airport evinces corruption problems at lower levels in the organization. The GN quickly removed the two soldiers and began an investigation of the unit.[73]

The Venezuelan judiciary's marginal ability to resist the corruptive influence of traffickers has hampered counternarcotics efforts. Although President Caldera has spoken out strongly against narco-corruption, most recently at the December 1995, Summit of the Americas, corruption in Venezuela remains a serious problem. A convicted trafficker, Larry Tovar Acuna, fled to Colombia after fraudulently obtaining a pardon, and the Venezuelan government made an extradition request to Colombia for Tovar. In addition, a corrupt judge released members of the Sinforoso Caballero money laundering organization. The Venezuelan Supreme Court reopened the case and investigated the judge. Venezuela has not yet approved its draft national counternarcotics strategy and has not begun to control precursor and essential chemicals.[74]

As is the case with the rest of South and Central America, drugs are not a primary concern in Venezuela. There are simply too many other pressing problems and issues. The narcotics budget allows only for officer's salaries. The officer in charge of the Venezuelan counternarcotics forces stated that more information about drug activities was needed before his country could get into counter drug activities. Venezuela appears destined to remain a major money laundering center as well as a major point of departure for European-bound cocaine. From an intelligence viewpoint, here, as in Ecuador, the value of the Tactical Assistance Team is unclear to joint US/Venezuelan counter drug plans. The level of the Venezuelan TAT activities is a reflection of low intelligence priorities.

The present financial crisis does not bode well for the country. The January 1994 failure of the Banco Latino, the country's second largest bank, has further exacerbated the continuing recession and spiraling inflation. Six other banks have asked for help to the tune of $2.6 billion. The combination of a shaky coalition government and the need for massive capital requirements appears to be a scenario nicely suited to equally massive transfusions of narcodollars and alliances.[75] Plagued by attempted coups, drug trafficking by members of the presidential family, and ultimately the resignation of the president—a whisper ahead of impeachment, Venezuela has dramatically moved to the forefront as a major drug transshipment location. Long rumored ties with the Mafia were confirmed in the apprehension, and deportation of the Cuntreras brothers, and the revelations of Operation Green Ice.

THE SOUTHERN CONE

The Southern Cone countries of Argentina, Chile, Paraguay, Suriname and Guyana have become "catch-alls" as the narcotraficantes seek new areas in which to operate. The common denominator in each country is the wherewithal to export drugs from port facilities to the United States and Europe. The trappings of drug trafficking are becoming clearly recognizable and it is but a matter of time before each country garners its share of both the profits and problems associated with the trafficking business.

Cocaine transshipment through Argentina has been showing a steady increase. Cocaine is smuggled into Argentina primarily from Bolivia by general aviation aircraft and containerized railway cargo. The drugs leave Argentina in containers bound principally to Europe. Aircraft smuggled cocaine also enters the country from Colombia. There has also been a steady flow of cocaine bound for Europe, via Italy, on Italian cruise ships, departing the port of Rio de Janeiro.[76]

Cocaine from Bolivia was transported to northern ports in Chile for transshipment in commercial cargo to the United States and Europe. Such shipments were facilitated by a bilateral agreement prohibiting the inspection of Bolivian goods routed through Chile for export to a third country. Some amounts of processing of Bolivian-produced cocaine base was also performed in Chile. In addition, Chile was a source of essential chemicals for traffickers in Peru and Bolivia. The country's financial institutions were used increasingly to launder drug proceeds.[77]

Paraguay is used as a transit route for cocaine shipped primarily from Bolivia, and increasingly from Colombia, to Argentina and Brazil for onward shipment to the United States and Canada. Paraguay is potentially a major money laundering center, based on its extensive re-export trade and its expanding and poorly regulated financial center. The record of former president Andres Rogriguez who was tainted by accusations of drug corruption did not help set the stage for his successor, Juan Carlos Wasmosy. The first democratically-elected civilian president in over five decades, Wasmosy has stressed his own personal commitment to combat drug trafficking.[78] The results, however, belie the promise. The US government accused him of failing to act decisively when provided with information relating to corruption within his government's counternarcotics leadership. One criminal investigation is believed to have been compromised due to corruption, and Wasmosy's overall lack of political will to uncover what is widely believed to be an extensive official corruption has led to a very weak drug control program.[79] When polled as to their perception of the effect of drug trafficking in the country in 1994, 84% of the people believed that the political system was partly or greatly influenced by traffickers.[80]

The year-end killing of the general in charge of the country's anti-drug unit—just after his announcement that he was going to release evidence linking business-men, military officers and police to drugs— points to further trouble for Paraguay.[81]

The situation in Guyana suggests that it has the potential to become a signifi-cant transshipment point for cocaine being transported from Venezuela, Brazil, and Suriname to Europe, the Caribbean, and the United States. Guyana's heavily forested and sparsely populated interior—with numerous small and virtually inac-cessible airfields—facilitated the transshipment of cocaine.[82]

THE CARIBBEAN

The deep-throated rumble of tri-engine powered "cigarette" boats in the Florida Keys signals the return of the Caribbean as a primary cocaine trafficking route. The re-emergence of the "go-fast" boats is proof positive of the ability of traffick-ers to react to changing market conditions, a combination of customer preferences and law enforcement tactics. Not since the early 1980's have the needle-shaped boats been in such abundance. US Customs says the return to speedboats indicates that inroads are being made in the traffickers clandestine corporate structure. They are "off-balance and not able to go through their more normal systems, like hiding the drugs within international cargo, commingling it with legitimate cargo enter-ing the US, which takes a great deal of coordination, a much broader network of individuals." But other experts say that the speedboats are being employed be-cause more shipments are being dropped off in Cuban waters. The boats "can go much faster than the Cuban Coast Guard or the Cuban Navy," says Bruce Bagley, an expert on the illegal drug trade at Miami University. Speedboats then run the contraband to the Florida Keys or other stretches of the South Florida coast. As the US-Mexican border has been tightened up and as Mexican traffickers have taken over the cocaine trade on their own territory, the Cali cartel has shifted its delivery routes back to the Caribbean, according to Mr. Bagley. "There's a kind of subdivi-sion of the United States taking place, with the [Mexican traffickers] increasingly important out West, particularly in the Southwest, and the Cali cartel dominating east of the Mississippi."[83]

The islands of the Caribbean form a natural chain which stretches from Trinidad and Tobago—a scant 7 miles off the coast of Venezuela, a short jaunt in a "go-fast"— and thence north through the Windward Islands—from Grenada to Barba-dos, St. Lucia, Martinique, and Dominica. Then, curving northwest to the Leewards—Guadaloupe, Monserrat, Antiqua-Barbuda, St. Barthelemy, St Maarten, Anguilla St. Kitts-Nevis, and then to the US Virgin Islands, Puerto Rico, Haiti and the Dominican Republic, Jamaica, Cuba, and the Bahamas—the closest of its is-lands also a short jaunt for "go-fast" boats to Florida.

Maritime traffickers made frequent use of Trinidad and Tobago during 1994 and 1995. A key staging point for waterborne shipments to Florida, the waters surrounding the island are also used as airdrop points. Trinidad, of late, has been terrorized by drug gangs. Just to the east of Trinidad and Tobago are the islands of Aruba, Bonaire, and Curacao. There, extensive maritime trafficking activities continued to grow in scope. Fishing vessels and pleasure craft carried much of the cocaine into the area and commercial vessels in turn took on the drugs for further transshipment. The three islands serve as bases for organizations of air couriers traveling to the US and Europe, as well as staging points for containerized cargo shipments. The Leeward Islands also registered increased activity during 1994 and into 1995. Seizures of cocaine exceeded 4 tons in 1994. Colombians reportedly have established bases of operations in St. Maarten and St. Kitts. Antiqua and Barbuda continued to be used as bases for maritime cocaine shipments destined for the US and Europe, as well as a site for air-drops to go-fast boats from Puerto Rico and the Virgin Islands. During the 1994-1995 time-frame, trafficking organizations from Trinidad, St. Lucia, and Dominica cooperated to smuggle hundred-kilogram quantities of cocaine to the United States.[84]

The situation in St. Kitts that broke into headlines during late 1994 and into 1995 is indicative of the tentacles of traffickers reaching into the political and law enforcement infrastructure on the island and throughout the region. A former St. Kitts UN ambassador who had been implicated in laundering drug money, disappeared with his wife and four friends.[85] The resignation of the deputy Prime Minister of St. Kitts, Sydney Morris after the arrest of two of his sons on drug trafficking and gun-possession charges, and the drug related killing of another son and his girlfriend—found burned to death in a canefield—suggest that traffickers have made deep in-roads there. Shortly after the resignation, a number of gun-related deaths—in particular the slaying of St. Kitts Police Intelligence Squad officer, Jude Matthew, who was assassinated while investigating the Morris case, points towards additional trouble with traffickers.[86]

French authorities in Paris have traced shipments of "crack" back to Guadaloupe and St. Maarten. The "crack" production is believed to be controlled by 6 crime families based in Dominica.[87] The island of St. Martin, which consists of French St. Martin and Dutch St. Maarten, serves as a transshipment point for cocaine. French and Dutch police seized 2 tons of cocaine in 1994. In August, 1994, 276 kilos seized from a boat arriving from Venezuela led to the seizure of another 717 kilos stored in St. Martin. The cocaine was to be transported by sailboat to the US Virgin Islands. Later in the year another 790 kilos was discovered in a cave along the shoreline of a small island known as Groopers, located between St. Martin and St. Barthelemy; the packaging of the cocaine suggested that it had been delivered by airdrop.[88] St. Martin is the new meeting place for the Colombian and Italian drug mafias—a real Star Wars bar of drug riffraff, claim DEA agents.[89]

The center of the Caribbean—the "new" Miami—is Puerto Rico. Felix Jimenez, the special agent in charge of DEA operations in San Juan argues that since 1990. Puerto Rico has been the focal point for the export of cocaine to the mainland from the Caribbean.[90] The island's status as a US commonwealth offers traffickers an extraordinary advantage, since passengers and cargo undergo only perfunctory customs checks to enter the US mainland. Once a shipment of cocaine is smuggled to the island, it can easily be transshipped to cities on the US mainland.

Puerto Rico has paid a step price for its leading role in the drug trade. Its murder rate has been higher than that of any state for three years straight. Ninety percent of all violence on the island is believed to be drug related. "San Juan has become what Miami used to be. You see 15-year olds with guns. People are afraid to go out at night," says US attorney Guillermo Gil, himself the victim of a carjacking by a teenager high on crack. In the summer of 1993, the drug trade had got so bad that Governor Pedro Rossello sent in the national guard to patrol housing projects where much of the business is conducted. Two years later not much has changed. Judges are lenient and bail is low, says Pedro Toledo, Puerto Rico's police superintendent. " We arrest people who have committed three four, five, six murders," he says, "and yet somehow they are free on the streets."[91]

Drug trafficking was down in Haiti because of the presence of US and UN forces in the country. Nonetheless, Haiti's central location in the Caribbean has, and will continue, to make the country a prime location for transshipment. The geographic factor, when coupled with an unstable political, and dismal economic, situation make Haiti in the center of trafficking activities. US law enforcement agencies have claimed for years that the Haitian military was deeply involved in trafficking, but this has never been substantiated. There is strong reason to believe that growing drug trafficker activities have greatly impeded the growth of more stable government in Haiti.[92]

In the Dominican Republic there are indications of an increased flow of drugs from maritime sources as well as some land smuggled cocaine entering from Haiti. Anti-drug legislation leaves much to be desired in the Dominican Republic particularly in the area of money laundering control. The legislature removed prison sentences, leaving only moderate fines for banks convicted of involvement in laundering activities.[93] The large Dominican community in New York City further aids the flow of drugs from Santo Domingo and other cities and ports in the republic.[94]

Jamaica remains a transshipment point for both maritime and air shipments of cocaine. Its long coast line and location near international sailing routes make Jamaica an ideal trafficking spot. A key source of ganja (marijuana) production, Jamaica lays directly astride a key flight path that begins in the Guajira Peninsula of Colombia and heads almost due north over the center of the island and thence on to and over Cuba and to the Bahamas or Florida. The Pedro Cays, which lie off the south coast of Jamaica, are a favorite spot for airdrops of cocaine. The new Jamaican Joint Information Coordination Center has been sharing information with US and neighboring drug law enforcement organizations.[95]

Trafficking in the Bahamas, site of the halycon days of Carlos Lehder, showed a decline in trafficking activity in 1994. Operation Bahamas, Turks and Caicos Islands (OPBAT) has been in operation for 12 years. Combining US and Bahamian forces, air and maritime operations continue to plague traffickers. In early 1995, Bahamian police arrested Ben Beneby and seven associates on drug-related conspiracy charges. Considered one of the most important trafficking groups in the Bahamas, the Beneby organization is suspected of having delivered numerous multihundred-kilo shipments of cocaine to the US. In one of the first tests of the island nation's 1994 Bail Bond Act, the Bahamian Supreme Court ordered Beneby held without bail, based upon a previous drug conviction.[96]

Cuba remains a concern, one that will undoubtedly grow exponentially if Fidel Castro steps down or when the country becomes open. Cocaine traffickers try to avoid law enforcement presence in The Bahamas by crossing Cuban air and sea space. Traffickers use international air corridors to blend with legitimate air traffic and thus avoid US interdiction. During 1993, Cuba seized 3,364 kilos, which was 104% higher than 1992 seizures, while in 1994, 238 kilos were seized.[97] In 1995, cocaine and marijuana drops in and near Cuban waters saw a "substantial increase" said Deputy Customs Chief Pablo Ferrer at a meeting of Latin American customs officers in November 1995. To make matters worse, fuel shortages have forced the military and border guards to cut back boat and airplane patrols around the island since 1991 when the Soviet Union stopped its subsidized oil sales to Cuba.[98]

With the evidence of increased drug trafficking building in Cuba, the Castro government has been quietly making overtures to the US for increased cooperation. So far, Washington has rebuffed the Cubans, calculating that any improvements in shared interdiction operations would be outweighed by the political implications of the enhanced teamwork.

In the Cayman Islands, long considered to be a key money laundering site, traffickers also use the island as a transshipment point for ganja from Jamaica and cocaine from Honduras.[99]

Today, the islands of the Caribbean are the center of a newly-revived, thriving transshipment point for cocaine. Stymied by economies that rely on a single crop or tourism, the islands are extremely vulnerable to business transactions—and in some cases like St. Kitts and Antiqua—domination by drug mafias. In 1994, 4 tons of cocaine were seized in the Lesser Antilles [Antiqua and Barbuda, Dominica, Grenada, St. Kitts and Nevis, St. Lucia, St. Vincent and the Grenadines, and Trinidad and Tobago].[100] St. Lucia has a growing population of cocaine addicts and the second highest murder rate in the world.[101]

Antigua is classic example of the "Colombianizacion" of the islands. With a population of 63,000 ruled for decades by the Bird Family, Antiqua is one of the most corrupt places in the Caribbean. Long regarded as a haven for drug traffickers and weapon's merchants, the island nation has most recently become a money laundering center. In one year, the number of offshore banks in Antiqua has doubled to nearly 50, which operate quite openly, and in some cases, quite legitimately. Ivor Bird, son of Vere Bird Sr. who ruled the country for over 15 years, denies that Antiqua is awash in trafficking. But Baldwin Spencer, head of the opposition United Progressive Party, states that "Antiqua has reached the stage where, if drug activities ceased to exist, the economy of the island would be in trouble. The talk is that if one or two ships don't reach our shores each month, it's serious." To add further fuel to the fire, US officials note that Americans and Russians are moving to Antiqua to set up money laundering operations for the new Russian Mafiya.[102]

Trinidad is another example of the onslaught of cocaine trafficking. Located seven miles from the Venezuelan coast, the island is a key transshipment point. During November 1995, Basdeo Panday, the leader of the sugar-industry trade union, became Prime Minister largely thanks to a campaign to stamp out the cocaine trade. However, US officials say that one of Panday's top advisors represents many of the island's accused traffickers, including the Dole Chadee group—believed to be the most important trafficking organization in the eastern Caribbean. Chadee is in jail in Port of Spain on suspicion of murdering one of his reputed drug associates, but witnesses against the group have a way of getting killed, their jaws shot off, their food poisoned or their families executed. In a bizarre situation in 1993, a Scotland Yard team investigating alleged police corruption, had to flee a Hilton Hotel after gunmen threatened them—inside local police headquarters.[103]

With payment being made in drugs to local traffickers and dealers by the Colombians, the increased competition results in more bloodshed. Concurrent with this is the decrease in counter-drug spending by the Clinton administration in the Caribbean, thanks to new emphasis on the South West Border. In 1992, budget cuts dramatically reduced US surveillance in the Caribbean. Nearly half of all ships and 80% of aircraft were diverted to other uses. Ironically, part of the reason for the cutbacks was the success of Operation Bahamas, Turks. In 1988, 28 tons of cocaine were seized in the Bahamas, in contrast to only 1.7 tons in 1995.[104]

EL CONDUCTO: THE TRANSIT OF COCAINE

The pass-through of cocaine has a major impact on the transit countries. Without exception, whether it be through Central America or through the islands of the Caribbean, the cocaine pipeline has had a devastating impact on each country that it touches. Following the processing of the coca leaf into cocaine hydrochloride, that portion of the finished product that is earmarked for entry into the United States follows several primary routes including four air corridors and four maritime routes.

Air

Originating primarily in Colombia, the first corridor follows the trace of the Pacific Coast of Mexico north to the trio-city area of Durango, Culican, and Matzatlan. The second corridor stretches north from Colombia, also along the Pacific Coast line, to the Isthmus of, then cuts sharply across Mexico to the gulf and then north along the coast to the Laguna Madre del Sur area. The third air corridor is oriented north over Panama to the Peten-Yucatan region of Mexico, Guatemala, or Belize. There the aircraft are refueled or off-loaded to smaller aircraft and the flights then continue toward various destinations in the northern states of Mexico. Once there, the cocaine is stored or prepared for shipment into the United States. The final corridor starts from Colombia and heads in a northeasterly direction to Jamaica, the Dominican Republic, Haiti, or to any of the thousand islands that dot the eastern Caribbean (see Figure 7.1).

Maritime

Maritime smuggling has steadily increased in popularity in both the Caribbean and eastern Pacific. Efforts to stem the flow of cocaine trafficking through the eastern Pacific have suffered from the lack of understanding of this vast ocean area as a major trafficking route from source countries in Latin America to first-stage

Figure 7.1
Major Cocaine Trafficking Routes

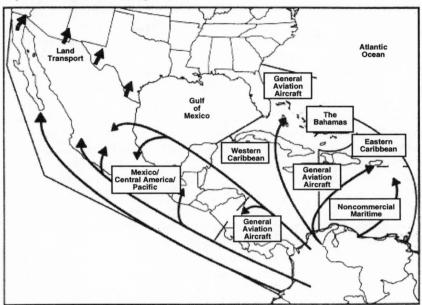

transshipment points in Mexico, Guatemala, and most recently Nicaragua. The yeoman maritime intelligence analysis performed by Joint Interagency Task Force West in Alameda, California, was for years dismissed by the intelligence and counter drug communities as not important. However with over 16 metric tons of cocaine seized in the eastern Pacific in October and November 1993 alone, the Washington Interagency Working Group has had to finally admit that Eastern Pacific route bears watching. Much of the credit for setting the stage goes to Admiral John Linnon, USCG, whose continued determination and intelligence driven operations have made the difference.[105]

Maritime cocaine trafficking really gained prominence as the Northern Border Response Force gained expertise in combating airborne trafficking into Mexico. As the trafficking seizures—of cocaine, aircraft, and men—continued to mount at record pace, the narcotraficantes did what they will always do; modify their operations so as to lessen loss. The primary option open to them was to turn to maritime transshipment. Initially, containerized shipments were favored to move large loads into Mexico. Multi-ton seizures in western Mexico in 1991 and in the Caribbean in 1992–1993 caused traffickers to look for alternative shipping routes. What they seized upon was the use of 60-to-180 foot fishing vessels and 25-to-45 foot sport fishing vessels. At approximately the same time, Latin American and Mexican traffickers began to move operations to southern Mexico and Guatemala in 1992, in the main driven to change by the response forces. But with seizures mounting in southern Mexico, the traficantes began to move eastern Pacific maritime shipments further north in early 1993. Clipperton Atoll and the Sea of Cortez, in particular, were used as the principal eastern Pacific rendezvous and off-loading areas for mother-ship operations. In contrast, traffickers concentrated the majority of Caribbean mothership operations in the area of the Yucatan Peninsula and Veracruz. Containerized ships, low-profile vessels (LPV's), "go-fast boats," and to a lesser extent, commercial fishing vessels were used to smuggle drugs in the Caribbean, while traditional fishing vessels and small coastal freighters were the preferred maritime conveyances in the eastern Pacific. Non container maritime cocaine shipments in the Caribbean tended to center on the frequent use of small vessels to move 500-to-1500-kilo loads, while shipments in the eastern Pacific were of larger size—6,000-to-8000-kilos, but were moved less frequently.

Much of the maritime cocaine shipments in the eastern Pacific have originated directly from or near the port of Buenaventura, Valle de Cauca Department, Colombia. The Cali families are the primary owners. Just "down the road" from Cali and the principal port in western Colombia, Buenaventura will continue to be the primary port of departure for maritime traffickers. This will be the case even if, as some believe, the surrender of key Cali traficantes takes place. Other locations which may increase in importance are Choco and Narino Departments. Ecuadorian ports such as Esmeraldas, Quito, and Guayaquil appear also to be taking on increased importance in eastern Pacific smuggling operations. Projecting out over the next five years, maritime trafficking will increase in importance with Mexico remaining key to drug transshipment. The NAFTA agreement has ensured that the South West Border will remain a primary entry point for drugs into the United States. The Sea of Cortez will likely see an increase in maritime trafficking in the form of commercial and non commercial vessels. Maritime trafficking is also expected to increase along the Central American isthmus, particularly if Mexican plans for a NAFTA-type agreement in Central America come to pass.[106]

PANAMA

Panama is a primary transshipment location for drugs, primarily maritime. Drug-laden vehicular traffic, headed north along the Pan American Highway, also begins in Panama. The Colon Free Zone is a key point of embarkation for large shipments of cocaine. Coco Solo, Balboa, Cristobal, and Bahias Las Minas are also centers for transshipment. Panama remains a prime money laundering location. The availability of cocaine on the streets of Panama City is the highest that it has ever been and this increase is reflected in a dramatic increase in drug addiction. The impact of drugs and of the money that follows are highly visible today. New luxury apartment buildings mark the skyline in Panama City. While the building boom may involve some legitimate financing, the rate of construction far outstrips the figures for building loans reported by local banks. Many of the buildings are paid for in cash, a sure sign of entrenched trafficking activities.

Shortly after the opening of the last session of the Panamanian parliament during which President Endara called for tough new legislation to counter the curse of drug trafficking, a DEA sting in Florida caught members of a major Colombian money laundering operation. Among the ten Panamanians caught were a vice-president and another senior employee of the Merrill Lynch, Panama branch office. Responding to US charges that Panama had not cracked down on drug trafficking, minister Raul Mulino told reporters that, "our dignity was offended and we will protest."[107]

The presidency of Guillermo Endara, suspected of trafficking activities before he ever took office was lack-luster. In a strange turn of fate, the party of Manuel Noriega, the Democratic Revolutionary Party (PRD), won the May 1994 election. While many thought that the PRD would fade from sight, Ernesto Perez Balladares ("El Torro") led the PRD return to power. Although he distanced himself from the Noriega years and claimed ties to the *rabiblanco* ("white tail") oligarchy, the Perez Balladares administration appeared to have little interest in cutting ties with narco-dollars. The victory was as much a credit to the organization of the PRD as the feeling in Panama that the Endara regime was "so bad that Noriega starts to look good."[108]

After taking office in 1994, Perez-Balladares acknowledged that narcotrafficking and narcotics-related money laundering threaten Panama's political and economic stability. In an effort to prevent abuse of incorporation laws, the new president issued a decree mandating attorneys to follow "know-your-customer" practices. He then established a special commission to develop money laundering controls. Several middle-and low-level officials were investigated for corruption, and, in a few cases, dismissed.[109] On August 27, 1995, Attorney General Valdes stated that the Judicial Technical Police (PTJ) was infiltrated by mafias. He pointed out that 24,154 case files dealing with trafficking offenses were frozen and 9,700 arrest warrants had not been served.[110] This followed earlier revelations by Jaime Abad, director of the PTJ, that some of his subordinates were involved in drug trafficking activities. Abad stated that " We have been able to detect a band, known as the Tumbadores (Tumblers), formed by some detectives, private individuals, and former members of the defunct Panama Defense Forces."[111]

For the foreseeable future, Panama will continue to be a key country in El Conducto, a country in which money laundering, drug transit, and the growth of coca plantations will continue.[112]

COSTA RICA

The "Switzerland of Latin America," Costa Rica has rapidly become a major transshipment point for cocaine. With no army and a small police force, the country has been inundated by air, land, and seaborne drug traffic. Astride the Pan American Highway and sharing a common border with Panama, Costa Rica has seen a tremendous increase in pass-through drug traffic. With only one radar with a 40-mile search radius located at the San Jose International Airport, drug aircraft can make undetected use of any of the 200 small airstrips throughout the country. Both the Atlantic and Pacific coastal areas are easily accessible to fishing, pleasure, and small to medium-sized coastal cargo vessels. One indicator of the depth of and strength of drug trafficking in the country is evidenced by an event in Guapiles in May 1993, in which an explosion and fire destroyed the mayor's office, causing the destruction of 525 criminal case files, many of which dealt with trafficking cases.[113] During the first 11 months of 1994, over 1.4 tons of cocaine were seized in Costa Rica. Most of the cocaine smuggled into the country was transported to US markets, often in containers from the port of Limon.[114]

As of yet, no senior government officials have been accused of narcotics corruption. There is reason to believe however, that large campaign contributions—tainted with cocaine dollars, have been made to both of the major Costa Rican political parties. A Costa Rican security minister argues that the majority of cocaine moves along land routes in the country, perhaps making it easier to spread through customs and police officers. Most of the drugs seized were from vessels which had attempted to land their cargoes on the Pacific coast. Most of these vessels were discovered and tracked by DEA radars located in Costa Rica and Panama.[115]

EL SALVADOR

On June, 12, 1993, the Executive Anti-Narcotics Unit seized more than 6 tons of cocaine—the largest seizure in the history of the country. Four Mexicans and one Colombian were arrested. This event gave truth to the belief that El Salvador was a major pathway in El Conducto. It is clear that there are well established links between Salvadoran traffickers and other trafficking organizations operating in Guatemala, Nicaragua, and Panama. Maritime trafficking appears to be well entrenched with the seaport of Acajutia the scene of one of the largest drug seizures in the country. Numerous airstrips in the San Miguel and La Union Departments, near the Pan-American Highway, provide convenient transshipment points for cocaine smuggled by aircraft.

With the Pan American Highway passing through the country, El Salvador has become a multimodal threat, as well as having an infrastructure already in place that allows for great expansion of drug trafficking activities. With attention directed toward bringing the lingering guerrilla war to a close, the Government of El Salvador only recently turned some attention toward counter drug programs. It is those guerrillas that could present problems in the future. With few opportunities to return to a life of normalcy, the guerrillas present a prime target for drug traffickers. Trained, experienced in clandestine movements, and with superb knowledge of the countryside, the former guerrilla, and his organization would be well suited to join in the trafficking business. While the Salvadoran government and the DEA have estimated that approximately 25 metric tons of cocaine transit the country each year, this figure appears to be unrealistically low. When one looks at the drugs passing through the countries on either side of El Salvador, the actual amount transiting El Salvador must be much higher.

The return to power of the Nationalist Republican Alliance, under the leadership of Armando Calderon Sol, raises questions as to whether or not the truce with the Farabundo Marti National Liberation Front will last. While the alliance continues to express the promise of reconciliation with the opposition in the twelve-year civil war, only time will tell if the rift can be healed. Until then, the potential for increased drug trafficking activities remains high.

In early 1995, government officials stated that the lack of radar to detect illegal aircraft and numerous illegal airfields make the country a "paradise stopover" for traffickers.[116]

NICARAGUA

Indictments handed down by the US attorney in Miami, in June 1993, document the fact that almost the entire Cuban government—from Raoul Castro on down—was involved in long-term drug trafficking. This information has cast new light on drug trafficking activities in Nicaragua. The allegations leveled against the Sandanistas in the mid-1980's appear to have been well founded. With the Sandinistas still firmly entrenched in the Chamorro government, the promise of more widespread drug trafficking in the country appears to be reality. The Nicaraguan military—with leaders trained by Cuba and the Palestine Liberation Organization—also controls the country's police force. In June, 1994, Humberto Ortega, petitioned the executive branch to transfer responsibility to the military.[117]

Drugs seized between January and October, 1994—1323 kilos of cocaine— surpassed all drugs seized from 1990 through 1993.[118] As was the case in Costa Rica, the Pacific coast in Nicaragua is favored by traffickers for ease of access, in particular in the movement of drugs toward Guatemala. Like El Salvador the presence of "out-of-work" guerrillas sets the stage for a new trafficking network in the country. Both the army chief of staff, Joaquin Cuadra, and the army intelligence chief have been accused of corruption, along with Interior Minister Lacayo, who allegedly receives $300,000 a month from drug traffickers. Of $225 million of foreign aid given by the United States in 1992, $100 to 180 million is unaccounted for. Noting that "After a decade in which drugs were almost unheard of in Nicaragua, drug trafficking and consumption have reached truly alarming levels, and the country has become a battleground in the fight against narcotics," *Barricada Internacional* went on to describe a recent joint operation conducted by the National Police and the DEA, in which 275 kilos of cocaine, bound for the United States, were seized near the Costa Rican border.[119]

All factors point toward a dramatic increase in trafficking activities in Nicaragua as the Chamorro government attempts to divest itself from the political and economic legacy of the Sandinistas.

HONDURAS

The situation in Honduras suggests that corruption and drug trafficking have deeply permeated the country. A tripartite customs agreement among Honduras, Guatemala, and El Salvador allows free transit for individuals from the three countries. The Honduran press has alleged that the military, which controls the police forces and the customs and immigration service, is closely tied to the narcotraficantes. General Luis Alonso Discua Elvir, commander of the 105th Infantry Brigade, has been accused of corruption, a series of bombings, and contract killing—all drug related. During April 1994, the Honduran army investigated a foiled plot to

assassinate President Carlos Roberto Reina and also an attempt to kidnap a prominent Honduran businessman. An army spokesman said a Honduran citizen with ties
to drug traffickers had offered the group $400,000 to kill the president.[120]

Honduras is the geographic midway point between Colombia and the United
States. In spite of the fact that there are 250 unmonitored air strips in the country,
airborne drug trafficking remains relatively low probably because of the 1992 shoot-
down of suspected drug aircraft by the Honduran Air Force. Adapting to the situation and terrain traffickers have made excellent use of the long Caribbean coast
line and the offshore Bay Islands. Honduran authorities seized 960 kilos of cocaine in 1994. Of this amount, 536 kilos were seized at a checkpoint near Puerto
Cortes. Police believe that the cocaine was delivered to Honduras from San Andres
Island and was to be transported to Guatemala by go-fast boat. In addition to drugs,
the Honduran government is faced with a steady flow of weapons from Nicaragua
and El Salvador. It is believed that the weapons go primarily to drug traffickers but
some are also believed to be destined for Zapatista rebels in Mexico.[121]

BELIZE

With a 30-mile radius for the one radar at the international airport, the country
is virtually wide open to drug aircraft that make use of the approximately 140
landing strips around the country. The new deep-draft container port at Bogwalk
further offers the opportunity to secret drugs in containers. The ease of approaching the coast in small vessels and coasters is such that a thriving maritime traffic
appears to be building.

There appears to be an increasing number of aircraft drug drops just off the
coastline and heavy truck traffic from Guatemala. Belize has increased in significance as a transit country for air and sea smuggling and also for its close links with
Guatemala, in particular the land routes from Belize City to Orange Walk to the
border; and, from Belize City via Belmopan to the Guatemalan border.[122]

In late 1994, the Police Special Branch came under investigation following the
disappearance of seized cocaine. Belizean authorities seized 141 kilos of cocaine
in 1994. This total was exceeded in a two day period in January 1995 when police
seized 636 kilos of cocaine.[123]

GUATEMALA

It is difficult to believe that in a small country like Guatemala which is absolutely milita-
rized to the smallest village, road and bridge, where the Air Force controls all the airspace
and the single radar in the country, the military cannot be involved in this drug trafficking.[124]

In the early morning hours of May 25, 1993, President Jorge Serrano set in
motion an autogolpe. A zealous evangelical Christian, Serrano declared that a "plot"
by a "mafia" of drug traffickers was about to take over the country. He stated that
drug corruption was now so prevalent that it had tainted the assembly, the courts,
the press and television. President Serrano argued that his duty was to save the

country from the scourge of traffickers. For almost 10 years, it has been clear that drug trafficking was making major inroads into the country. In reality, Guatemala ranks second only to Mexico in terms of importance in El Conducto. It is the springboard in the pipeline, a strategic location that dramatically reflects growing air, sea, and land smuggling, as well its role as a narco-communications center.

The growth of drug trafficking in Guatemala took place with little outside attention. In retrospect, it now appears that the use of Guatemala as a primary drug transit country began in the late 1960's and early 1970's, with marijuana the first pipeline commodity and cocaine soon to follow. In 1977, the United States appropriated $347,000 to eradicate drug production and to train special security units to combat drug trafficking. In 1986, a bilateral agreement between Guatemala and the United States enabled the Guatemala military to begin marijuana eradication. However by this time the framework for El Conducto was firmly entrenched. The primary issue continues to be the on-again off-again peace talks that are aimed towards ending the "Thirty Years War," three decades of brutal guerrilla warfare. Once peace talks began, political posturing and public sniping appeared to have become the rule of thumb. Taking office on January 6, 1991, President Jorge Serrano declared his intention to achieve "total peace" in Guatemala. He insisted that the goal was not merely a ceasefire but something that would "go beyond the scope of Esquipulas." He added that halting the military actions had never been stipulated as a condition for talks with the country's armed forces.

On April 26, 1991, the Guatemalan National Revolutionary Unity—a melding of the four primary guerrilla organizations—and the Guatemalan government opened the way for serious negotiations during a three-day meeting in Mexico City. During this meeting, URNG leaked information to the press that the Guatemalan army planned to launch a major offensive in early May, in an attempt to force the insurgents to surrender. However, it appears that during the final night of the meeting, serious negotiations took place, for an Agreement on General Topics of Discussion was soon released. Since that time three events have focused further attention on Guatemala; the selection of Rigoberta Menchu for the Nobel Peace Prize, the largely ineffective but high-profile peace talks, and the short- lived autogolpe of President Jorge Serrano. These events have overshadowed the dramatic increase of drug trafficking in Guatemala.

Guatemala's central location on the Central American isthmus lends itself to the transit of cocaine and drug production—opium and some coca. The country is divided into two basic regions: the lowlands, which extend from the Gulf of Mexico inland to the highlands, and the Chiapas highlands. The lowlands consist of swamps, marshes and dense forest. The highlands consist of dense forest. The southern coast has numerous shallow lagoons and swamps through which small craft can move undetected. The departments of Quiche, Huehuetenango, San Marcos, Quezaltenango and the western half of Peten, are areas in which numerous illegal airfields and marijuana and opium fields are found. Marijuana is grown primarily in the Peten Department, while opium poppies are grown in the northwestern mountains of San Marcos and Huehuetenango.

The 962-kilometer-long border between Mexico and Guatemala is defined by both natural features and negotiated boundaries and is sparsely populated. Guatemala lost the state of Chiapas, much of which is now the Mexican state of Tabasco, and areas along its Peten Department border to Mexico in the 19th century. The northern continues to be an area of contention between Guatemala and Mexico. Collusion between Mexican narcotraficantes and growers in Guatemala and low level corruption between military and police officials on both sides of the border add to the fertile drug trafficking climate. Guatemalan refugees pose a problem for both sides. Guatemala claims they support the insurgents, while Mexico claims the presence of the refugees is a threat to Mexican sovereignty. In fact, the insurgents train on the Mexican side of the border and use the refugee camps as safe-havens and sources of recruits. There is much collusion between narcotraficantes, local drug producers, and Mexican and Guatemalan border authorities, all of which adds to the fertile drug trafficking climate.

There is clear evidence that the guerrilla forces, the military, and the business elite are involved in drug trafficking. In spite of the eloquent protestations of Commander Monsanto, there is solid evidence to confirm that the insurgent forces are involved in the drug trade. Ideological reasons aside, the fact remains that external funding from Cuba and Nicaragua is drying up. Faced with the loss of support, the insurgents have opted to turn to cocaine, heroin, and marijuana for the production of hard currency. Conversely, arguments are made that such is not the case. Accusations of such ties, claims Commander Monsanto are being made by "members of the US government who have links to the Guatemalan army and government. The accusations are made for the primary purposes of concealing US intervention in anti-guerrilla combat and camouflaging military aid under the pretext of fighting drug trafficking." The evidence, however, speaks to increased ties between narcotrafficking and the insurgents.

The type of drug which each of the guerrilla groups that constitute URNG traffics in is a reflection of their geographic area of operation. The Organization of People in Arms [ORPA] appears to be involved in opium trade in the Culico Valley, Huehuetenango Province, and in the region of Mt. Tajumulco in San Marcos. Irrigation systems have been installed there, and because accessibility to the area is easiest through Mexico, the region appears to be an extension of Mexico territory. There is also reason to believe that attempts to grow coca were under way in this same area as early as 1988. The Rebel Armed Forces is involved in cultivating, smuggling, and protecting marijuana fields in the Melchor de Menos district in the northern Peten area, in an area known as Tres Banderas. This area is located near the Guatemala, Mexico, and Belize border. The Guerrilla Army of the Poor, like ORPA, is involved in opium production and protection in the Huehuetenago area.

The newsletter *CERI-GUA* suggests that government involvement in drug trafficking is an open secret. The upstart newspaper *Siglo Veintiuno*, which attacked head on the "delicate" issue of drug trafficking and the alleged participation of Guatemalan officials, found itself on the receiving end of a midnight raid by armed men who burned thousands of copies of the next day's papers. The newspaper went on to suggest that the hierarchy of the Christian Democratic Party was also deeply involved. Interior Minister Carlos Morales stated that, "there is a long and revealing list of persons not only from the business and commercial sectors but also government officials who are linked to narcotics trafficking." In the same vein, the president of the congressional committee that oversees internal security, Roberto Valle, said that "a number of businessmen and well-known persons take part in the business." Along the Passion River in Peten Province, extensive marijuana fields were found on the plantations owned by former president Carlos Arena.

There are abundant indicators that point to the in-depth involvement of Guatemalan army intelligence in drug trafficking. The valve of an intelligence network that literally touches every element of life in the country is clear. With the wherewithal to "feel the pulse" of the nation, army intelligence has the ability to monitor the full range of drug production and trafficking activities. This knowledge also gives them the option of playing in selected arenas. No other sector of society can match the army's capabilities. It dominates the other services and controls the national police and many of the so-called private police forces hired by the wealthy, as well as various right-wing vigilante groups. The business and agricultural elite seek to make money with a minimum of interference from the government. Political parties have been weak in ideology and leadership, and labor has not been well organized. The Catholic Church has largely refrained from politics. None of these institutions poses a threat to the army's dominance. At the heart of the matter is the Esquema Politico, "a tacit understanding among the military, the private sector, and the political parties to create a democratic facade. They want to avoid the twin threats of mobilized politicized labor and campesino populations, and an unpredictable and unmanageable political processes."[125]

During August 1989, Lieutenant Jose Fernando Mineras Navas was arrested when he tried to ship 25 kilos of cocaine to the United States. Mineras testified that La Aurora International Airport was used by drug traffickers who had protection all the way to the presidency. Mineras furthered accused the brother of then president Cerezo of permitting the illegal entry and departure of foreigners to and from the country. The arrest and murder, in Pavon Penitentiary, of Gary Elliot, an American pilot smuggling cocaine through Guatemala raises further questions. Prepared to testify in early 1990, Elliot appears to have been silenced to prevent damaging testimony.

Guatemala is an important location for money laundering. "Drug trafficking interests now have large investments in real estate and no longer have problems laundering money since they have their own banking contacts." Indications that Guatemala is a regional money laundering center are suggested by the fact that in 1991, in spite of a recession, new construction increased 60%. On one day alone, in early March 1992, $41 million entered the central banking system.

In 1987, the US government estimated that approximately 750 hectares of marijuana were under production and 675 hectares were under cultivation in Guatemala. A year later, the published figures suggest that earlier estimates were extremely low. Claims of over 17,000 acres of opium poppies under cultivation in the San Marcos and Huehuetenango regions were made by the US embassy in 1988. New York Times journalist Lindsey Gruson wrote in 1987 that Guatemala had "become the sixth largest producer of poppies in the world."[126]

In 1989, approximately 3.1 metric tons of cocaine were seized. In 1990, 15.5 metric tons were seized. According to other sources, one ton of cocaine a week passed through Guatemala every week during the same year. In 1991, it is estimated that 150 metric tons of cocaine passed through the country. During the period from January 1992 through January 1993, 9,508 kilos of cocaine were seized. During the period from January 1993 to May 1993, period, another 335 kilos were seized. In 1994, 1.9 tons of cocaine were seized.[127]

It is of some interest to note that the National Narcotic Intelligence Consumers Committee Report: The Supply of Illicit Drugs to the United States, August 1995, states that "transshipment of cocaine through Guatemala continued, although the volume has decreased slightly in the past several years."[128] When one compares the increasing quantities of drugs reported south of Guatemala and also north in Mexico, it is apparent that something is amiss with the NNICC Report.[129]

It is estimated that today there are 640 legal airfields, and 1,600 clandestine landing fields, most of which are located along the southwest coastal areas. These fields service approximately 145 drug flights per month. Guatemala is the location of large cocaine "stash" sites which are constantly being replenished by twin-engine aircraft from northern South America. A steady stream of utility flights by single engine aircraft fly from the stash sites to southern Mexico, where they off load or drop their cargo and return. Accidents among drug aircraft that operate to and from Guatemala are the highest in the entire transit pipeline. Guatemala is the location for large "stashes" of cocaine, the repositories of which are kept filled by a constant stream of drug aircraft from South America, and increasing maritime deliveries.[130]

MEXICO

The modus operandi has been: the trafficker first buys a Bronco, then a Mercedes, then a mansion, then a politico. Some would reverse the order and change the official, claiming that none of the material goods is within the smugglers budget if he does not first own a judge.[131]

Mexico is the linchpin in El Conducto. By years end, 1995, it had became quite clear that Mexico was poised to become a driving force in drug trafficking in the Western Hemisphere. Driven by events in Colombia and Mexico, the cocaine trafficking business has evolved to a new plateau. No longer is Mexico a business agent for Colombian traffickers. Mexico has become a prime mover in the business of cocaine and in the directed growing of opium poppies in Peru. Integral to this evolution are events that reach back to the first days of the Salinas administration. One cannot understand the situation today without reflection on the past.

Assuming power in 1988, President Carlos Salinas de Gortari was faced with the legacy of the "lost years" of the de La Madrid administration. State ownership and control of the public infrastructure was marred with blatant inefficiency and corruption. Reliance on Mexico's petroleum reserves, heavy borrowing of overseas capital, and little reinvestment that would benefit the country. By 1982, Mexico was threatening to default on its $120 billion debt. By 1987, capital flight was taking place on a large scale and inflation had risen to 159%. Perhaps the most telling fact was that the tortilla, the basic foodstuff, had to be subsidized by the government.

The campaign was a hotly contested event with the National Action Party (PAN) doggedly hounding the Party of Institutionalized Revolution (PRI). Following an election in which the PRI juggled votes—there are many who believe with good reason that the PAN was again deprived of its victory thanks to a last minute "purchase" of votes—Carlos Salinas de Gortari took the reins of government. Surrounding himself with "technos"—Mexico's best and brightest technocrats—many of who had received advanced degrees at the best US universities, the Mexican miracle took root. Inflation was the first order of business. Creating innovative agreements between business and organized labor, Salinas instituted tough, tight fiscal policies. The budget crisis was handled by curtailing government spending rather than increasing taxes, subsidies to state firms were reduced, and political patronage was reined in. Through the vehicle of the "pacto"— a working agreement between government, business and unions, prices and wages were limited, price controls on basic staples was instituted, and of the greatest importance, government, business, and the unions came together to discuss the future. The results were little short of a "milagro." Major structural reforms, privatization, deregulation, tax reform, and foreign investments laws dramatically liberalized. Monies from the cost cutting exercises were applied to debt service, and to politically popular moves to fund rural electrification and sanitation. With tax reform came something that had never been seen in Mexico before, people went to jail for tax evasion. By 1991, a Gallup Survey indicated that 70% of those queried felt that the Salinas Administration had gotten things on track. Capital flight had been reversed, the national debt had been restructured and a truce drawn up with the international banking community.

However, the cost of the "pacto" was high. Salinas found it prudent to agree to a series of compromises with the PRI old-guard. The message was clear: the "PRIistas" and the "technos" had to be counter-balanced. Thus, Enrique Alvarez Castillo, who was the Governor of Jalisco when the Guadalajara cartel freely operated there and DEA agent KiKi Camarena was kidnapped and murdered, became the Mexican attorney general. Pablo Diaz, who had been chief of state of the Jalisco State police under Governor Alvarez, became the Chief of the Mexican federal Judicial Police (MFJP). Javier Garcia Paniagua, ex-Director of the Direccion Federal de Seguridad (DFS) and President of the PRI, who was accused of being present at the Guadalajara cartel meetings at which the Camarena kidnapping was planned was appointed as the Chief of Police for the Federal District of Mexico City. And, a Colegio Militar classmate of Garcia and Nazar Haro and another ex-DFS Director, Fernando Gutierrez Barrios, became Secretary of Gobernacion (roughly the equivalent of the CIA). With these linkages, it is not surprising that when Colombian and Mexican drug traffickers sought mutually agreeable arrangements, the full range of Mexican government agencies quickly became parties to the agreements. Attorney General Jorge Carpizo Macgregor summed it up with eloquent simplicity, "We have traitors."[132]

Bedazzled by the success of his economic miracle, Carlos Salinas wrongly assumed that he was in control of the massive drug-induced corruption that was growing just beneath the surface of his government. It was the slaying of Cardinal Juan Jesus Posadas Ocampo on June 21, 1993 that peeled back the covers just enough to reveal the depth to which drugs and corruption had permeated Mexican government and society—a situation that reached to the very top of the Salinas administration. Cut down in a hail of bullets, the death of Posados brought to center stage the specter of the "Colombianizacion" of Mexico.

Within hours of the attack on the cardinal in Guadalajara, the official statements issued by the Mexican government began to be questioned. Coroner Mario Rivas Souza told newsmen that some of the shots that hit Posados were as close as three feet away, and that the attack appeared to be premeditated. "Powerful political and economic interests are related to the death of Posadas Ocampo," said Nicolas Lopez, president of the Latin American Bishops Council. State Attorney General Leobardo Larios Guzman stated that the cardinals' vehicle unfortunately had arrived at the airport "at the moment of confrontation" between gangs of two prominent drug dealers from Tijuana and Sinaloa. The cardinal was probably confused as one of them." The chief prosecutor in Mexico City argued that the cardinal's death was an aberration, since violence is not predominant in Mexico. The facts, however, belie his statement. The recent killing of a witness in the Posados Ocampo case further raises the issue of the real facts behind the Cardinal's death. Ramon Torres Mendez, one of eight suspects, was found smothered to death—with his own pillow—in his cell in Guadalajara.

While the country basked in the light of the "new" Mexico, the losers, at least from their own perception, were the "dinosaurs" of the PRI. The promise of "institutionalized revolution" had been tried, it had succeeded, and that success had shaken the PRI to its very roots. The seemingly senseless killing of the chief Catholic prelate in Mexico, gave cause to many who had held their criticism in check. Laura Castillo, spokeswoman for the Democratic Revolutionary Party (PRD) stated that "the president knows very well where the drug trafficker's landing strips are, when they come and go, and who they are, and they haven't acted until now."[133]

The final bubble burst with the assassination/murder of presidential candidate Luis Donaldo Colosio on March 23 1994. In a comic-opera setting, much like the murder of Cardinal Posados Ocampo, Mexico was sent into a tail spin. When everything was shaken out, the single-gun, lone assassin theory was supplanted by the multiple-weapons, conspiracy truth. With former PJF officers deeply involved in a plot that appears to have strong links with the dinosaurs of the PRI and narcotraficantes, the murder cast a new light on the inner workings of the PRI.

In appointing a fact-finding commission to investigate the killing, President Salinas said the commission would play a vital role in helping to "open the investigation and avoid a climate of suspicion" in the wake of the killing. Six weeks after the commission was appointed they resigned because they were not given access to certain reports and evidence compiled by government investigators. Any doubts as to a cover-up were ended.[134]

Commenting on the killing of Colosio, the respected Mexican news journal, El Financiero, claimed that it had acquired a copy of a report from a US intelligence agency that revealed that Colosio had made the decision to strike a strong blow against drug trafficking in manner similar to the tactics used by former president Salinas when he attempted to break the power of the Trade Union of Petroleum Workers of the Mexican Republic, early in his administration.[135] The paper went on to quote at length, Eduardo Valle Espinosa, "El Buho" (the Owl). A former government investigator who fled the country, "El Buho" claims that Colosio was assassinated because he refused to attend a dinner in his honor sponsored by narcotraffickers in Tamaulipas who sought to bring him into the Mexican version of La Empresa.[136] Tamaulipas State is the home of the Gulf Coast family of Juan Garcia Abrego. It will be interesting in the months ahead to learn what role if any Garcia Abrego might have played in these accusations as there appears to have been close ties between the Gulf Coast family, the PRI, the Mexican government and the Colosio campaign in the form of family members who appeared on the presidential candidates logistics and security teams just a few weeks before the assassination.[137]

In an event less publicized but of great significance, the police chief of Tijuana—a man who disputed the single gun theory—was ambushed and murdered as he responded to what was later determined to be a false call to police headquarters. All indications point to the murder as an act to ensure that anyone close to the truth would be silenced.

Colosio's death left a severe power vacuum. Selected by the outgoing president, the new candidate bears the PRI's stamp of approval. The destape (the unveiling) of the presidential candidate is the result of years of intense behind the scenes political work. Forced to go through a second destape of only a week's duration, the choice of Ernesto Sedillo Ponce de Leon was a stop-gap measure. A techno with little political experience, Zedillo was placed into a situation in which he was clearly over his head. As the selection of Zedillo was announced, the elder statesmen the PRI put out the word that they were there to help. The price that would have to be paid for that help was for Zedillo to keep things "in balance."

The dust had barely settled when Jose Francisco Ruiz Massieu, deputy leader of the PRI was killed. Within a short period of time 12 persons were suspected of involvement. They included a former congressman and a former federal government official. Mario Ruiz Massieu, brother of the slain politician, theorized that the killing was a "political affair with aid or financing from drug traffickers."[138] In short order, Mario Ruiz Massieu would soon be accused of accepting more than $6 million from Humberto Garcia Abrego—brother of Juan—for securing his release from federal authorities.[139] Shortly thereafter, in a precedent breaking series of events, Raul Salinas—brother of the former president—would be arrested for the death of Massieu.

It is the rule of law that binds together democratic institutions into a cohesive state. The absence of law or the flagrant abuse of the law signals trouble. Such is the case in Mexico. Of the 60,000 people arrested on drug related charges in the past 8 years, between 60 to 70 percent of them have been freed through bail or bond. This is the reflection of a judicial system that is so corrupt as to be totally ineffective. From the Attorney General's office (PGR) to the lowest courts in Mexico, law and justice is an illusion. At the pinnacle of this void is the Office of the Attorney General. Three Attorneys General were disgraced and fired during the Salinas administration. Enrique Alverez del Castillo, the former Governor of Jalisco State—the first of the corruptos—was deeply involved with the Garcia Abrego Tamaulipas trafficking family before he took office. During his tenure as governor, drug trafficking thrived in Jalisco. Miguel Felix Gallardo operated there with impunity—Alvarez del Castillo failed to execute 14 arrest warrants against him. The governor was also implicated in the kidnapping and death of DEA agent Camerena. During his tenure, police acted with singular impunity as a wave of kidnappings and rapes became the order of the day. During this period, Norma Corona Sapien, President of the Human Right's Commission of Siniloa State brought pressure on President Salinas to form a national Human Rights effort. Shortly after the commission was formed Corona was assassinated.

Next in line was Ignacio Morales Lechuga, who was appointed in May 1991, and was forced to resign in January 1994. With instructions to get a handle on the drug trafficking problem, Morales stepped into a war between Hector Palma, "El Guero," and Miguel Felix. A series of shoot-outs in Sinaloa and Tijuana ensued with no resolution of the problem. In fact, "El Chapo" Guzman and the Arellano Felix gang also engaged in open warfare after a disagreement over a shipment of cocaine. Morales made no headway in attempting to curtail the growing power of Juan Garcia Abrego who, by that point in time was designating those who should serve as deputies in the PGR.

The Garcia Abrego "appointments" were sealed with enormous sums of money which ensured that the Tamaulipas operations would go untouched by law enforcement. Morales was also involved in the Alvarez Machain affair. (Humberto Alvarez Machain was the doctor that kept DEA Agent Camerena alive while he was being tortured for information on US and Mexican government country drug operations.) It was the Christina discotheque incident in Iguala and a series of bombings in Culican that were the final straws that led to him being sacked. In May, 1994, Morales Lechuga was presented with criminal prosecution charges for his links with the incident at Tlalixcoyan—a shoot out between PJF forces and the Army, where 7 policemen were executed by soldiers who were guarding a delivery of drugs.

Following Morales, from January 1993 to January 1994, Jorge Carpizo McGregor brought a heretofore missing sense of integrity to the PGR's office. He let it be known that anyone who did not toe the line was going to jail. He fired over 100 PGR agents and fired the chief of the PJF—Rodolfo Leon Aragon. When Carpizo indicted four congressmen on corruption charges the courts refused to prosecute them. He then accused the judiciary of "acting suspiciously." He also sought to bring charges against journalists that he believed were involved in drug trafficking. In his zeal to clean up corruption, he appears to have given short shrift to a wave of kidnappings that were sweeping the country. His efforts to break the back of corruption in the judicial and police agencies was viewed as too threatening to many within the government. It appears that it was the kidnappings and the Chiapas rebellion that was used by the "dinosaurs" to demand his resignation.

Carpizo was replaced by Diego Valades who had been with the Federal Prosecutor's office. A political hack whose appointees were believed to be largely corrupt, Valades bungled attempts to bring additional charges in the Colosio killing. His final straw was a altercation with the National Action Party in Baja California that left the already embattled office further tarnished.

Humberto Benitez Trevino followed Valades and embarked upon a total restructuring of the Federal Judicial Police (PJF). Five commanders were discharged and the files of all 2,000 employees were reviewed. He dismantled a number of special investigation's groups and the General Operations Coordinating Office. Two weeks after the investigation began, PJF commander Jose Luis Fortuna was found in his car— executed—on the outskirts of Mexico City.

In accusations that could prove damning if substantiated, Eduardo Valle Espinosa argues that "the group led by the top representative of the Colombian cartels in Mexico had been on the verge of arrest when, quite mysteriously, all evidence disappeared, all evidence disappeared from the PGR offices in Matamoros, documents, weapons, and even the cocaine. Pilar Silva Arroyo, head of the PGR offices was later removed from office. Later, her involvement in the matter was also dismissed. How can one explain the existence of these individuals? Very simply, because they were protected for 15 years by the PGR, protected by the best commanders, the best communications system, the best intelligence systems. The PGR adopted them and made them what they are. That office is an intermediary of the federal government with the drug traffickers."[140]

At this same point time, the Catholic bishops of the country delivered a particularly forceful message to the country, declaring that "40% of the PGR's office was involved in drug trafficking."[141] The bishops went on to suggest that arrest of the Attorney General of Baja California "represents an advance" in the investigation of Cardinal Posados Ocampo. Calling it "narco-sacrilege"—"incompetence, concealment, and complicity by silence"— the bishops claimed that the murder of Posados Ocampo had not been solved because "certain officials are in collusion with drug trafficking. There is no other explanation for the killers being fugitives at large."[142]

The Mexican Catholic hierarchy has also accused members of the Army of being involved in drug trafficking. In a document entitled *Pastoral Instruction on Violence and Peace*, prelate Hector Gonzalez argued that the "drug trafficking Mafia has bought or become associated with a large number of public officials and members of the military." Gonzalez was forced to retract the statement by the Vatican, but the damage had been successfully inflicted.[143]

Further research into these statements suggest that the Bishops appeared to believe that with Benitiz in the PGR's office there might be hope for at least a lessening of corruption. Looking even deeper, it is apparent that since 1988 the Catholic bishops had been coming down hard on the drug trafficking threat in the country through a series of low-key, but pointed statements. This threat may well have been the driving force behind the assassination of Posados. Ironically, his successor—Cardinal Juan Sandoval Iniquez— appears to be even more the fire-brand.

In researching drug trafficking in Mexico, it become clear early on, that the military is deeply involved in drugs. From the Mexican admiral, who was in charge of the Veracruz area—the very waters that waterborne cocaine shipments passed through to Garcia Abrego's organization—with three large estates in the Houston, Texas area, to the generals who control "la plaza" in their military regions—the Tlalixcoyan debacle of 1991 is the classic example of army involvement—the military is a key player in the Mexican drug connection.

Once peaceful Mexico, rocked by political upheaval and economic crisis, is in the grip of a crime wave that analysts say is tearing at the fabric of a society already stretched to its limit. Nationwide, robberies are up by 50 percent from a year ago, according to a survey of Mexican states by the newspaper Reforma. While homicides declined slightly overall, they rose in the Mexico City, Guadalajara, and Cuidad Juarez, where 13 people were slain in one week. In Juarez, following the order that all police officers must submit to random drug testing, 300 of the city's 1,700 police officers resigned. Many of them are now believed to be on the streets, preying on the populace.[144]

The present wave of violence in many ways reflects a similar period during the Salinas administration. More than 80 people were killed during 1992 in the city of Culiacan, "little Medellin," the capital of Sinaloa state. The level and intensity of the violence was exemplified by the killings instigated by the Sinaloa "capos," Joaquin Guzman Loera—"El Chapo," and Hector Luis Palma—"El Cuero Palma." Beginning in early 1990, they murdered the human right's director Norma Corona Sapien and then executed all those individuals who could bear witness. Shortly thereafter they murdered Rudolfo Sanchez Duarte, son of the ex-governor of Sinaloa. In Guadalajara, they tortured and killed Marco Toledo, son of a another ex-governor. Turning then to settle accounts with rival trafficker Miguel Angel Felix Gallardo, they kidnapped, tortured and executed Gallardo's seven nephews. A cousin of Gallardo's, Chalino Sanchez Felix, a noted Sinaloa singer was also executed. In Puerto Vallarta, 50 Guzman henchmen assaulted the Christina discotheque and massacred eight people. Quickening the pace in early 1993, they ambushed and killed Cuidad Juarez "capo" Rafael Aguilar Guajardo, and a nearby US tourist. Following up on a threat shortly thereafter they executed the former Sinaloa state attorney Rodolfo Alvarez Farber in front of his wife.

"Its a symptom of the end of a political regime, the end of a historical period that began after the revolution," noted Lorenzo Meyer, a prominent historian and political commentator. "The incapacity of the government to fight crime is only one element of this decline. In fact, the government is incapable of doing anything. Just look at the economy, at the political system, at the impunity of drug-traffickers." This sentiment is echoed by William Olsen, former deputy assistant secretary of state in the Bureau of International Narcotics Matters. "It's no longer this old-time corruption that people understood. It's a new kind of corruption that's following a path right to the heart of the political system."[145] A further indication of the breadth and depth of the violence is the fact that over the past 7 years, nearly 500 people have disappeared in Mexico—usually labor figures, minor political activists, human-rights activists and journalists.

What many outsiders fail to understand is that law enforcement in Mexico is considered a career of last choice. Mexican police have a reputation for committing abuses, such as extortion and brutality against the public with impunity. When the judicial police began looking for new offices in Roma, a neighborhood in Mexico City, residents in the neighborhood mounted a storm of resistance, arguing that in order to save the neighborhood they had to kick the police out.[146] Mexico City has had three patrol police chiefs in the past six years and during the same period, four chiefs of the Judicial Police. Corruption involving drug traffickers or organized crime has sometimes reached all the way to the top. Recent investigations have shown just how widespread the corruption has become. While the *mordida* (bribe) is well known, the *entre* (tribute) is deeply ingrained in the system. The *entre* is paid to senior police officers to keep patrol-car assignments or other perks.

The ties between Mexican law enforcement agencies—in particular the PGR and the PJF— and drug trafficking are best exemplified in a link analysis which is focused on the operations of Juan Garcia Abrego. It becomes abundantly clear that both active and former members of each of the federal agencies were involved with the Tamaulipas drug mafia (see Figure 7.2).

In the case of ties between traffickers and the Federal Highway Police—an agency that has jurisdiction over the large trucks that travel through Mexico to the US border from Central America—"El Buho" argues that its parent organization— the Communications and Transportation Secretariat with pilots, airports, aircraft, maritime transport companies, and gasoline—is, by commission or omission, in the service of the drug traffickers.[147]

Upon the capture of the second in command of the Carillo Fuentes family, Moises Juarez Ledezma, a small arsenal was discovered along with an equally large number of police uniforms all with PJF and PGR insignia, confirming in part that the traffickers were not only tied in with law enforcement but also dress like them.[148]

In a report from the Attorney General's office in late 1994 entitled *Evaluation and Follow-up of the National Drug Program*—in what must be considered the understatement of the 1990's—the authors noted that counter drug efforts had been less successful towards the end of the Salinas regime. It noted that "crime related to the production, trafficking, and sales of drugs had assumed proportions to an extent that it was beginning to look like a power parallel to the state of law." The study went on to note that drug trafficking had the capability to penetrate Mexican government structures as well as private institutions and both factors called out the risks to the national security of the country.[149]

Figures for aircraft seized in Mexico show a downward spiral from 1989 to the present:

1989–78
1990–66
1991–40
1992–26
1993–24
1994–14

Figure 7.2
Link Analysis

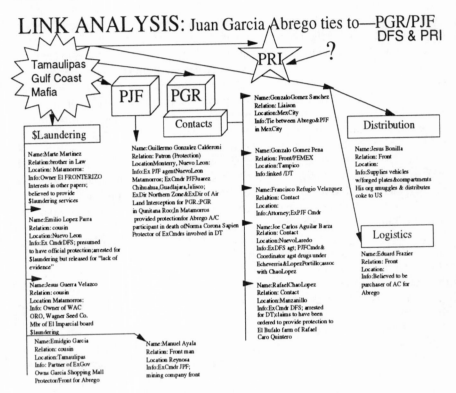

LINK ANALYSIS: Juan Garcia Abrego ties to—PGR/PJF
DFS & PRI

Tamaulipas
Gulf Coast
Mafia

PRI ?

PJF   PGR

Contacts

Distribution

$Laundering

Name:GonzaloGomez Sanchez
Relation: Liaison
Location:MexCity
Info:Tie between Abrego&PJF
in MexCity

Name:Marte Martinez
Relation:brother in Law
Location: Matamorros:
Info:Owner El FRONTERIZO
Interests in other papers;
believed to provide
$laundering services

Name:Guillermo Gonzalez Calderoni
Relation: Patron (Protection)
Location:Monterry, Nuevo Leon:
Info:Ex PJF agentNuevoLeon
Matamorros; ExCmdr PJFJuarez
Chihuahua,Guadlajara,Jalisco;
ExDir Northern Zone&ExDir of Air
Land Interception for PGR.;PGR
in Qunitana Roo;In Matamorros
provided protectionfor Abrego A/C
participant in death ofNorma Corona Sapien
Protector of ExCmdrs involved in DT

Name:Gonzalo Gomez Pena
Relation: Front/PEMEX
Location:Tampico
Info:linked /DT

Name:Jesus Bonilla
Relation: Front
Location:
Info:Supplies vehicles
w/forged plates&compartments
His org smuggles & distributes
coke to US

Name:Emilio Lopez Parra
Relation: cousin
Location:Nuevo Leon
Info:Ex CmdrDFS; presumed
to have official protection;arrested for
$laundering but released for "lack of
evidence"

Name:Francisco Refugio Velazquez
Relation: Contact
Location:
Info:Attorney;ExPJF Cmdr

Name:Joe Carlos Aguilar Barza
Relation: Contact
Location:NuevoLaredo
Info:ExDFS agt; PJFCmdr&
Coordinator agst drugs under
Echeverria&LopezPortillo;assoc
with ChaoLopez

Logistics

Name:Eduard Frazier
Relation: Front
Location:
Info:Believed to be
purchaser of AC for
Abrego

Name:Jesus Guerra Velazco
Relation: cousin
Location Matamorros:
Info: Owner of WAC
ORO, Wagner Seed Co.
Mbr of El Imparcial board
$laundering

Name:RafaelChaoLopez
Relation: Contact
Location:Manzanillo
Info:ExCmdr DFS; arrested
for DT;claims to have been
ordered to provide protection to
El Bufalo farm of Rafael
Caro Quintero

Name:Emidgio Garcia
Relation: cousin
Location:Tamaulipas
Info: Partner of ExGov
Owns Garcia Shopping Mall
Protector/Front for Abrego

Name:Manuel Ayala
Relation: Front man
Location Reynosa
Info:ExCmdr JPF;
mining company front

Also, according to Mexican figures the amount of cocaine seized, dropped after 1990: 1989—39,523 kilos; 1990—46,000 kilos; 1991—11,000 kilos; 1992—unknown; 1993—20,000 kilos; and 1994—10,00 kilos.

If it is true that 6 out of 10 kilos of cocaine seized by government agencies reenter the market through government agencies, then Mexican seizure figures are but a drop in the bucket and a measure of effectiveness that bears close scrutiny.[150] Conversely, drug profits appear to have increased from a 1991 high of $500 billion, to $800 billion in 1993.[151] Extrapolating out to 1995 and 1996, it would appear that drug profits in Mexico might have reached to a figure just short of a trillion dollars. In light of the foregoing, one cannot help but wonder just how much of the start-up costs of the Mexican economic miracle was underwritten with drug dollars.[152]

Mañana in Mexico

The much heralded capture of Juan Garcia Abrego in early January 1996, may well have a number of unanticipated consequences. A billionaire trafficker, it is believed that he controlled approximately 50 percent of the cocaine that flowed to Mexico and then on to the United States. US and Mexican authorities believe that Garcia Abrego had close ties to Raul Salinas. They believe that one factor in the death of Massieu may have been falling out between Salinas and Massieu over a real estate deal that was to have been funded by drug-dollars from the trafficker.[153]

Everything points to a war in which the drug trafficking organizations will fight for territory and control of "la plaza." Two days after Garcia Abrego's apprehension, federal agents in Monterrey were met by heavy gun-fire when they attempted to arrest another drug dealer. A day later, an unknown gunman walked into a Monterey cafe and executed a lawyer who had accused a northern states' attorney general of drug ties.[154] The war may well have begun.

It appears at this time, that by default, Garcia Abrego has ceded much of his multibillion-dollar empire to rival Amado Carrillo Fuentes, the "Lord of the Skies." Carrillo Fuentes pioneered the use of 727 cargo jets to carry his drugs and was believed to have moved 20 tons of cocaine during the month of November 1995. However, this could turn out to be a bloody affair similar to the open warfare that wracked Mexico in the early 1990's. Those in Garcia Abrego's organization will soon turn to guns and explosives to thwart the Carrillo Fuentes family.

It is curious that Mexico allowed the immediate extradition of Garcia Abrego to the United States. Although he is a US citizen, the narcotraficante's testimony could be extremely damaging to many Salinas holdovers in the Zedillo government. Following Garcia Abrego's arrest, many Mexicans angrily asked why the government did not question him about his many alleged crimes in Mexico, dozens of killings and his apparent ties with the former Salinas administration. US officials say that he has refused to cooperate with his American interrogators.

Getting to the bottom of what Mexicans call "narcopolitics" has proved virtually impossible because of the code of secrecy that politicians and drug lords obey. The Mexican government does its best to keep those in the know from talking. When a reporter passed a written questionnaire to Felix Gallardo through the drug lord's lawyer, he gave only evasive answers. The lawyer noted privately that the authorities would punish him if he talked more freely. In a similar event involving Raul Salinas, the result was virtually the same. Amid 5,000 words of eloquent philosophizing about prison existence, Salinas alluded only vaguely to the charges against him.[155]

In the United States, Garcia Abrego will probably receive life imprisonment even though he has been charged with collusion in several murders. Had he been held in Mexico, the chances of an "accident" or "suicide" taking place would have allowed him to be silenced. It may well be that President Zedillo has taken a bold step and decided to distance his administration from the Salinas years and the rampant corruption. If this is the case, such a move will no doubt anger the already embattled and isolated PRI which could attempt to reach out to Zedillo in the same manner that they did to Luis Donaldo Colosio.

From the moment of his taking office, Ernesto Zedillo stumbled on to a rollercoaster ride that still continues. The economy nose-dived requiring a bail-out by the United States. Today, it is estimated that $5.2 billion has fled the country since the Colosio murder. The "errors of December"—the disastrous devaluation of the peso—still have the country reeling. Add to that, the smoldering insurgency in Chiapas and the seemingly never-ending scandals of the Salinas years, the future looks bleak. Looking beyond the headlines, it is apparent that the primary threat from drug trafficking is not so much the Colombianizacion of Mexico. The real threat is the depth of the corruption that appears to reach into the very soul of Mexico. While Colombia may have a chance to reverse the trend, positive change may well be out of the reach of the Mexican government.

With the war of words heating up on both sides of the border, many experts say the rhetoric is irrelevant: whether by using praise or taking a hard line, the United States can do little to make Mexico's fight against drugs more effective. "The problem with US pressure about drugs is knowing where to stop," said Jorge G. Castaneda, a political analyst at the National Autonomous University of Mexico. "The corruption is so huge and so deep that if you keep digging, you will undermine this government—and that's something the Clinton administration clearly has no interest in doing."[156]

A series of events that occurred during the last weeks of February 1996 appear to have revealed more of the iceberg. The drug corruption case against Raul Salina was severely damaged when several top businessmen said they had given him most of the $100 million found in his Swiss bank accounts. Although the charges still stand against Salinas relating to the 1994 assassination of Ruiz Massieu, it may well be that the whole issue of drug corruption in the Salinas administration may be swept under the rug. In another set-back, a US magistrate in New Jersey, where Mario Ruiz Massieu has been jailed since last March, has rejected repeated attempts to extradite him to Mexico to face trial on drug corruption charges. US diplomats now admit that both governments have botched the case.[157] The broad package of legislation to reform Mexico's notoriously lax laws on money laundering, government corruption and the sale of precursor chemicals used in processing drugs has been stalled in the Mexican congress since November 1995. While the proposed legislation was hailed by both the Mexican and US governments—the bill was proposed by Attorney General Antonio Lozano, a member of the conservative National Action Party—it has been twisting in the wind, thanks to opposition from Mexican businessmen who argue that it would increase government control of the economy. The bill is not expected to be reconsidered until fall, 1996—if then.[158]

Today, rumors abound about a huge pre-election "donation" of $40 million Colombian narco-dollars that was deposited in PRI coffers. The money is alleged to have been used to swing the election for the PRI. In the past, the PRI "bag-men" made the rounds prior to each election, "fertilizing" the electorate with pesos. Such occurrences are the way things are done. It is estimated today that as much as $500 million a year is paid by traficantes to bribe Mexican officials. What is different about the $40 million is this: if it can be proved that it came from Colombian narcotraficantes—in a set of circumstances akin to the presidential election-crisis in Colombia—the resulting uproar could be the boost needed to drive the PRI into a crisis from which it will not recover.[159]

A REGIONAL OVERVIEW: PRODUCTION AND TRANSIT

Obedezco Pero No Cumplo (I Obey, But I Do Not Comply)

As 1995 drew to a close, it appeared that contrary to US government figures, cocaine production continues to rise with production up approximately 13% to 15% over the past two years. A growing percentage of that increase is being directed to European markets. US-sponsored programs for the eradication of coca plants, an exercise in futility in the past, will continue to falter in the production countries since it is not in their best interests to eradicate, nor are they capable of implementing the programs. Colombia and Bolivia will continue their efforts to both commercialize and legalize coca products. Coca cultivation will continue to expand in the Yungas and Apolo regions, with the new crops coming on line in the 1996–1997 time frame. Recent planting in the central and lower Huallaga, the Ucayli, and the Apurimac valleys will also be ready for harvest in late 1996. There has been a shift in the ratio of coca paste and base being shipped, suggesting that the regional use of basuco is also on the upswing. Without exception, the consumption of drugs in both the production and transit countries is on the rise, dramatically so. With no mechanisms to cope with the scourge of basuco, marijuana, and heroin, everything points to a drug epidemic in late 1996, similar in nature to the crack epidemic that wracked the US during the late 1980's.

The cultivation of marijuana to create *aceite de marijuana* (oil of marijuana) is on the increase. All indicators point to this being an export product. The cultivation and production of *amapola* (opium) will continue to increase thanks to the high profit margin and the growing market.

It appears to be but a matter of time before the onslaught of "designer" drugs is felt. The tremendous amounts of ephrindrine being seized in Mexico were first thought to be used to "cut" cocaine before shipping it on to the United States, thus increasing profits. What appears to be the case, however, is that the production of methamphetamines in Mexico, all aimed at the US market, is growing dramatically. With the strides that narcotraficante *cocineros* and *quimicos* (cooks and chemists) have made (for example, agua rica and the cocaine machine) the synthesizing of a wide range of "designer" drugs appears easy.

Throughout the region, following the example of the production countries, new laws prohibiting extradition for trafficking-related crimes have been codified. The repatriation of money, no questions asked, continues to be encouraged. In 1991, Colombia removed the $10,000 limitation, allowing its citizens to bring in or take out of the country any amount of foreign currency. Repentance decrees and lessened penalties for drug trafficking are the rule of thumb throughout the production region. A quiet accommodation with drug traffickers is under way. The key to the latter appears to be widespread growth of corruption, thanks to the liberal application of drug dollars coupled with the understanding that trafficking without violence is acceptable.

Of future importance is the legitimization of traffickers. Much like Michael Corleone in the *Godfather*, the first tier of traffickers have been buying their way into proper society. Through strategic investments in public utilities and infrastructure, positioning of assets in legitimate businesses, and the use of ready dollars to buy acceptance, today's narcotraficantes will become tomorrow's business and political leaders.

With the exception of Brazil and Haiti, the entire region has shown positive economic growth. But this growth will be difficult to sustain, particularly in light of the fact that per capita income has not maintained the same pace. Trade liberalization throughout the region is widespread, but the downside is that this hurts small and medium sized businesses by depriving them of ready access to capital. The result is a ready market for drug dollars that can provide the impetus for growth and an ideal situation for money laundering and narco-legitimization efforts.

For the campesinos throughout the production and transit countries, the situation continues to look grim. Coffee prices recently hit a 20-year low, and the threat of a banana quota by the European Community could hurt exports. The impact of both events will be to further encourage the growth of coca and amapola.

The overall political situation throughout the region is one that suggests change and turmoil. In the 1988–1989 elections, every governing party in the region, with the exception of Mexico, was ousted. With the results of the elections 1993 and 1994 complete, the promise of continued change is in the air.

One of the most pronounced trends throughout the South and Central America is the growth of multilateral counter drug accords which do not include the United States. They range from the United Nations agreement to supervise the implementation of bilateral anti-drug agreements between the US and Peru, a move to alleviate "repressive" US tactics; to Venezuela's proposal for a pact that will "allow Latin America to discuss the issue with the same voice," in order to "deal with our needs or relations with the industrialized countries of the North." An exemplar of this trend was a December 1995 joint operation involving Panama, El Salvador, Mexico, Belize, Guatemala, Honduras, Nicaragua, and Costa Rica. During Operation United, 6.23 tons of cocaine were seized along with weapons, counterfeit cash, and vehicles throughout the week long operation. The bulk of the cocaine was seized in Mexico and most of the rest in Panama. The operation came on the heels of a regional security pact signed by the Central American nations aimed at boosting the war against drugs.[160]

It is clear that the US role in regional counter drug efforts, at least in the manner in which they have been force-fed to date, is no longer desired. The growing importance of the Inter-American Drug Abuse Control Commission is clearly the harbinger of things to come. Such moves will of necessity force the United States to rethink its programs. Today, in spite of the havoc caused by drug trafficking, the production countries have attempted to come to grips with the problem in their own way. US counter-drug efforts have failed. A further distancing from United States policies and strategies will continue, thus precluding any US policy that does not take into account the new order of things.

What is clear is that the smug attitude that was directed against the Spanish crown for two hundred years by Latin Americans will continue to be directed against

United States drug policy. "Obedezco pero no cumplo—I obey, but I do not comply"—has been and will continue to be the rule of thumb.

THE ANDEAN STRATEGY: A BRIDGE TOO FAR

> *Senator Kerry*: What would your principal criticism be of the strategy at this point?
> *Sherman Funk*: Aside from the goal, which I said is unmeasurable, it is assumed there is a kind of monolithic, inflexible situation applied to the entire Andean Region.
>
> —US Senate Hearings[161]

The primary elements of the Andean Strategy are:

1. To strengthen the political institutions of the Andean nations, a policy essential for the promotion of accountable government and protection of human rights;
2. To promote the general economic interests of the Latin American nations, along with the particular economic needs of the former coca growers;
3. To assist the security forces in the region so that their interests are tied to the democratic regime generally and to assist democratic policies aimed at specific security, legal, and economic threats to the society.

In February 1991, the Committee on Foreign Affairs of the House of Representatives held its first meeting on the Andean Strategy. Opening the session, Chairman Robert G. Torricelli stated that the basic question to be asked about the strategy was whether the drug war was "being conducted with full regard for local realities, in genuine consultation with our allies, or is the strategy made in Washington and designed more for sound bites than for policy."[162] With the implementation of the Andean Strategy barely begun, the questions and testimony were relatively benign. Such was not the case one year later. After welcoming the speakers from the State Department and the US Southern Command, Senator John Kerry set the stage for the hearing by expressing his concern that "a lot of this may be like holding a bucket under a waterfall. Back in 1987 the DEA set a goal of reducing United States cocaine supplies by 50 percent in three years. That goal has been abandoned. In 1990, the President announced a new goal-reducing imports of cocaine and other drugs by 15 percent. That goal, too, has been abandoned. The production is at record levels."[163]

Responding to Senator Kerry, Melvyn Levitsky, assistant secretary of state for International Matters, stated that the Andean Strategy was being implemented "by focusing on working with producer and transit countries to attack drug trafficking from its point of origin and in dealing with every link of the drug chain from leaf to street." Secretary Levitsky commented that the increased political will in the production and transit countries was up, and argued that coca production was down, with seizures up. He stated that "our progress to date by no means won the war, but we have made substantial progress. It remains for us to sustain those gains."[164]

The testimony of Bernard Aronson, assistant secretary of state for inter-American affairs, was in the same vein. Noting that alternative development had started to succeed in Bolivia, he threw in the comment that inflation in Bolivia was down, but failed to mention that the influx of narcodollars was probably the primary cause.

Senate and House hearings have in the main reflected a Washington view of the drug war. Nowhere is this more pronounced than when one compares and contrasts the statements of Levitsky and Aronson, against the reality from the "front lines" of the drug war.

In a cable from the US Embassy in Bogota, a strikingly different picture of the Andean Strategy appears. In a remarkably candid report, the US ambassador described the strategy from his viewpoint:

Some of us involved in Counternarcotics (CN) programs in the Andean Region must face the prospect that we no longer engage in CN activities. Rather, most of our time is spent fighting bureaucracy. Upon close inspection, we find that more of our time is expended planning and replanning; preparing for conferences; attending meetings to evaluate and reevaluate programs; entertaining visitors; explaining, revising, and defending positions, reformatting budgets, executing procurement actions; negotiating contracts; and preparing periodic reports rather than actually implementing programs. The result is that we're rapidly approaching our second anniversary of the Andean Initiative with little to show that can be attributed to the hundreds of millions of dollars allocated, only a fraction of which is "on-line." Sadly, many of the first echelon (chronologically speaking) policy planners and many intermediate officials have already departed the CN scene. Others will be moving on this coming summer cycle without seeing much in the way of results. More disturbing is the prospect that in two more years we'll find that we haven't made any real progress in the Cocaine War. We'll only find that it is costing more.[165]

The cable went on to suggest (somewhat tongue in cheek) that the fifth objective of the Andean Strategy should be to minimize CN bureaucracy, both inter- and interagency.

Every agency involved in CN (there are too many to name-a part of the problem) has its own pet peeves. It's the system that's broken, and we recognize that some issues go well beyond the CN realm, per se. The time sensitive nature of CN programs, however, accents the problems we face day to day, and heightens everyone's frustrations. Typically, these frustrations lead to reevaluations, second guessing by outsiders, and endless reviews or inspections trying to figure out why implementation is so slow. The field typically responds we don't have enough resources as everyone tries to clamber aboard the money wagon. Washington retorts that they've already provided hundreds of millions of dollars, where's the results? And so it goes on.[166]

Thinking about solutions, the ambassador noted that "the answer is not so much a question of total resources as it is one of unclogging the system. Speed of action can be a resource multiplier."[167] The ambassador went on to lament the situation wherein the embassy faced a no-win situation in trying to explain to the Bogota government the dichotomy of the US being able to execute a miracle in six months in the Gulf War, while CN programs languish for 6 years. Turning to the issue of airborne drug traffic, which appeared to be the entire focus of SOUTHCOM operations, the embassy cable noted that air trafficking is a real problem.

We're investing and exploring the application of hundreds of millions of dollars in expensive equipment and attendant systems to identify, monitor, and intercept airborne traffickers. So then what? At some point we're going to have to face the reality that the USG and/or host countries don't have a consensus on shoot/down, force/down policy. Maybe we should do that first before we become too committed in terms of money and time in developing expensive systems (including the host nation aircraft) which will be of limited use. We suspect that thousands of hours and countless dollars already have been expended on the radar issue and operational implications.[168]

It is of the greatest interest at this point to note the interchange between Senator Kerry and Levitsky, following the reading of the foregoing cable to the hearing. Levitsky was extremely reluctant to have the cable placed into the official record, noting that "we do not agree with the conclusions in the cable. It was an extreme case of, as I say bureaucratic frustration.[169]

The testimony of Sherman Funk, inspector general of the State Department, appears to bolster the comments made by the Bogota embassy. One of the difficulties with the Andean Strategy, he noted, was the fact that it "fails to come to grips with what SOUTHCOM calls the tier 2 countries, the countries surrounding the Andean area." Taking it one step further, Funk stated that there "is an almost Alice in Wonderland approach" in regards to the strategy. In reference to Bolivia and the continuation of the myth of coca eradication, Funk argued that "eradication is an extraordinarily unpopular process, to put it mildly. Just as it is likely that Congress would raise taxes in an election year, Bolivia has a big election coming up in the early part of next year, and yet we are expecting the Bolivians to enforce mandatory eradication."[170]

NUMBERS, POLICY, AND REALITY

We publish these numbers with an important caveat:, the yield figures are potential, not actual numbers.... The actual quantity of final product remains elusive
—*International Narcotics Control Strategy Report*
March 1992

There is no way of arriving at reliable estimates owing to the absence of official data.... A number of guesses and estimates have been used in the absence of precise information. Resulting values are very approximate and should be interpreted accordingly.
—Joint State-USAID Cable
US Embassy in LaPaz, February 1992

In addressing the research aspect of the intelligence process, Sherman Kent argued that "when improperly guided the knowledge which it purveys may be inappropriate to the use it is supposed to serve, incomplete, inaccurate, and late."[171] Nowhere is this more the case than with the efforts directed toward quantifying drug trafficking activities. Section 1005 of the Anti-Drug Abuse Act of 1988 requires that each National Drug Control Strategy include "comprehensive, re-search based, long-range goals for reducing drug abuse in the United States," along with "short-term measurable objectives which the Director determines may be realistically achieved."[172]

There are two primary documents that address the policy quantification-the National Narcotics Intelligence Consumers Committee Report (NNICC) and the International Narcotics Control Strategy Report (INCSR). In fact, they have become the bibles of the drug war although there is no evidence to suggest that there was divine intervention in their creation and perpetuation. Unfortunately, the INCSR and the NNICC have been cloaked in the guise of "a scientific approach, "validated," and dogmatically cast in stone, and trotted out as the final word on the amount of drugs that is produced.

The NNICC, "based on the best data currently available and on the combined available expertise of NNICC member agencies, is a comprehensive assessment prepared for the federal government."[173] The INCSR, prepared by the Department of State, is a "primary source for production estimates and drug control efforts in foreign countries."[174] The NNICC Report was established in 1978 to coordinate the collection, analysis, dissemination, and evaluation of strategic drug-related intelligence. The purpose was to support and gauge policy development, resource deployment and operational planning.[175] The agencies that contribute to the semi-annual creation of the NNICC report are

- Central Intelligence Agency
- Coast Guard, Customs Service
- Department of Defense
- Drug Enforcement Administration
- Federal Bureau of Investigation
- Immigration and Naturalization Service
- Internal Revenue Service
- National Institute on Drug Abuse
- Department of State
- Department of the Treasury

The Office of National Drug Control Policy is an observer. The Deputy Assistant Administrator for Intelligence for the Drug Enforcement Administration served as the committee chairman.

Five years later, the situation described in the first NDCS—"scarce or unreliable drug-related data currently hamper policy planning on a number of important fronts"—continues to be the rule. The truth of the matter is that in spite of expenditures that may well have reached to the tune of $12 to $15 million we still don't know exactly how much cocaine is being produced and shipped into this country. But the real issue is this: how accurate does our knowledge have to be?

How Much Do We Know?

The numbers represent the US government's "best effort to sketch" the international drug problem. That picture is "not as precise as we would like it to be." The numbers range from cultivation figures, relatively hard data derived by proven means from crop production and drug yield estimates, to much softer figures where many more variables come into play. Yield figures are "potential, not actual" numbers.[176]

We know the following with reasonable certainty:

The most reliable information we have on illicit drugs is how many hectares are under cultivation. For more than a decade, the USG has estimated the extent of illicit cultivation in a dozen nations using proven methods similar to those used to estimate the size of licit crops at home and abroad. We can thus estimate the size of crops with reasonable accuracy.[177]

We know the following with less certainty:

Where crop yields are concerned, the picture is less clear. How much of a finished product a given area will produce is difficult to estimate, since small changes in such factors as soil fertility, weather, farming techniques, and disease can produce widely varying results from year to year and place to place. In addition, most illicit drug crop areas are inaccessible to the USG, making scientific information difficult to obtain. The actual quantity of final product remains elusive.[178]

This obsession with numbers for the sake of quantification alone was best exemplified by a series of events that took place in early January 1993. During a presentation at a conference dealing with the war against drugs sponsored by the Army War College and the Ridgeway Center of the University of Pittsburgh, Admiral John Linnon of Joint Task Force 5, briefing with "working numbers" provided by the Los Alamos CD Intelligence Team, stated that total cocaine output could reach as high as 1,300 metric tons. In the audience were representatives from the DEA, DIA, and other government agencies. The "official numbers" used by the US government were a range of 700 to 900 metric tons. Within days, the CD Intelligence Team was "invited" to Washington to "explain" both the numbers and the methodology that produced them. Four meetings took place, one at the Pentagon, one at ONDCP, one at the Central Intelligence Agency, and one at the Drug Enforcement Administration headquarters. The first three meetings went well, with the Los Alamos methodology being accepted. In spite of a detailed description, the 1,300 metric tons remained a matter of concern. The same approach was taken during the final meeting at the DEA. After what was by then a well-rehearsed "dog and pony show," David Westrate, Chief of Intelligence, cut to the chase. Reluctantly admitting that the methodology appeared logical, and that the 1,300 metric tons might be considered "reasonable," Westrate hastened to add that it had taken the CD community three years and millions upon millions of dollars to produce "their" numbers. Where the problem lay, he suggested, was that the Los Alamos team was not a "member of the community" and "clearly out of step." His real but unspoken concern was that the Los Alamos effort had cost less than the estimated millions of dollars and years of work by the government. The message was abundantly clear—"don't upset the apple cart."[179]

Within a short period of time the "official numbers" were raised to reflect a range of 900 to 1,100 metric tons. Westrate and the CD community were never told that a convincing argument could have been presented to show that cocaine tonnage was probably closer to 1,500 metric tons. The Los Alamos numbers had been produced from open sources at a cost closer to $10,000—a staggering differ- ence from the $12-15 million that it is estimated it cost to produce the government product.

The obsession with the "official numbers" is not soon to die. Operation Break- through, an attempt to establish reliable coca crop estimates "through the applica- tion of scientific field survey methodologies and laboratory analyses," is alive and well. Presently underway in Peru and Bolivia, Operation Breakthrough was ex- tended into Colombia in 1995.[180]

What should be understood here is that we can never know the precise number of hectares under plant, the yield therefrom, or the exact amount of cocaine pro- duced and shipped to the United States. Perfect numbers are not the real issue. What is important is to quickly get close-enough. However, with the "body count" mindset of the CD community— part of the continuing legacy of Vietnam—the qualitative approach becomes all important. Building upon the fallacy of the early RAND work, the importance of qualitative measures of effectiveness is still dismissed out of hand. Afraid of standing up to the congressman from Detroit or New York who constantly demands to know why the level of crack is so high in his district, the US government has taken the easy way out. In so doing, the government is caught in a trap of its own making. It speaks to the paucity of policy and strategy that the obsession with the "correct" numbers is nothing more than a failure to devise realistic measures of effectiveness—and have the guts to stick with them.

Performance Working Group

Nowhere is the production of "correct numbers" more pronounced than in the ongoing DoD attempts to measure its effectiveness in detection and monitor- ing. Once each quarter, the Performance Assessment Working Group, convenes for a four day session in which numbers are collated and "blessed." Representa- tives from the Defense Intelligence Agency, National Security Agency, Customs Service, all JTF's, DEA/EPIC, Commander in Chief Atlantic, Commander in Chief Pacific, 12th Air Force, and NORAD go through a laborious exercise in which the numbers from each of the agencies are discussed and a determination made as to their use in the production of a single, consensus driven, classified document.[181]

The main thrust of this process is directed to air events, even though maritime trafficking is admittedly the largest mode of drug transportation.[182] The process is "body count" oriented with trend analysis and other methodologies that would provide predictive, actionable intelligence specifically not within the mission char- ter. Land events are not discussed. There is no baseline against which to compare the numbers produced since the total number of events is unknown. This exercise is done to produce numbers and percentages so as to "feed" the Washington scene. Nothing is done with the products in terms of trend analysis over the long term or the "so what" questions. Nothing is done to address "splash and crash" events, even though it is estimated that as much as 30 metric tons of cocaine are lost when thrown overboard or destroyed in plane crashes.[183]

US Southern Command

> Strategy in SOUTHCOM is based on support to our ambassadors and their country teams in developing host nation support capability and host nation public and political will. My focus is operational or regional because of the extent of the narcotrafficking process.
>
> —General George Joulwan, Commander in Chief, South
> Testimony before the US Senate

In attempting to provide a framework for venturing into the unknown of counter drug strategy, the Strategic Studies Institute of the US Army War College drafted a document entitled *Campaign Planning and the Drug War.* Military strategy they argued, is composed of three essential elements: military strategic objectives (ends)—the protection of national interests; military concepts (ways)—how the job will get done; and the military resources (means)—what it will take to support the concept. Military strategy enjoins the leader to seek a disciplined balance of ends, ways, and means. The degree to which balance is not achieved indicates the risk accepted by the strategy.

If the foregoing is correct, the US Southern Command appears to have been willing to accept almost 100% risk. In applying the campaign planning process, the military leader is required to answer the following questions: What conditions must be produced to achieve the strategic objective; what sequence of actions is most likely to produce that condition; how should resources be applied to accomplish that sequence of actions?

In order to answer those campaign questions, it is necessary to heed George S. Pettee's advice and turn to the "study of the detailed record of wartime intelligence" to see "how well we have learned the lessons of the war." This is accomplished by reviewing a May 1992 evaluation of SOUTHCOM counter drug activities. Below I use the Pettee framework to compare the After Action Report against the Army War College campaign strategy.

Ends: What Condition Must Be Produced to Achieve the Strategic Objective?

The primary Southern Command mission is in support of drug law enforcement agencies through the detection and monitoring of drug trafficking activities in Central and South America and adjacent waters in the Pacific and the Caribbean. The strategic objective, which is to be executed by the law enforcement agencies, is the interdiction and apprehension of the drug traffickers.

1. The military minds in SOUTHCOM continue to ignore the fact that their number one reason for being involved in counter drugs is to provide support to the Drug Enforcement Administration. In a number of areas in the theater, DoD is barely on speaking terms with its number one customer—DEA.
2. The average military man finds it repugnant to be handed a mission task list by a civilian. It was not uncommon for SOUTHCOM to plan a large-scale mission/exercise and bring DEA into the loop at the last minute to "chop" on it for political reasons.

3. SOUTHCOM frequently included DEA operations in its large-scale operations, attempting to reap whatever credit might be forthcoming.
4. DEA, bemused and befuddled at the machinations that it takes to simply get one military helicopter to move from point A to point B, appears to have given up on trying to forge any kind of meaningful command-wide partnership. The division of assets has proven fatal thus far. On one side is the military with all of the personnel, equipment, money, and technical assets and on the other side sits DEA with all of the expertise, experience and legal mandate. It is the equivalent of two battalions going into combat, with one having the bullets and the other having the guns.
5. The SOUTHCOM response to a "mission" is to arbitrarily decide to mount a "surge" or "operational exercise" and hope that some hapless drug runner gets snared. This is what SOUTHCOM calls the "Linear Strategy."
6. The military decision cycle is far too slow to play in the dynamic CD arena. The problem is acute on the lieutenant colonel level. In the world of counter drugs, decisions must be made in three hours, not three days or three weeks. Late is absent. Julio is in the wind. The average peacetime American military officer is an overly cautious creature of the system. Decisions are made with one finger firmly planted on the lineal list. Decisions must be staffed up and down the chain of command regardless of whether they fall easily within the purview and mission of an action officer or commander. Unfortunately, the drug cartels build success on the very attributes shunned by the drug-fighters: initiative, imagination and risk.
7. SOUTHCOM has forcibly impressed a structured, static overlay onto the dynamic arena of drug manufacture and movement. The Fulda Gap mentality is alive and well. Again and again the Petrolera Complex and the Guajira Peninsula are photographed. One photo looks like another. Sorties are run, the system is engaged, people are working, assessments are made and nothing happens. Drug Law Enforcement Agencies laugh among themselves. Off the North Coast in the Caribbean, naval vessels run regular routes, aerostats are put up, suspect tracks are noted, the system is engaged and paperwork is generated while the drugs keep moving. The hidden tragedy is that the military has created an impressive system of technology, deployed assets and task-oriented personnel, which produces considerable activity and almost no results. It generates intelligence that is virtually worthless to the operational side of the house, but that is not the priority. The real priority is to show active employment of all assets and personnel.
8. There is no one location at US Southern Command in which a person can get the complete picture. At present there are five mini-command centers, each of which provides a piece of the puzzle. It is clear that this situation will not be rectified until an overall CD commander is created.
9. In the main, host nation CD commanders have never been systematically debriefed and surveyed in terms of what intelligence or equipment they need. There is a casual disregard for translating Operation Plans into Spanish. All too often the host nation commanders are "patted on the head, and told to sit in the back of the helicopter" while the "Big Gringo" directs the show. The irony here is that we are constantly telling the world that we are helping host nation forces to get out in front on the drug war and take the initiative themselves. This is difficult when they have little say in formulating the operation or cannot read the OPLAN or Intelligence Annex.

Ways: What Sequence of Actions Is Most Likely to Produce That Condition?

1. The CD community in the Command is badly fractured. Failure of the last two J2's to aggressively bring all CD elements in line with a well-defined strategy has resulted in a

Balkanization of the CD assets at Southern Command. Part of the problem is the command structure, which does not provide the J2 with a First Among Equals 06 (colonel) whose only job would be to ramrod CD. The J2 and his deputy have much of their time drained off with other issues. What has happened then is that Colonel X instructs his analysts not to talk to any member of Colonel Y's unit without permission. Colonel Y puts out an order that no member of Colonel X's unit can be briefed on ongoing operations without his personal approval. Colonels X and Y refuse to disclose anything of a sensitive nature to Colonel Z, whom they consider to be a complete bumbler. Colonel Z, in turn, drags his feet on mission requests from Colonel's X and Y personnel or ignores them altogether. Rarely do the three main CD elements know what the other is engaged in. There is mutual cooperation only in times of personal crisis, such as when the CINC wants a briefing and all 06 behinds are on the line. The end result is that there is no coordination or cooperation on a level required to mount a serious intelligence-gathering program.

2. No one has ever seriously looked at the operational security situation at SOUTHCOM. An intercepted message indicated that the narcotraficantes were considering disabling a P3, but then thought better of it. Why bother, we are not a serious threat to their operations.

3. No system has yet been put in place at SOUTHCOM for effective document exploitation. The common complaint among SOUTHCOM analysts is that they could not get access to documents seized by the DEA or host nations. Much of what is seized in a raid can be used by analysts without compromising a prosecution.

4. The theater is rich in Human Intelligence (HUMINT) potential. DEA regularly debriefs individuals, pilots, mules (humans carry drugs), etc. Very little of this reached SOUTHCOM analysts who are ultimately expected to provide operational intelligence back to DEA. Not surprisingly, most senior military intelligence officers in the CD business come from a signals intelligence background, and their inclination is to hide behind the legal restrictions. There is much that could be done in securing HUMINT and still stay well within the law.

5. There is a shortage of officers with backgrounds in analysis, HUMINT, and operations available to work in counter drugs. The overriding requirement should be an officer who wants to work in CD.

6. The Tactical Analysis Teams (TAT) at the various embassies are operating at about 30 percent of their potential. They will never get any better until SOUTHCOM elevates them beyond the status of messenger boys/girls for the Military Group commanders. In effect, the TAT's are the forward element of the DoD effort, an arms reach from the host nations and Country Teams. But they will only become effective when they are recognized and "plugged-in" to SOUTHCOM.

7. There has been no use of deception operations by SOUTHCOM, although it is quite clear that the traffickers regularly practice such measures. If SOUTHCOM were to deploy aerostat-type balloons, for example, they could effectively funnel drug air flights into corridors in which they could be made more vulnerable.

Means: How Should Resources Be Applied to Accomplish That Sequence of Actions?

1. Drug LEA's in Latin America see the threat. They see a flood of cheap narcotics moving unchecked. They see the cartels expanding with better equipment and employees. What the US/host nations seize or disrupt is "the cost of doing business," and at a very small cost at that. The drugs seized so close to the production source has

no real dollar value. A major seizure is not a $3 million loss to the cartel. It might as well be 30 kilos of baking powder compared to the amount being produced. A loss to the traffickers occurs when their profits begin shrinking, not when a small dent is made in their inventory.

2. All factors point to the only real area of vulnerability that can be exploited by SOUTHCOM and DEA is the transshipment phase in Central America. Presently, there are too many political, cultural, and military factors at play which prevent any kind of success in the eradication of the growing fields. Host nation intelligence is not good enough yet to catch up to the labs which can be set up and folded within a seven day processing cycle. Once the drugs cross the southern Mexico border, they are home free.

3. The North Coast (Colombia) and the Caribbean is the SOUTHCOM Fulda Gap. The area is well known, most of our assets are there, and we feel comfortable. The traffickers are doing an end run through the Eastern Pacific by sea, air, and sea/air. Normally US assets there consist of only one cruiser or destroyer, a cutter, and maybe one aerostat.

4. The longer a plane is airborne, or a ship at sea, the greater the exposure to US technical assets, which the narcotraficantes really do respect. Therefore most of their transshipments are in three legs: Venezuela/Colombia to Central America, to Mexico, to the United States. As you would guess, CD assets are thinly dispersed in this area, especially on the Pacific side, where they are virtually nonexistent. There is a good reason for this, aside from stupidity; deployment of US assets would require a coordinated effort between US Southern Command, Country Teams, and host nations.

5. There is strong reason to believe that there are significant supply hubs, owned and operated by Colombians, in two Central American countries. This is a part of the pipeline inventory. These hubs are strategically placed storage areas where large caches could be safely maintained. Once the Colombian laboratory produces finished cocaine, it must be moved. Moving it to a storage site that would be one-third of the way up the pipeline would almost ensure the safety of the product. Interestingly, DEA did not place great stock in this theory. To do so would be to admit that the cocaine is there under their nose, though they are so understaffed and little resourced, that little time could be spent pursuing this without first-rate HUMINT.

6. If the transshipment of drugs could be seriously disrupted over an extended period of time, what would be the result? The first to "jump ship" would be the pilots. Some pilot/coordinators control 10 to 20 other pilots. If the money began to be tight, they would be gone. The result would be the requirement to find and enlist second-string pilots and equipment. The risk of losing a load would be greatly increased. As the loads were aborted or intercepted, with the concurrent loss of revenue, the narcotraficantes would be forced to move larger loads over longer distances, thus presenting a fatter target. Undoubtedly this would drive them to move by ship and cargo container, but this would also entail risk, not the least of which is being forced to utilize more people who are not a part of the organization. Individuals who provide support service to the traffickers outside of the CentAm area might well shift their loyalties to other organizations.

7. Lastly, sustained losses would almost ensure that ruptures and divisions within the primary trafficking organizations would take place. The major traffickers have never had to operate in a prolonged crunch situation. What would it mean to break the back of one the organizations? Everything! It would be a first. It would show that it is possible and provide a real boost to everyone involved in what is now a quagmire.

8. There is little doubt that there is a cause/effect relationship between the present deployment of US assets and the schedules and routes of the narcotraficantes.[184]

Military Misfortunes

The answer to the conundrum of the Western Front... entailed developing
new techniques and developing a doctrine that emphasized flexibility over
rigidity and innovation over obedience to long established principles.

—Eliot A. Cohen and John Gooch
Military Misfortunes: The Anatomy of Failure in War

By July 1993, a year after the foregoing report was delivered to the
SOUTHCOM J2, many hoped that some progress might have occurred. Unfortunately, such was not the case. Cohen and Gooch's three fatal maladies—the failure
to learn, the failure to anticipate, and the failure to adapt—appeared to have a
death grip on SOUTHCOM.[185]

SOUTHCOM's anticipatory failures are linked to an institutional inability or
refusal to foresee and take appropriate measures to deal with the narcotraficantes
probable strategy and tactics. In spite of four years of constant indications and warnings SOUTHCOM still failed to adapt its strategy and tactics to reflect the reality of
the intentions, capabilities, and operations of the drug trafficking industry.

Cohen and Gooch argue that of all the forms of institutional failure, the failure
to learn is the least excusable. After two years of work with SOUTHCOM, this
failure remained devilishly puzzling. A steady diet of information was provided
from the modeling and simulation exercises to the CINC, Deputy CINC, J-2, J-3,
J-5, and J-6. In spite of additional information from a number of other agencies,
the thrust of which was that present strategy and tactics were not effective,
SOUTHCOM continued to move ahead in a monolithic lock-step. The following
anecdote portrays this situation.

On July 2, 1993, in what appears to have been an eleventh-hour attempt to
come up with something that would pass for a strategy, the SOUTHCOM J5 sought
to examine a number of scenarios in order to examine capabilities and the placement of assets; consider specific alternatives and options; and, attempt to develop
a game plan that would consider a number of options. Melded together, the foregoing factors should have formed the framework for building a strategy. But, as in
the past, SOUTHCOM approached strategy building by refusing to address the
strategic trilogy of ends, ways, and means and by placing caveats and restrictions
on the evaluation and planning process that ensured failure from the start.

For reasons that are still unclear, the exercise was to be done by the Los Alamos
team.[186] The following restrictions were levied against the planning process:

1. Three days were allotted for completion of the project;
2. Focus was to be directed to the production countries with the transit areas and Central
   America specifically excluded;
3. No consideration was to be given to the provisions of PRD-18, nor the initial readings
   from Washington that suggested that major drug policy changes would soon be
   forthcoming;
4. No consideration was to be given to the mushrooming growth of opium/poppy cultivation.

Three scenarios were to be developed:

1. A base case with no additional SOUTHCOM activity-business as usual;
2. A case with activity that equated to a level of activity that Operation Supporting Justice IV; and,
3. One in which massive US military assets (primarily large numbers of fixed and rotary wing aircraft) would be added to the SOUTHCOM inventory with the addition of division-sized military units from the Andean Ridge countries. It was made clear that the third scenario was the favored one and that it was here that emphasis was to be placed.[187] Although the recommendations were completed in the allotted time and briefed to the CINC, what became of them is unknown.

The Drug Enforcement Administration (DEA)

> *Egbert*: This is the direction the agency has chosen to go and anyone who doesn't believe in it does not belong in the agency. What you don't understand, Levine, is that the Congress asked DEA what our answer to the cocaine problem was. Snowcap is our answer. If Snowcap fails, DEA is down the tubes.
> *Levine*: It's the Bolivians—not me! They are saying Snowcap has no effect whatsoever. They say they've got landing fields that planes land on every ten minutes around the clock, picking up cocaine.
> *Egbert*: Snowcap may not be the best game in town, but it's the only game in town.
> *—Deep Cover*

Shortly after the foregoing dialogue took place, DEA Administrator John Lawn sent an all-hands teletype stating that talking an agent out of volunteering for Operation Snowcap would not be tolerated. The irony of the situation is to be found in further statements by DEA staff coordinator Art Egbert:

1. The DEA did not have aircraft with "near enough range" to reach cocaine labs;
2. The corruption problem was "insurmountable;"
3. The Bolivian cocaine traffickers were warned three days before every recon flight and that every cocaine seizure that Snowcap did make was "a gift to keep us happy;"
4. "They are making so much cocaine down there that just seizing another ten, twenty or thirty thousand kilos isn't going to make any difference whatsoever."[188]

With virtually no support from SOUTHCOM, the DEA waged its own war in the Andean region until late 1994. Committed to the Kingpin Strategy—a targeting of the vulnerabilities, i.e., production, transportation, communications, finances, and leadership of the major drug trafficking organizations—the DEA remained blindly focused, like SOUTHCOM, on the Andean Ridge. While the DEA wistfully hoped for "a realistic, flexible, and effective interagency operations plan for the region that will successfully affect the trafficking organization's ability to operate," DEA internal documents speak to the fact that "United States Government (USG) efforts suffer in the long term due to a lack of cohesive, comprehensive strategic planning and synchronized execution." They make no mention of the lack of reality in their own design.[189]

The selection of Thomas Constantine, former superintendent of the New York State Police, to lead the DEA was the handwriting on the wall. Constantine brings a "uniformed cop" approach to the game. Today, everything points towards a downsizing and pull-out of DEA in Latin America. While many had hoped that the DEA would be tucked back under the protective and professional wing of the FBI, the decision in 1993 not to do so, does not mean that all is lost.[190] Constantine, a member of the "New York cop mafia," has close ties to FBI Director Louis Freeh. Ties between the two agencies are expected to grow. For the DEA, the era of the suits and the cowboys appears to be coming to an end. The frontline "grunts" deserve better. Constantine may not be the man to pull the agency back together. If the DEA could combine the street smarts of its agents with a new culture of intelligence and develop mid and upper level leadership, then it might be possible to enhance the professionalism and performance of the agency. The DEA like the rest of the drug community must understand that we can never hurt the drug trafficking industry by "nickel and diming" them. What is needed is large-scale, long-term, high-impact intelligence-driven operations that will make La Empresa hurt.

Failure and Success in the Production and Transit Zones

As the Los Alamos CD Intelligence Team learned more and more about the drug production and transit areas, La Empresa business practices, and US and host nation counter drug operations, it became clear that we could draw up a ledger sheet showing success and failure for both sides.

We were surprised that US agencies had little idea of their own successes, never mind of the balance sheet for all agencies. In 1993, we estimated that La Empresa losses were approximately 30% of finished product throughout the entire delivery chain—from production countries, through the transit zone, up to and across the South West Border. This included all interdiction efforts as well as "splash and crash."[191] It is of some interest to note that it was not until January 1996 that US Southern Command would announce—for the first time—the same percentage.[192] In addition, we noted the following trends in the production area and El Conducto are noted for the time-frame 1993 through mid 1994:

1. Profits are down for coca cultivators;
2. The coca grower is now producing both pasta basica and cocaine base;
3. There have been no dramatic increases in hectares planted with coca;
4. Cultivators are leaving old areas to seek new growing areas in which higher profits might be produced;
5. Laboratories are constantly being moved;
6. 1st-tier associates of La Empresa Coordinadora are purchasing long range jet aircraft capable of high altitude flights;
7. The dramatic increase in the use of Global Positioning Systems and radio silence for drug aircraft;
8. The recycling of chemicals and the use of reoxidation in the laboratory process;
9. The use of aqua rica, the one-step process, and more efficient production methods;
10. A dramatic increase in payment for services in drugs, instead of dollars;

11. Diversifying into new product lines-heroin and legitimate businesses;
12. Developing new markets;
13. Stockpiling/stashing of finished product in "neutral" or safer countries;
14. Attempts to increase profits by lowering the purity of the product.

The ledger for US operations is as follows:

1. Operations conducted by US Southern Command, DEA, and production country forces have caused the traffickers to shift their transportation routes, moving from the primary production countries into the "squish" countries, and thus increasing the cost of doing business. But that initial cost increase is soon offset by the fact that lab sites in the "squish" countries require less security and overhead costs. It is important to note that the actual cost of a finished laboratory operation is "small change" for La Empresa.
2. The most profound actions to date have taken place in increased cooperation and coordination of CD efforts principally in the Andean Ridge countries. Peru and Ecuador, for example, virtually in a state of war since the seizure by Peru of contested land on their mutual border have sent observers to sit, side by side, in aircraft, monitoring narcotrafficker aircraft. Bolivia and Brazil, and Colombia and Venezuela, have all joined in cross-border operations, even though the operations were initially shaky. As mentioned earlier, multilateral operations will soon hasten the push-out of US operations.
3. The placement and use of ground-based radars to track drug aircraft brought about unexpected results. Pushed by US Southern Command to allow the radars to be used, in spite of the ineffectiveness of the radars and the lack of end-game resulted in the realization by the host countries that it was *their* airspace and sovereignty that were being pierced by the narcotraficantes. Despite scarce resources, those countries sought to acquire their own radars and interceptors.
4. The 76-longitude, 30-latitude "Corridor," running parallel to the Andes "spine," which for so long had been the primary airborne narco route, was disrupted from time to time enough to cause the narcotraficantes to shift some of their flights to new and longer flight routes, south and east into Brazil and then north into the Vaupes area in Colombia. Such disruptions did not cause major problems for the narcotraficantes.
5. The announcement in mid-May 1994 that the US military had stopped sharing intelligence with Colombia and Peru may be attributed to several reasons. First, it is clear that the DoD is trying to extricate itself from what it considers to be a "lose-lose" situation. Knowing full well that the Clinton administration has little interest in the wars on drugs, the DoD does not want to be in a position to take the "hit" when the Congress calls for answers. Pentagon officials have been heard arguing that the United States is at risk if foreign governments shoot down suspected drug aircraft thanks to information supplied by US intelligence. Secondly, this may well be the first move of the newly appointed CINCSOUTH, to pull back and consolidate his position, perhaps with "backchannel" pressure from the Pentagon and the White House. On the job in March 1994, General Barry McCaffrey completed his reconnaissance of the region and moved counter drug activities to a third-tier position on the "things to do list" at US Southern Command. Cutting off intelligence to the production countries appears to contradict the thrust of PRD-18, which sought to place more emphasis on attempting to stop drugs at their source. The State Department opposes the move fearing the loss of a "valuable tool." Whatever the reason, the move is not in the best interests of the United States. We have known for years that some of the information that was passed on to production country governments was either handed off to the narcotraficantes or simply disregarded.

However, we also know that not all the officials and agencies that are dealt with are "dirty." Even though the pace has been slow over the past four years, there has been a definite trend towards the creation of a skeleton corps of trusted agents in the production countries. These people are not spies, but rather citizens within the government, police, intelligence services, and military who believe that it is in the best interest of their respective countries to break with the corruption of the past.

6. Due to the lack of centralized counter drug command and control, and decentralized intelligence driven operations, any successes in the production and transit zones have not been recognized even by the agencies that have achieved them. Looking at the detection rate of drug aircraft by the US military that resulted in aircraft seizures over a three year period, it is clear that the wherewithal to detect airborne narcotraficantes has greatly increased in 1989, 9%; in 1990, 24%; and in 1991, 40%. Admiral Nick Gee of Joint Task Force-4, noted that in 1993, 85% of all airborne drug traffickers entering Caribbean and Eastern Pacific airspace were detected. Of that number, 65% are trailed and monitored. This number plummets to 30% when it comes to maritime traffic.[193] Unfortunately, there is no "end game." As noted by the US Embassy in La Paz, all the monitoring and tracking in the world is for naught if the drug aircraft cannot be driven to ground or apprehended on the ground.

7. After an intensive review of US Southern Command and DEA "successes," the bottom line suggests that published "successes" are grossly overshadowed by the costs. US efforts to date have simply helped La Empresa fine-tune their operations at relatively low cost.

8. The argument that "nation building" and detection and monitoring go hand in hand is patently false. The former requires at least a generation of critical activities to make democracy take hold, and then only with great luck. The curse of the Spanish colonial system in Latin America is a heavy cross to bear and attempts to shrug it off will more often than not fail. Writing in *The Madness of Things Peruvian: Democracy Under Siege*, Alvaro Vargas Llosa argues that the failure of democracy in Peru, and for that matter throughout Latin America, is a result of historic vices and deficiencies in institutions that virtually stayed frozen during the long years of dictatorship in Latin America. During the short intervals of democratic government that interrupted those years, elected leaders never dared to attempt reform of state institutions or state/society relationships. The resulting absence of political, economic, or cultural freedoms in all respects of Latin American society is the root cause of the region's failure to build a democratic tradition. SOUTHCOM attempts to bring the Latin American military into the drug war simply perpetuates this instability.[194]

9. What the US Southern Command attempted to palm off as strategy is not. That this approach is faulty was demonstrated in 1986, three years before the National Drug Control Strategy was drafted. A totally military response, Operation Blast Furnace was executed, nearly bringing the Bolivian cocaine industry to a standstill—and almost causing the collapse of the Bolivian government with it. As David Westrate of the DEA noted, "what we learned at the end ultimately, is that we cannot do that again. I do not see the US military being deployed in an enforcement context, particularly in Latin American countries, in the future." But purely military interdiction attempts remain the rule of thumb, much to the continuing frustration of the DEA, and the production country governments.

Clueless, SOUTHCOM failed to understand that detection and monitoring is a reconnaissance and warning mission which has nothing to do with whether or not the average Central or South American will grasp the concept of democracy. As long as SOUTHCOM continues to interpret its mission as drug interdiction, rather than providing detection and monitoring support to the federal law enforcement agencies, then what Barbara Tuchman has referred to as the "march of folly" will continue.

Favors Returned

Seven years after Operation Blast Furnace, the Drug Enforcement Agency turned the tables on SOUTHCOM. In January 1993, following a SOUTHCOM "dog and pony show" in which the merits of an upcoming CD wargame were being touted, DEA, in the person of David Westrate, now Director of DEA Intelligence, demanded that DEA should become the "supported CINC" and argued that the game scenario should be built around DEA. Oblivious to the message, SOUTHCOM failed to heed the warning and proceeded with a "business as usual" mode. At the counter drug wargame that was conducted at the National Defense University in June 1993, the DEA launched a well-planned, publicly executed frontal assault which took SOUTHCOM totally by surprise, leaving CINCSOUTH "twisting in the wind." Flanked by a phalanx of DEA "suits"—including Judge William Bonner—Westrate launched the attack in front of the 45 agencies that had been assembled to play the game. In professorial fashion, Westrate reminded the assembled group that interdiction was a law enforcement mission, not a military mission, and that it was the law enforcement that should be running the show. Not briefed by his staff as to the seriousness of the DEA threat, General George Joulwan was left to grasp for answers.[195]

OFFICE OF NATIONAL DRUG CONTROL POLICY (ONDCP)

Created in 1988 to develop a national drug control policy, the ONDCP was charged with the missions of coordinating and overseeing implementation of the NDCS and evaluating and revising the strategy on a yearly basis. Its tenure has been marked by continued controversy. Under constant criticism, ONDCP appears to be on unstable ground. With the promise of renewed attention to the wars on drugs, the Clinton administration dashed all hopes for a stronger Office of National Drug Control by cutting back on its budget and staff. An attempt to enhance the administration's drug agenda by making ONDCP a cabinet position did not work. The appointment of Lee Brown as the "drug czar" proved to be a lackluster choice. Thanks to budget and staffing cuts and Brown's apparent lack of knowledge, imagination, and drive, ONDCP status has dropped even lower. A congressman suggested that Brown had "managed to skillfully undo the relationships" between ONDCP and the Congress.[196]

Haunted at ONDCP by what in part appeared to be a repeat of his apparent "less than satisfactory" actions during the Crown Height riots when he was police commissioner, Brown appeared as odd man out during his service as the third drug czar. In balance, some law enforcement officials spoke highly of Brown's work and complained with some truth that his hands had been tied by the Clinton White House.[197]

The nomination of General Barry McCaffrey as the fourth drug czar is something to get excited about. In a surprise move—one that could enable the Clinton administration to seize the initiative on the drug issue in an election year—McCaffrey could put life into the seemingly lifeless national drug strategy.

The most decorated officer serving in the US Army today, he was badly wounded while assaulting a bunker-complex in Vietnam. A hard-driving warrior—a trait that does not endear him to the political generals—McCaffrey is noted for pushing his staff beyond accepted limits. Articulate, but sometimes overbearing to a fault with those junior to him—to include those wearing stars—he is known to choose a course of action and drive toward it with a vengeance[198] As a warrior, McCaffrey has never been a charter member of the "general's club," a place where predators are not welcome.[199] As the general officer commanding the 24th Mechanized Infantry Division in the Gulf War, he lead the "Left Hook" which swept north, leaving large numbers of Iraqi units decimated and trapped. He was said to be unhappy with the political decision to stop the fighting after 100 hours.[200]

After receiving his third star for his exploits in the Gulf many felt that his career was finished. However, an insult at the hands of a White House staff member early in the Clinton administration brought forth an apology and what appears to have been a new lease on life. On the departure of George Joulwan from Panama back to his NATO stamping-grounds, McCaffrey was appointed as the Commander in Chief, US Southern Command.

The general's comments at the Heritage Foundation, in a talk entitled, US Interests in Latin America, are revealing and provide clues to the future. Following his graduation from West Point, he served as a rifle platoon leader in the Dominican Republic in 1966. After service as company commander in Vietnam, he was posted to Panama for duty as aide de camp to the CINC South. As a plans officer he performed studies on low intensity conflict, looking at the Sandanista regime and was also involved in the planning for Operation Just Cause. It is clear from the text of his speech that he understands the nuances of the southern hemisphere. Going beyond that, he is clearly *simpatico* (sympathetic)—but not in a fawning manner.

Senator Orrin Hatch raised the key question that must be answered before McCaffrey's selection as drug czar: does McCaffrey's nomination "signal the administration's new found commitment to lead in drug war, or is it, more simply, an election-year makeover."[201] Part of the answer may have been found when Washington newspapers suggested that his earlier remarks—"when he publicly criticized the current drug interdiction strategy, saying that then had been poor interagency coordination and that it had not reduced the cocaine flow northward, despite some recent spectacular arrests of cocaine cartel chiefs"—reflect an independent thinker. He stated further that "we lack an international coalition" and "we lack effective cooperation" among the numerous federal agencies involved in the anti-drug effort."[202] McCaffrey said that he had been assured by the White House that he will get the resources he needs to coordinate more than $13 billion in federal anti-drug efforts. He expects to ask for funding to increase the size of ONCP staff from its current 45 positions to about 150 posts.[203]

The general went on to note that Americans were simply unaware of the reality of the region and how it has changed in the last 25 years. Moving to the military involvement and drug strategy, he stated the US Armed Forces are not the lead agency in struggle against the drug menace. He suggested that "we've got a decent strategy. It's sort of a coherent attempt to take a coherent look at source country operations, interdiction, demand reduction, and to move ahead on a broad front. There are some things that are we are doing that are working. There are a bunch of them we are doing that are working but make no difference." In reference to cocaine production in Colombia he pointed out that "we've been just enough effective that they are now moving to other systems."

Reflecting on intelligence he said that "our intelligence isn't that bad. We're doing okay, we've busted some of these international criminals 800 miles at sea and taken 27 tons away from them. We're playing some sophisticated operations against these people, and we are forcing them out to sea."

In thoughts that most certainly reflect on where he plans to aim his efforts, McCaffrey noted that

- "It seems to me we ought to have a very humble view of what the United States role can and ought to be. We're not going to instruct Latin American sovereign nations in how they should organize themselves to address their internal drug menace."
- "We need a better construct in which congressional and federal government cooperation will address the external problem, and then we need to see a renewed commitment on the domestic front to reduce demand."
- "I think we're achieving tactical successes without making an operational difference."

In closing he said that "I think you can engage this problem. We know where the drugs are grown. We know how it's moved. We know how the international money laundering system works. We know the names of a lot of people are involved in it, and we're after them, so I think we need a long-term solution. We all want to knock this thing dead in two years. Its not going to happen. This is a 10-year struggle to protect our children."[204]

It will of great interest to see if the new drug czar can move beyond the confines of military thinking and do another successful "left hook"— into the swamp that is filled with alligators from the drug law enforcement community. He may get sorely needed congressional support in the form of proposed legislation by Senators Dianne Feinstein and Alfonse D'Amato who want to block the extension of the $20 billion US bailout of the Mexican economy. There is other legislation pending that ranges from anti-grant legislation to a bill to drastically renegotiate NAFTA. It is this last bill, sponsored by Representative Marcy Kaptur—with 77 co-sponsors from across the political spectrum—that could used to work with Mexico on a more responsive approach to border problems—in particular, drug trafficking.[205]

As mentioned earlier in this case study, McCaffrey went to SouthCom with marching orders from the White House to quickly move beyond the policies of George Joulwan. Initially, McCaffrey distanced himself from federal law enforcement agencies in Panama—in a knee-jerk manner—much like his predecessor.[206]

If confirmed, McCaffrey will have to deal with the drug law enforcement community up close. His force of personality and character will be crucial in bringing them to the table. It is those two traits—something that Mr.'s Bennett, Martinez, and Brown lacked, that will be the keystone to some modicum of success.

Senator Joseph R. Biden, Jr., the author of the legislation that created the Office of National Drug Control Policy clearly drew the line in the sand: "You have this administration by the ears. If they don't step up and give you some authority, you're in a position to say, I resign. This is an election year. Being a man of your standing gives you a credibility that they'll have to listen to."[207]

LA FRONTERA: THE SOUTH WEST BORDER

> You think the norteamericanos are fools because they are unable to stop your smuggling. Their weakness is a political failing, not one of professional expertise. You do not understand that, and so I will explain it to you. Their borders are easy to violate because the Americans have a tradition of open borders. You confuse that with inefficiency. It is not. They have highly efficient police with the best scientific methods in the world—do you know that the Russian KGB reads American police textbooks? And copies their techniques? The American police are hamstrung because their political leadership does not allow them to act as they wish to act—and as they could act, in a moment, if those restrictions were ever eased.
>
> —Felix Cortez to narcotraficante Escobedo
> *A Clear and Present Danger*

During the third week of September 1993, in a scene reminiscent of Operation Intercept a quarter century earlier, the U.S. Border Patrol put into effect what amounted to a 20—mile blockade of the border along the Rio Grande between Mexico and El Paso, Texas. Border Patrol officers literally brought the stream of illegal immigrants to a halt. Arrests dropped from an average of 1,000 per day to slightly over 100. Crime in El Paso dropped off dramatically, and citizens can once again walk the streets. But the money allocated for the Border Patrol's "full-court press" has been expended and new funds do not appear to be forthcoming. And, as with Operation Intercept, there is a hue and cry that such a blockade would seriously damage the area's economic and social balance. It is unclear what impact this round of sealing of the border will have upon drug trafficking. Traditionally, the seizures of large quantities of drugs have not taken place at ports of entry. Rather seizures have taken place, inland in what might be called a zone, approximately 20 miles north of the border.[208]

Of the greatest concern along the South West Border is the performance—or lack of performance—of the US Customs Service. In an attempt to blunt growing criticism that it fails to stop drugs from being shipped into the United States in cargo trucks, the Customs Service announced that its drug seizures had jumped 25 percent in 1995. The report on the year-old Operation Hard Line came after widespread criticism of agency Commissioner George Weiss, and after several recent allegations of agency corruption. Both the FBI and a grand jury are looking into the charges that some Customs Inspectors allowed cocaine into the United States. In addition, some former employees have charged that a Customs program called "Line Release," that allows firms to pass a background check to send cargo trucks across the US border with little or no inspection has aided large-scale drug trafficking.[209]

The present sealing of the border was driven by political pressure to stop the flow of illegal aliens and a growing concern of drug trafficking. This situation is indicative both of the past and most certainly of the NAFTA-shaped future. For drug law enforcement agencies, it raises again the issue of the lack of a coordinated drug strategy along the South West Border. It must be remembered that a "gag-order"—demanding silence on the drug trafficking implications of the treaty— was passed to all law enforcement agencies prior to signing the NAFTA accord with Mexico.[210] It is quite clear that political considerations in the form of further "gag-orders" will ensure that trafficking issues will be checkmated by trade priorities.

The National Drug Control Strategy calls for the inclusion and active participation of state and local law enforcement in the war on drugs. It does not suggest how this is to be accomplished. There is almost a feeling of deja vu when comparing the NDCS and earlier federal attempts at implementation of the Safe Streets Act of 1968. Describing that act, Feeley and Sarat wrote that "by leaving so much open and by inviting, or rather requiring, the joint action of officials responsible to many different constituencies, the Act promoted conceptual confusion and did not provide a clearly legitimate device for solving it." Reflecting upon the design of the Safe Streets Act, and the problem of complexity built into the act, Feeley and Sarat noted further that:

At the time of the passage of the Safe Streets Act, there was wide-spread concern about the problem of crime. Congress and the president responded by developing a program which enlisted the federal government in aid of state and local law enforcement but assigned the major responsibility for deciding how to use that aid to officials at the state and local levels. The Act tried to take advantage of federalism to establish a partnership among government agencies, some new and some ongoing, at three levels. Congress established procedures through which programs could be developed without specifying the precise details of the programs. As a result, the Act had built into it unusual complexity, complexity which made efficient and effective implementation almost impossible.[211]

THE NEW MEXICO CRACKDOWN

The real keys to success in stemming the flow of drugs are long-term, intelligence driven operations, executed jointly by federal, state, and local law enforcement agencies. One of the most promising efforts directed toward bringing state and local law enforcement and the public together for the purpose of developing drug information and intelligence was conducted by the New Mexico Crimestoppers Commission on May 3, 1990. It used a highly publicized statewide telethon, "The New Mexico Crackdown" in the hope that some public interest would be stirred. Following the television and radio broadcast of "New Mexico Crackdown," the tremendous public response caused the New Mexico Crimestoppers Commission to take stock of the approximately eight hundred "tips" that were received. The decision was made to take these tips" and build a database, the purpose of which would be to create an initial picture of drug use and drug-related activities in New Mexico. The findings were published under the title, *Drugs in New Mexico: The First Report.*[212]

The criteria for the project were five fold: strict confidentiality of informants who provided the tips adherence to the intent of the National Drug Control Strategy-sharing drug information; an intelligence production approach; end products oriented toward both supply and demand reduction programs; and to establish the basis for further research and understanding of the drug problem in New Mexico.

Because of the nature of the tips—incomplete to detailed information provided by informants who had the option to remain anonymous—*The First Report* would be subject to close scrutiny by both the public and law enforcement agencies. Ultimately, the findings of *The First Report* would have to be "validated" by law enforcement communities across the state. Thus, a quantitative and qualitative approach, following the sequence of the Intelligence Production Cycle was used.

The tips were compiled by incident, community, "lines of communication," and region and coded for later computerized analytical procedures. Statistics were drawn from the findings so as to create the basis for a quantitative manner as the first step toward the creation of drug related intelligence. The analysis produced a series of indications and warnings, which were derived in a format similar to that which is used in the production of strategic intelligence.

While designed along the basic framework of a social science study, the approach was focused in the direction of intelligence research. The analysis sought to pull together related pieces of information that might become the basis for furtheir analysis. The end result was a series of products that would enable law enforcement and policymakers to better address drug supply and demand issues in New Mexico. The findings represent a picture, an initial baseline, of drug use and drug-related activities in New Mexico for a specific slice of time.

In building the research approach, the following assumptions concerning the state of New Mexico were articulated:

1. Proximity to Mexico, a prime producer of drugs and, of late, a prime transshipment point for cocaine.
2. A large portion of the state consists of public lands and forests, in which large quantities of marijuana are cultivated or through which cocaine, heroin, and marijuana are smuggled or transshipped.
3. A large number of methamphetamine laboratories.
4. Intrastate drug trafficking for local consumption.
5. Interstate drug trafficking pass-through for other national markets.

As indicated by the 545 tips, drawn from 51 communities around the state, drug abuse and drug-related activities cut through and permeated New Mexico society from the home to the classroom and into the work place. Indications of drug dealing and use from a place of residence appears to be matched if not exceeded by drug use in the workplace. Cocaine and marijuana clearly stood out as the drugs of choice. Approximately 13% of drug users were alleged to be armed, and 19% were alleged to have had prior arrests. Findings indicate that New Mexicans from age 12 through 60 were engaged in drug use or related activities. Men were more often identified as drug users than women by a ratio of almost 4 to 1. Statewide, approximately 22% of "Crackdown" informants were willing to be identified. (see Table 7.1)

Table 7.1
Statistical Summary

1.	Total tips used as the basis for *The First Report*:	545
2.	Drugs of choice in New Mexico (in order of use):	
	Meth labs	13
	Marijuana plantations	3
3.	Businesses identified as having substantial employee drug use or classified as an establishment in which illicit drug activity takes place:	59
4.	Indications of weapons involved with drug activities:	13%
5.	Indications of prior arrest by tips suspects:	19%
6.	Number of informants who identified themselves:	22%
7.	Links* established by qualitative analysis: 46/97 (tips)	18%
8.	Chains* established by qualitative analysis: 17/50 (tips)	9%

*A "link" is two or more tips, and a chain is three or more tips which show a strong relationship to a specific person or activity.

There are several things to note about the statistics from the "Crackdown":

1. The tips which form the basis for this work were allegations of the presence or use of drugs or drug-related activity. Such allegations would be considered fact only after law enforcement agencies went through a formal procedure to ensure the validity of the tips.
2. It is important to note that drug use/abuse baselines that were postulated to date, nationally, have been built upon what many contend to be questionable survey populations and methods of collection of that date, primarily the NIRA Household Drug Abuse Survey. Drug control officials have acknowledged the substantial under-reporting of the NIRA Household Drug Abuse Survey. A recent Senate Judiciary Committee report, criticized the NIRA for not only not polling those most likely to be addicted to cocaine but also for relying on the accuracy of respondent's self-reported drug use.
3. Many people who give information have been victims or witnesses of crimes, or they may have a strong desire to aid law enforcement. There are others motivated purely by selfish interests. However, regardless of their motivation, the use of information is basic weapon in the fight against crime, and they are a judicially recognized source of information.[213]

Indications and Warnings

The following indications and warnings were drawn from the study:

1. The presence of weapons as part of drug activities. The implications for law enforcement officers and concern for their safety, particularly in light of the dramatic increase in the presence of automatic weapons, strongly suggested a review and update of patrol, vehicle stop, and search and raid procedures.

2. There were indications of the use of police radio scanners for drug-related activities. New Mexico law enforcement agencies do not have secure voice communications.

3. There were strong indications of the presence of drug abusing personnel with access to law enforcement information in sensitive positions such as police and sheriff radio dispatchers, courthouse personnel, and personnel in district attorney's offices. Background checks and drug testing should be considered for personnel in sensitive positions. If "Crackdown" revealed only one thing, it was that of drugs have permeated all walks of life.

4. There were strong indications of illegal drug related activities on the part of law enforcement agencies, particularly outside of the Albuquerque area (no mention of drug related police corruption appeared with the Albuquerque tips).

5. Indications of money laundering were present. Such indicators were well below the level that had been anticipated. This suggested that money laundering activities need to be considered from a pass-through approach and from a much more decentralized viewpoint than anticipated in the past.

6. There appeared to be logical lines of communications for drug trafficking. These roadways and networks are unique to both the type of drug and the barriers i.e., effective law enforcement agencies, between the dealer the marketplace. An initial "sense" of a series of patterns for drug deliveries was noted. (There are indicators of increasing use of the US Postal Service and private sector delivery—UPS, etc., for drug transportation.) There appeared to be no indicators of a monolithic drug trafficking network. Rather, the case appeared to be a series of networks, each operating independently of the others. While numerous examples of what appears to be individual "narco-entrepreneurs" were evident, drugs are a business in the fullest sense of the word and there are clear indications of the presence of major drug trafficking businesses in New Mexico.

7. While drug supply trafficking from the southern part of the state to other parts of the state was expected (and was clearly evident), there were strong indications that drugs are coming out of Colorado and into New Mexico. Prior experience in this area suggested that drug traffickers would react within 5 to 7 days to any interference with their network by changing routes and methods of delivery.

8. Indications were that approximately 20% of those identified as engaging in drug activities had prior arrests. This raises potential questions from both the supply and the demand sides of the drug problem.

AREAS OF FURTHER RESEARCH

The "Crackdown" findings suggest additional areas that could be studied in the future:

1. The absence, presence, and number of tips from certain communities within the state raised questions about the absence or presence of drugs and drug related activities in certain areas. Why, for example, did a community which was previously identified as having heavy drug activity, produce so few tips? There appeared to be several reasons for this, each of which might give local policymakers a better understanding of the presence or absence of drugs.

2. "Crackdown" data lends itself to further social research and answers. Is it possible to determine why a certain neighborhood is a den of activity while three streets away, drug activity is greatly lessened?

3. Consideration should be given as to how to meld, match, and compare "Crackdown" data with other sources of local and regional information, as well as further "Crackdown" programs.

The New Mexico Crackdown is a realistic example of how state and local law enforcement agencies might coordinate their efforts with the public. It is an exercise that could be replicated throughout the country. What is missing in the Crackdown operation is the infusion of federally generated counter drug information and intelligence so as to sharpen the focus where a difference can really be made. (For a detailed view of "Crackdown" statistics, see Appendix)

THE INFORMATION/INTELLIGENCE SHARING SYSTEM

During July 1990, a quiet meeting took place in a downtown hotel in El Paso, Texas, home to the El Paso Intelligence Center (EPIC). Seven people were in attendance—one from the state of California, two from the state of New Mexico, two from Arizona, and two from the state of Texas.[214] The purpose of the meeting was straightforward. Disgusted with attempts by the federal government to provide counter drug intelligence to the border states and convinced that the feds would never get their act together, the seven participants decided to circumvent the federal government develop They planned to develop a South West Border counter drug intelligence system which was to be called the Information/Intelligence Sharing System.[215]

Initially, each state would build its own intelligence database. Once they were completed, an intelligence communication network would link the states together. That this meeting took place less than a year after the 1989 declaration of the war on drugs speaks eloquently to the fact that the failure of previous federally driven counter drug intelligence plans was well known along La Frontera. Early on, the hopes for predictive, actionable intelligence from EPIC had been dashed. The appointment of Ed Heath, a man who didn't believe in analysis, as EPIC's director precluded any hope that SWB intelligence might be improved. Blindly clinging to the idea that only the DEA, and EPIC in particular, had been blessed by the gods to "do intelligence," Heath ensured that drug related information would enter EPIC, but drug intelligence would never leave.[216]

BUILDING A COUNTER DRUG STRATEGY: HOW DO WE WIN?

Open source intelligence can provide the evaluated information that is the grist of strategy making. Strategy very simply is the answer to the question: How do we win? The underlying reason for the failure of the wars against drugs is the continuing refusal to come to grips with the strategic trilogy of ends, ways, and means. Intelligence must give substance and shape to those three elements.

In *War, Peace, and Victory: Strategy and Statecraft for the Next Century*, Colin Gray provides a framework around which strategy may be constructed. With certain modifications, Gray's work serves as a superb template around which to structure the findings of the counter drug intelligence model. The framework has five primary elements:

1. The unity of strategy—its purpose, policy design, policy implementation, strategic concepts, doctrine, command and control, planning and operational coordination, role and expectation of intelligence, measures of effectiveness, the role of technology on strategy and operations;

2. The *influence of geography*, for political and strategic relationships;
3. The *value of historical experience*;
4. The *power and value of national culture*, to help shape expectations,beliefs, and behavior;
5. The *relationship between strategy and technology*.

In this section I discuss the various factors that are involved in the first element, that of strategy.

PURPOSE

A national drug control strategy should address what the United States can reasonably be expected to accomplish, in a manner that is consistent with our national interests. The still-smoldering partisan struggle over how best to address the drug issue is not new. In fact, this phenomenon is to be found whenever the US government has attempted to implement a large-scale program. The war on drugs, like the Vietnam debacle before it, is a case in which "almost from the beginning, the program was beset with disputes over exactly what it was to accomplish."[217] The National Drug Control Strategy is primarily to blame because it set goals that were unobtainable, thus creating unrealistic expectations. When these factors are combined with the struggle within the legislative branch and a disinterested White House, the result is the present state of chaos in drug policy and strategy.

POLICY

The simple fact remains that the United States cannot have a national policy comparable to its commitments unless it has the means to form such a policy and to base it upon the best possible knowledge of the facts and circumstances.[218] National drug policy should present a definite course or method of action selected from among alternatives that reflect present conditions. This policy should guide and determine present and future decisions. Present drug policy is a reflection of the antiquated concept of internationalism. Disciples of this school espouse a policy that holds that the United States will never know real security unless the rest of the world is also secure and prosperous. The internationalists argue that security is indivisible, and that threats to security are highly contagious and will spread around the world regardless of where they break out. Hence, they argue that the only way to achieve stability is to eliminate those conditions that caused them—wherever they existed. The end result has been that internationalism has insisted that US foreign policy should aim at manipulating and shaping the global environment as a whole rather than at securing or protecting a finite number of assets within that environment.[219]

It is no surprise then, that the "Americanization of the war on drugs" is a reflection of the failed school of internationalism. Present-day policy, driven by the internationalists has as its basis four primary elements.

Extradition

With perhaps one or two exceptions—those in other than the production countries—extradition is a pipe dream. There is every reason to believe that Carlos

Lehder was "offered" up by the Medellin families when he became a liability rather than an asset. While extradition is the greatest fear of the narcotraficantes, they have aggressively rejected any movements for same in the production countries, using the threat of terror to "convince" the government otherwise. Legislation in the production countries has been enacted to ensure that extradition of narcotraficantes will not take place.

Income Replacement

The continuing dilemma of income replacement is the issue of getting crops—any crops—to market. Coca is contracted for, paid for, and picked up by the narcotraficantes, thus ensuring a completed production cycle that puts money in the hands of the campesino. Any crop that is recommended as a worthy substitute has to meet the test of ability to get to market; this in itself is the very heart of the core/periphery issue in Latin America. The lack of a transportation network is endemic throughout South America. The narcotraficantes have solved the problem.

Sanctions

Much favored by the US Congress, without exception they have failed as a tool. Such efforts have never affected the drug traffickers. Rather, the sanctions have alienated the country against which they are directed, causing at least a symbolic tie between the campeñsino and the narcotraficantes.

Negotiated Drug Cutbacks

The issue here is not the cutback, but who one negotiates with—the production country governments or the coca producers. Like the sanctions, negotiated drug cut backs are unrealistic. Such a move fails to take into consideration the failure of five previous drug "wars" to solve the problem from this angle. Since 1989, the cocaleros have pressed not only to increase coca production, but also to legalize certain coca based products. Present day "drug policy suffers from an excess of wishful thinking and over-simplification. Policy is much more responsive to deeply-held, but largely unexamined beliefs and political agendas than to the complexities of the drug problem."[220]

INTEREST-BASED POLICY

What is required is a drug policy that reflects our national interests. Such an approach would distinguish between what is absolutely necessary to achieve essential objectives, and those things that are not essential. This approach would force decision-makers to continually examine policy within a definitive time frame and modify that policy accordingly. The basic tenets of this policy approach are as follows.

First, the drug problem is a threat to our national interests (our national security) and well-being in the realm of law enforcement/criminal justice, public health, and productivity. It is a cyclical, long-term issue, and it is first and foremost the long-term responsibility of state and local government.

Slowing the distribution or sale of drugs at the street level is principally the responsibility of state and local governments. Disrupting trafficking operations by interdicting their shipments between the source countries and our border likewise requires the considerable resources, unique capabilities, and national scope of the federal government.[221] A past program which most clearly is akin to the wars on drugs, and which would at least provide a conceptual starting point for realistic policy planning, is the Law Enforcement Assistance Administration (LEAA). The processes and procedures through which the federal government became a major player in state and local efforts to fight crime are instructive about the strengths and weaknesses of federal policy activity.[222] Referring to broad-based criticism that the LEAA was "overly bureaucratized, lacking firm leadership, political and overall ineffective," Feeley and Sarat look at a program on which the war on Drug appears to be modeled. It is apparent that the federal government learned little from the shortcomings of the LEAA. In 1992, the NDCS was modified to include a federal strategy that encompassed the arrest and imprisonment of street dealers in their plan rather than leaving that task to the local authorities.[223]

Second, drug use and crime should be acknowledged to be an intractable social problem. There is no technology for, nor very many convincing ideas on how to go about eliminating crime. Policies, like those embodied in the Safe Streets Act, like the present NDCS are usually aimed at improving the capability of government to manage continuing and complex social processes rather than obtaining specific goals in the pursuit of soluble social problems; they have multifaceted and ambiguous goals rather than precise and definite objectives. As a consequence, their impact is long in coming, indirect, and intertwined with a host of other disparate efforts.

A more realistic policy approach might well follow along the lines that James Q. Wilson has described. Wilson argues that crime policy (read drug policy) should be tailored to the achievement of attainable ends and that it should be concentrated on the manipulation of objective goods or conditions which are easily within the government's control. "Rational" policy, he suggests, does not ask what is the cause of the problem, but what is the condition one wants to bring into being, what measures do we have that will tell when that condition exists, and what policy tools does a government possess that might produce at reasonable cost a desired alteration in the present condition and progress toward the desired condition? In this case, the desired condition is a reduction in specified forms of crime. The government has at its disposal certain policy instruments. A policy analyst would ask what feasible changes in which of those instruments would, at what cost produce how much change in the rate of a given crime.[224]

Third, supply and demand programs are mutually complimentary—the purpose of supply side programs is to buy time so that demand reduction programs can drive the use of drugs to an "acceptable" level—what constitutes an "acceptable" level of drug consumption is a domestic political issue, one that American society must ultimately anguish over.

Fourth, we cannot stop drugs at their source. We can, however, monitor drug production and provide early warning in the production zone so as to inflict real losses on the narcotraficantes in the transit zone, along our borders, and within our borders, and ultimately at the state and local level—if that makes the most strategic sense. To accomplish this, we need strategic drug intelligence. The analysis that would be derived from such intelligence products would tell what is possible and what is not. What is needed is detailed, up-to-date information on the structure and performance of drug markets, on the economic, social, and political features of source countries that constrain their responses to the drug problem, and on effects of different policy mixes on the behavior of both markets and countries—in short, the sort of information which is necessary for a comprehensive and sophisticated analysis which provided policy-makers with a better understanding of the complexities they face and a basis for novel and bold policy-making."[225] However as Grant Wardlaw has noted, "almost certainly, strategic analysis will defy accepted wisdom, lead to policy prescriptions which do not fit the current American mood, and be seen as a threat by law enforcement agencies (federal) because the assessment can be used as an evaluation of their operations."[226]

Fifth, present policy is built around the concept of a "war" on drugs. While this approach provides the opportunity for creative rhetoric on the part of politicians so that they can respond to their constituents and argue for large-scale appropriations, it is a "cop-out," a failure to respond to the real issues, and a convenient ploy to foist the responsibility and ultimately the blame for their own failure on someone else. The "wars on drugs" is little more than a "metaphor crafted primarily for political and propaganda purposes."[227] The war on drugs was the result of a "sky is falling" approach that was reflected in the "panic selling" on the part of the Congress in 1988–1989. This last-stand effort grasped at the military establishment and cast the blame on other countries, rather than facing the facts. It is clear that the military should only be involved in the implementation and execution of drug policy, where it can provide unique support.

Policy Implementation

Historically, the planning and implementation of large government projects have had mixed success. The success, for example, of the Marshall Plan, has been off-set by the questionable results of the Great Society and the War on Poverty. The litany is endless. The wherewithal to design and implement programs of such size and complexity has eluded us to date. More often than not we demand that somebody:

[Do] something! [Do] anything! Do it right away! [we] are in trouble. [We] need so much so fast time is running out; hence, [we] are always tempted to engage in short run expedience to overcome long term problems combining undue pessimism about the past with wild optimism about the future if only [we] could contribute to the one big project that would turn the tide.[228]

Instead, the search for a solution is "to make difficulties of implementation a part of the initial formulation of policy. Implementation must not be conceived as a process that takes place after, and independent of, the design of policy. Means and ends can be brought into somewhat closer correspondence only by making each particularly dependent on the other.[229] The "bottom-up" school of policy implementation offers an explicit and replicable methodology for identifying an implementation structure and it could well offer methods for offsetting potential implementation problems. Richard Elmore argues that policymakers need to consider both the policy instruments and other resources at their disposal (what he calls forward mapping) and the incentive structure of the ultimate target groups (backward mapping)—in this case state and local law enforcement agencies—because program success is contingent on meshing the two.[230]

The goal of federal criminal justice policy might be to foster a research and development capacity to experiment with, test, and develop new and innovative ideas. If this is the case, then there is a need for a federal agency to exercise firm control over the expenditure of federal dollars. Once a demonstration project has proven itself, it would then be left to sink or swim on its own in the marketplace of ideas in the political competition for sources at the state level. Such a reformulated federal effort is consistent with the concept that states are appropriate laboratories in the federal system.[231]

A Theory of Counter Drug Operations

If purpose and policy determine that actions directed against drug trafficking are best framed in the context of "war," then we must have a theory as to how that war is to be waged. After reflecting upon the OSINT findings, it is clear that we cannot "win" in the sense of traditional military campaigns. This is because we cannot completely stop the flow of drugs. We can harass and deter, channalize, and raise the "cost of doing business"—but no more than that. Ultimately, it is demand reduction which will make the difference.

Doctrine

Doctrine is simply a description of how we are to fight the threat of drug trafficking. Doctrine would provide us with ground rules, the likes of which would provide a common base from which to work. Doctrine would specify how agencies would effectively work together. A spirited series of arguments, fueled, and evaluated by OSINT, at each of the tiers should cause us to come close to an acceptable "road map."

Command and Control

This OSINT-driven case study clearly shows that no one is in charge of the present wars on drugs. Because there is no leadership—centralized command and control which directs counter drug activities through strong decentralized operations—the drug war has become plural. With this plurality of interests, the war has degenerated into a series of wars conducted by each agency with a counter drug mission. A number of uncoordinated, desultory skirmishes with drug traffickers have ensued, the sum of which could never effect a positive final outcome. The end result is that without command and control, the reason why we "went to war" was lost. In addressing the failure of the US attempt to bomb North Vietnam into submission through Operation Rolling Thunder, James Thompson spoke to the ridiculously long lines of command and control and the nit picking direction of the war from Washington—to include selection of targets by the president and his close advisors. Such is the case today with the war on drugs.[232]

At present, there is no centralized command and control in the war on drugs. The findings of this case study suggest that resolution of this issue would quickly clear up many problems in Washington, along the SWB, and in the transit and production zones. Whoever is in overall command should be capable of working in a federal politico/military and state and local environment, both commanding the respect of and guiding law enforcement and military support operations. The distance between the Office of National Drug Control Policy and the sheriff of Doña Ana County, New Mexico, is substantial. For the sheriff on the front lines, Washington is light years away. Faced with local problems and pressure, he will be hard put to answer to many masters. There is no way that the federal government can expect to direct and control the battle from afar. The central problem is this: "the selection, preparation, and direction of means appropriate to secure the objectives instrumental to achieving the purposes of policy" cannot be done from afar, nor by committee."[233]

Coordination

Looking at the war on drugs through an intelligence focus, one is reminded of the complexity of the problem of coordination between intelligence agencies. Reflecting upon the failure of strategic bombing in Vietnam, James Thompson argued that "the division in the intelligence community must be noted. Those agencies closely connected with the military—DIA, NSA, and army, navy, and air force intelligence—agreed with JCS estimates. The agencies identified more closely with civilian bureaucracies—the Bureau of Intelligence and Research and the CIA—raised important questions about the JCS arguments."[234] It is of the utmost importance to remember that these same agencies have been brought into the war on drugs and have again "formed sides."

The Role and Expectations of Counter Drug Intelligence

To date, counter drug intelligence has been poorly organized and under-funded, in particular, the analysis element. The emphasis upon tactical intelligence as exemplified by most federal law enforcement agencies, has masked the failure of the very limited attempts at the creation of strategic intelligence. While the singular area of consensus amongst law enforcement agencies is the need for "more intelligence," that belief overshadows the reality of the situation. Clearly what is needed is to define what may be expected of CD intelligence in the areas of drug production, transshipment, border entry, and state and local activities. Such a requirement would address:

1. A policy that emphasizes that counter drug operations must be guided by intelligence.
2. The need to develop intelligence measures of effectiveness at the national, state, and local level.
3. The adaptation of a decentralized approach to intelligence. This approach would stress a regional and state emphasis. It would push analysts down to positions closer to the intelligence customer; create regional, state, and local information mini databases; and use off-the-shelf artificial intelligence software to manipulate the information, emphasizing the use of appropriate technology versus "high" technology.
4. A system to make classified information available to state and local law enforcement intelligence units. Since the process of "desanitizing" intelligence is laborious and the end result frequently removes the meat and cancels out the time value of the information, this may well prove to be impossible. It is unrealistic to expect that every law enforcement officer will be given, or could qualify for a DoD security clearance. The fact is that such a requirement is not necessary. With open source developed information, a high level of accuracy and depth of subject matter may be achieved. It is not trite to suggest that knowledge is power. The implication here is that with open source derived CDI—complemented where appropriate with classified information—the knowledge level of both analysts and managers could be dramatically upgraded. As mentioned earlier, a security/personnel screening system, similar to that used by the Western States Intelligence Network could be used as a prototype.
5. A policy that ensures that intelligence and the secure means to transmit it are one package.
6. The creation and implementation of operational security and counterintelligence programs for federal, state and local law enforcement agencies. While police corruption is viewed as being a "south of the border thing," the reality of the situation is that drug trafficking has made and will continue to make inroads amongst US law enforcement.
7. The production of strategic intelligence products so as to provide policymakers with an accurate assessment of the situation.

Operations

Operations, whether they be federal, state, or local, should be driven by intelligence, and reflect policy goals. The diverse nature of the drug trafficking threat, the geography of the drug "theater," and the variety of the agencies involved suggest that operational control should be decentralized, yet coordinated with provisions that ensure complementary, single, and multizone operations. It should be clearly recognized that drug "interdiction" has not been a failure, since an effective program of interdiction has never been attempted. In spite of the recent statement by Timothy Worth of the State Department as to "interdiction failure," the botched detection and monitoring attempts by US Southern Command— which were never coordinated with Pacific Command, US Atlantic Command, JTF-4, JTF-5, JTF-6, or any law enforcement agencies—do not constitute a failure. The case is that no one has yet to accurately assess the design and impact of a clearly defined, flexibly executed interdiction strategy.

Measures of Effectiveness

Nowhere has the failure to address measures of effectiveness on the wars on drugs been more pronounced then by the General Accounting Office (GAO). As

Colin Gray notes, the "rigorous and highly repetitive quest after detailed sins of official[s]—[those of] commission and omission— displaces the consideration of strategy. Politicians and journalists would seem to find better reward in the minute examination of the procurement process than in the investigation of the suitability of hardware and procedures for the objectives of operations and strategy and the purposes of policy."[235]

Current measures of effectiveness (MOE's) include the drugs seized, the interdiction rate, the price of drugs, and the support factor. In the future, MOE's should include:

1. Qualitative and quantitative measures of effectiveness
2. Intelligence sharing
3. Centralized command, decentralized operations
4. An emphasis on developing and more and better human intelligence sources
5. Directing support to State and Local LEA's

Success or failure must be measured to ascertain the strengths or weaknesses of policy, strategy, and operations. To date, no measures of effectiveness have been devised to gauge the progress, or lack thereof, in the wars on drugs. The primary indicators of success in use today are the fluctuation of the street price of cocaine and the amount of drugs seized or the interdiction rate. Neither method provides an accurate measure of success or failure. In the former case, as argued erroneously by Peter Reiter of RAND, common wisdom holds that as an interdiction program improves, the supply of drugs will go down, resulting in a rise in prices. Since prices have gone down, then it follows that interdiction programs must be failing. In reality, this is not true. Drug prices are not directly and solely related to supply. If one looks at and understands the unusual factors involved in the drug industry, then it is painfully clear that the present mathematical approach to price is a poor indicator of effectiveness. The attempt to devise measures of effectiveness exclusively by quantification, is a throw-back to the McNamara/Vietnam era. Succumbing to what Colin Gray calls the "sin of technicism," the propensity to attempt to reduce issues of means and ends to the promise of a new machine or accounting system, attempts at building a suite of realistic MOE's has been deemed to be a task that is too difficult. Instead, attempts which fall far short of the mark have been accepted.

A major concern of the MOE dilemma is that no one set of measures can be applied to the wars on drugs. Each agency has special requirements, hence the need for evaluation techniques that accurately weigh actions against mission and produce a picture of performance. Trial and error strongly underline the fact that there is no one best approach to MOE's. Rather, as the commandant of the Coast Guard stated to a congressional inquiry on measuring effectiveness, "drug interdiction evaluations must also consider qualitative indicators of deterrence, disruption, and displacement."[236]

The Role of Technology

Technology is the bête noire that continues to haunt and cripple the search for effective counter drug strategy. The "sin of technicism" continues to be endemic in the wars on drugs. Characterized by the proclivity to reduce the issues of means and ends to the hope of some new software or "black box," the history of drug wars technology "fixes" is littered with failure. A major problem is the arrogance of technology. This is best exemplified by a 1991 attempt by a consortium of the national laboratories to address Integrated Analytical/Computer Models To Support National Counter Narcotics Activities. In spite of the fact that the needs of the user community were as "yet undefined," the National Laboratory Consortium— Battelle, Lawrence Livermore, Los Alamos, Oak Ridge, and Sandia, submitted a "consensus approach" to the Office of National Drug Control Policy. Refusing to first recognize and then address national and front-line requirements, the consortium members each sought to contort their "pet" projects into something that might fit the unknown issues of the counter drug community. Fortunately, the proposal met a quiet death, preceded by murmurs of disbelief at ONDCP.[237]

In Puerto Rico, federal officials have been attempting to sell the Relocatable Over The Horizon Radar (ROTHR). A $9 million project that proponents claim could track low-flying aircraft a well as boats carrying drugs throughout the Caribbean. In spite of claims by the Department of Defense that the ROTHR is its biggest tool in the fight against drug traffickers, most Puerto Ricans are opposed to it. The ROTHR consists of a huge transmitter and receiver at least 50 miles apart. It also makes use of 744 receiving antennas that stand 19 feet high. Over 200 acres would have to be acquired to house the operation. Puerto Rican farmers and environmental groups oppose the radar, claiming that its antenna system would produce a high level of electronic emissions that would harm the health of nearby residents. There is little reason to believe that this radar would be any different from two other systems that are located in Texas and Virginia. Absent an end game, it makes no difference how many boats or aircraft are tracked if they can not be acted upon. Again, technology is proffered as strategy, a belief that has cursed the drug war since day one.[238]

The problem of searching containers for illegal drugs is being addressed through a project that is being prototyped for DoD's Advanced Research Projects Agency by Analytical Systems Engineering Corporation of Alexandria, Virginia. Using horizontal and vertical x-rays beams, it is possible to create a digitized computer image of cargo within any container. The images are so clear that an inspector can find a handgun packed inside a bag of dog food. Inspectors can also tell how much fuel is in the truck hauling the container and whether anything is hidden in the fuel tank or secret compartments. Up to 35 containers per hour can be check for contraband.[239]

On the other hand, there have been cases where the national laboratories have refused to apply their claimed expertise to the counter drug arena. In one case dealing with LIDAR, one of the most promising but least addressed devices which could make an impact on drug trafficking, the Los Alamos National Laboratory LIDAR section leader, launched into a hysterical tirade. Screaming that the drug traffickers would kill him and his family if he worked on such a project, he refused to even address the issue.[240] In the main, however, the national laboratories have simply refused to seriously address the drug issues, arguing that such work is "beneath" them and certainly ill-suited to such prestigious institutions where only "good science" is done.

If technology is to be successfully applied to counter drug operations it must be required to show cause as to the soundness of theory and application. This would ensure that expensive and nonsensical devices, such as AWACS, aerostats, EMERALD, and certainly General George Joulwan's "Hollywood Squares" would be weeded out early on. As events in the past have shown, technology all too often fosters a managerial mindset, the very antithesis of solid analysis and realistic strategic thinking. The rule of thumb should be *appropriate* technology with emphasis on using "off-the-shelf" devices for state and local law enforcement.

This move would coincide with limitations upon the size of federal databases. I would discourage and limit the growth of large intelligence databases, encouraging instead regional, state and local mini databases. What is clear to date is that the present fixation on counter drug databases has more to do with data "turfism" than with amassing useful information for the creation of counter drug intelligence. Simply put, technology cannot substitute for strategy or analysis.

AN ALTERNATIVE COURSE OF ACTION

Concept

As was discussed earlier, the basis for a drug strategy should be formulated through a unitary approach. It should reflect the influence of geography—as it impacts both traffickers and US efforts to stymie them. A strategy must reflect the knowledge of historical experience—something that would clearly show that present day drug policy and strategy is nonsense. Our strategy must be a reflection of our national culture—a reflection of those things that are acceptable to the body politic. Whatever the strategy, it must be supported by technology—not driven by it. Above all, the strategy must be shaped by realistic expectations of what can be accomplished in the long-term. Combining these elements with an interest-driven policy approach, the following is suggested as an alternative course of action for a US supply-side strategy.

Federal Government

1. Place someone in charge at the federal level—a cabinet level director of the Office of National Drug Control Strategy—who has the power, stature, command presence, and imagination to pull all agencies together to directly *support* state and local counter drug efforts. Provide this individual with the power of the purse string to ensure compliance from federal agencies.

2. Make OSINT the intelligence of first choice. Use OSINT in the production of strategic intelligence—the driver to support policy and strategy. Emphasize the analytical element of intelligence production. One of the dilemmas is the issue of what may be expected from the intelligence process. More often than not, expectations that are too high cast the intelligence process in an unrealistic light. Part of that may be overcome by making the intelligence process more professional. In addition to the selection and training of intelligence personnel, I believe that there is another important consideration that has been overlooked. Writing in the *Secrets of the Vietnam War*, Lieutenant General Philip B. Davidson, the chief Army Intelligence officer in Vietnam from May 1967 until May 1969, raised the issue of quantity versus quality in intelligence

production: [S]omewhere along the line, increased numbers of people just get in each other's way. Sheer numbers obscure the fact that the really valuable intelligence is produced by a few talented analysts and estimators. These people sit back, slightly removed from the day by day process of intelligence, projecting the information of the enemy's past and present into the future. Without these gifted estimators—and they are rare birds indeed—the intelligence presented to the commander is little more than the recent history of enemy strength and activities.[241]

3. Ensure that supply-side intelligence directly supports demand-side programs and also draws information from them.

4. Inform the American public. In *The Burdensome Concept of Failure*, Mark M. Lowenthal argues that:

there is a public role to be played by the intelligence community, albeit a difficult one given that it will always appear self-serving—and at some level it is. Nevertheless, the intelligence community can be allowed occasionally to release data or analyses to indicate areas of success. I am not suggesting that the intelligence community release a report card or batting average at the end of each year. But the price of public support is evidence of success. I would argue that a few successes could be noted, without risk of sources and methods, and without necessarily going overboard.[242]

Production Countries

It has been and will continue to be contrary to the best national interests and ability of production-zone governments—Peru, Bolivia, and Colombia to attempt stem the flow of drugs.

Recommendations: Monitor the growth, production and preparation of drugs in order to provide actionable "departure" intelligence to agencies located in strategic positions along the drug pipeline that can effect "end game." Recognize that while difficult to monitor, maritime trafficking routes are of primary importance and must be addressed. This will require greater HUMINT assets and the coherent use of national technical assets.

"Squish Countries"

As with the production countries, it is contrary to the interests and the ability of those countries that border the cocaine production to engage in much more than counter drug rhetoric. Problems caused by corruption and internal drug consumption are not yet severe enough for these countries to shift drug issues higher on the list of national priorities.

Recommendation: Monitor the movement of drugs through these countries in order to provide actionable "departure" intelligence to agencies located in strategic positions further down the drug pipeline that can effect "end game." This will also require HUMINT assets and the expanded use of national technical assets.

El Conducto: The Transit Countries

A sound strategy should weigh the value of forcing airborne traffickers to ground. It may well prove to be more advantageous to develop plans to capitalize upon the weak spots in airborne smuggling, than to drive them to ground and see a shift to greater maritime smuggling. The strategy should reflect a dramatic increase in maritime detection and monitoring operations.

Panama

Panama will continue to be a primary maritime drug transshipment location as well as a major money laundering location. There is no reason to believe that the political situation there will change in the near future.

Recommendation: While little can be done to curtail the money laundering activities, low-key HUMINT operations should be directed against the Colon Free Zone and other key locations to monitor and detect container and maritime activity for the purpose of providing early warning and "departure" information and intelligence to agencies further down the pipeline.

Belize

Rapidly coming on line as a primary drug smuggling, pass-through location, Belize should be used as a window to look into Mexico and Guatemala.

Recommendation: Locate radar and signals intelligence assets in Belize to monitor movement of drugs west and north.

Guatemala

Second only to Mexico in trafficking activities, Guatemala is a location where trafficking organizations are vulnerable. With finished product, aircraft, vehicles, communications centers, and oceangoing vessels all found there, strikes directed against narco assets there—or just prior to arrival could dramatically raise the "cost of doing business."

Recommendations: The place to begin "end game" execution since it is susceptible to US political pressure. Counter drug operations directed against drug trafficking would include the following:

1. Concerted political pressure directed against the business elite and the Guatemalan military. Such pressure would raise the "cost of doing business" for both groups; apply pressure on the government—similar to what was done in El Salvador—to come to terms with the guerrillas thus negating the continued incentive of these groups to turn to trafficking as their only means of support.
2. If it is advantageous to the overall strategy, attack the "stretch" point for drug aircraft arriving from northern South America. At present, drug-laden aircraft arrive at Guatemala low on fuel, and with pilots tired after the trip from Colombia. With the highest number of airplanes crashes in central America, Guatemala could prove to be prime location for constricting airborne drug routes.
3. Active deception directed against trafficking organizations could start internecine warfare that would disrupt lines of communications, transit, and, of the greatest importance, the command and management nodes.
4 Address multimodal transit—maritime-land; air-land: airdrop-maritime-land.
5. Provide warning and alert to US "end game" agencies.

Caribbean

The strategy should be to work in conjunction with Canadian, British, French, and Dutch military and law enforcement agencies toward immediate efforts to professionalize island police and military forces and to apply political pressure from all the aforementioned governments to attempt to get the island governments to develop stronger laws directed against trafficking and money laundering.

Mexico

The opportunity to apply political pressure and extract specific intelligence requirements still exists as NAFTA trade policies are still being implemented. The ground swell of opposition parties that would support such a move could further add pressure to the PRI to support US counter drug efforts.

Recommendation: Execute end game setup. Apply political pressure to shape post-NAFTA agreements to include specific requirements dealing with counter drug activities. The strategy here should consist of the detection, monitoring, and advance warning of drug departures, from Mexico, toward the South West Border. This would consist of three tiers: a working relationship with the new Mexican Drug Intelligence Center, development of a HUMINT network in Mexico; and, the positioning of signals intercept devices, radar, and other national assets on the US side of the South West Border to look and listen in Mexico.

South West Border

The entry point for approximately 70% of the cocaine that enters the United States, the SWB remains a disjointed collection of law enforcement and military agencies. The strategy here should be oriented toward a centralized command and control situation, with decentralized, intelligence driven, long-term sustainable state and local activities.

Recommendations:
1. Four state operated, federally funded and supported drug intelligence centers (California, Arizona, New Mexico, and Texas) operating primarily with OSINT supported by secure communications. Expansion of a personnel security system along the lines of that used by the Western States Intelligence Network. Direct—onsite—analytical support from federal intelligence and law enforcement agencies.
2. Offense in depth, i.e., a series of law enforcement "belts," unobtrusive to the public, that would force drug traffickers to work their way through at least three law enforcement barriers by the time they have traversed 75 miles into the United States. These belts would be non static and would change locations in accordance with the reaction of the drug traffickers.
3. Forward looking signals, RADAR, and LIDAR situated to provide early warning by looking into Mexico to the depth of at least 400 miles.
4. Re-evaluate asset forfeiture seizures. While the trafficker's pocketbook is vulnerable, so, too, are the US citizens who have been injured by the misguided execution of asset seizure at the hands of law enforcement agencies. The damage from "claim-jumping" and intelligence hoarding far outweighs the monetary benefits of the program. [243]

Epilogue: Turning Points

In December 1992, I drew up a five-year forecast of key events—turning points—that I thought would come to pass in the cocaine trafficking arena (see Figure E.1). The idea for this came from a quote by James Schlesinger, former Director of Central Intelligence. Schlesinger noted that "Intelligence is good at monitoring day to day activities, but it is not so good a discerning turning points." I wondered at that time if my work would enable me to discover any milestones. The forecast would serve a test of how well I had analyzed and evaluated the drug related information. Having studied that evaluated knowledge from 1990 to 1992, I then dared to venture into what Sherman Kent called the "speculative-evaluative" function of Intelligence.[1]

FORECAST 1993–1997

A review of the events suggests that the forecast was quite accurate. Summarizing those events from 1993 to the present it is clear that extradition is a non-starter. Tied to a series of repentance degrees that are aimed at lessening the level of drug violence in the source countries, extradition is something that only exists in the fogged minds of US policymakers.

The repatriation of drug tainted dollars is a non-issue. It will remain in the best interest of Latin American governments to encourage the flow of drug tainted dollars through their economic systems. Always cash-short, cocaine-dollars will help growing economies do what the Alliance for Progress could never do.[2] Better economic conditions will strengthen most of Latin America and—ironically—speed the legitimization of a large numbers of the traficantes.

Multi-lateral counter drug accords—without the US—regardless of their seemingly initial ineffectiveness, are now the rule rather than the exception. The arrogance of United States drug policy has ensured that the 'big gringos" will be excluded from critical compacts in the future.

Figure E.1
Turning Points

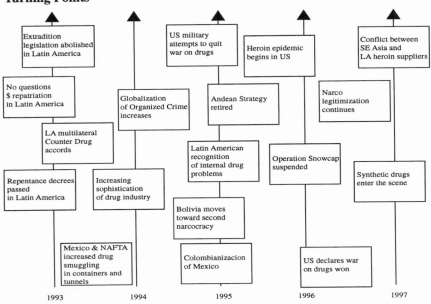

It was apparent in 1993 that drug traffickers were becoming more and more sophisticated. Now, writ in large script—in what must clearly be considered a turning point—drug traffickers have moved beyond the pale in their business operations. The primary reason behind their success has been their institutionalization of intelligence. Simply stated, the traficantes do intelligence better than us.

After five years of multibillion dollar investments directed to programs to counter the traficantes, it is all too clear that the US drug policy is a long-term disaster. It will take a major shift in policy and strategy to inflict telling wounds that will make a difference. Nowhere is this more apparent than in Mexico where the sophistication of traffickers and organized crime have Mexico teetering on the brink of chaos. The NAFTA agreement—ratified in the US only after law enforcement agencies were gagged—is an invitation to large-volume drug smuggling.

I believe that I was off target in the forecast in arguing that the "Colombianizacion of Mexico" would be complete by the 1995–1996 time frame. What I did not see was that the corruption in Mexico is primarily self-induced. The influence of the Colombian traffickers merely speeded up a process in Mexico in which the PRI had become the thief in the night. The issue now, is this: can the opposition parties such as PAN, rise above the morass and seize control of the country in a manner that will vilify the corruption and thus lead Mexico out of the swamp; or, has the corruption become so endemic that it cements Mexico into the framework of narcocracy? I believe that US policy could tip the scales either way. We must stay engaged in Mexico. This engagement should be a positive one that supports those elements in Mexico that are trying to chart a new course for the future.[3] It appears that while Colombia and Bolivia will have a long uphill struggle, they are in a much better condition to win their battles. Unlike Mexico, they have both recognized the problem and have started to attempt to cope with the curse of cocaine. Not the least of this recognition is driven by the realization that Latin America has a drug consumption problem.

The gradual withdrawal of the US military from the drug arena is all too apparent. As argued earlier, the military can—and should—provide those unique services that they alone have the wherewithal to bring to the drug arena. The military must be seconded to counter drug duties in such a manner that their fitness reports reflect the support they provide. The disengagement of the military coincides with the demise of Operation Snowcap and the Andean Strategy—both monuments to the continuing nonsense that characterizes thinking in Washington.

In a scene repeated during the late 1970's and early 1980's as cocaine and crack reached epidemic proportions while the DEA was focused upon heroin, the obsession with the current drug of choice in the United States has resulted in a failure to recognize the significance of the next drug in the pipeline. Heroin is now making its way into this country in large, pure-grade shipments. It remains to be seen who will seize control of the heroin market. What is clear is that there will be open-warfare between suppliers in southeast Asia and the new generation of Latin American opium traffickers. By the time that we recognize that the heroin epidemic that is now upon us, we will have lost sight of the onslaught that will begin with a new generation of designer drugs that will be manufactured in the United States, in home laboratories.

Everything points toward the US government declaring the war on drugs won by 1997. It is my sense that the drug issue, closely tied to law and order, will become one of the major issues in the 1996 presidential campaign. From this viewpoint, neither political party appears to have the slightest knowledge of what it will take to mount a long-term campaign against drugs. Today, despite the provisions of the 1995 Anti-Crime Bill, little of real substance is being done to address, plan, and attack the drug problem today. Any hope that was held out for an enlightened Clinton administration drug policy was lost with the implementation of Presidential Review Document-18 (PRD-18). The hope that prior to casting new policy, policymakers would take the time to study the whole problem of how well we have learned the lessons of the war did not come to pass. Instead of evaluating the war on drugs and asking the ends/ways/means questions, PRD-18 appears to have been blindly aimed toward options that a realistic policy evaluation performed by intelligence, would have discounted. The record of the Clinton Administration appears to be a step backwards. The record is as follows:

- Slashed the staff of the Office of National Drug Control Policy by 80%;
- Issued an executive order reducing military interdiction, including the elimination of 1,000 anti-drug positions;
- Cut interdiction funds for the Customs Service and the DEA;
- Shortened mandatory minimum sentences for drug traffickers;
- Eliminated 355 DEA agents and 102 personnel from the Justice Department's organized crime drug enforcement task force;

- Dropped the drug issue from the top to the bottom of the National Security Council's list of 29 priorities;
- Disbanded Operation Snowcap which assigned DEA agents to cocaine producing countries to aid police.[4]

In the case of the last element, little was lost by closing down Operation Snowcap. But in the items previous to Snowcap, it is clear that those moves were driven by the perception that the drug issue was "too difficult" and thus the monies were transferred to other programs.

Casting further light on the Clinton administration drug policy, a 1995 GAO report noted serious problems in many aspects of drug strategy, policy, and leadership issues.

First, the executive branch has changed the focus of its international strategy for cocaine from law enforcement and drug seizures in the transit zone to stopping drugs in the source countries before they reach the transit zone. However, the executive branch has had difficulties implementing a key part of its strategy shifting resources from the transit zone to the source countries.

- US Southern Command is now flying fewer sorties than it did in 1993 and counternarcotics assistance to each of the three primary source countries is expected to be less in 1995 than in 1991 or 1992.
- Shifting resources between and within agencies is problematic. In mid-1994 the DEA Attaché in Mexico City cautioned that the Northern Border Response Force had been jeopardized by the loss of detection and monitoring coverage in the transit zone. In addition, the senior officer at the US Atlantic Command stated that he saw a need to continue detection, monitoring, and interdiction efforts in the transit zone and believes that shifting resources to the source countries would adversely affect this coverage.
- The Office of National Drug Control Policy has designated Mexico as the second most important country in the international narcotics program—behind Colombia—even though Mexico is listed as a transit-zone country. The DEA has recommended that Mexico be reclassified as a source country so it can be considered for more resources.
- In November 1993, the executive branch announced that within four months it would develop a strategy to combat the heroin trade. As of July 27, 1995, about 20 months later, there still was no heroin strategy.

Second, in addition to combating drugs, the United States has other important objectives that compete for US attention and resources. As a result, the United States must make tough choices as to which objectives to pursue most vigorously.

- The drug trade in Mexico is the fourth highest priority in the US Mission Action Plan. The US Ambassador to Mexico stated that he had focused his attention during the past year and a half on trade and commerce—NAFTA and financial support for the Mexican peso.

Third, the many US agencies are not always well managed. In the past, we have recommended improvements in how US counternarcotics assistance funds are managed. We find that the extent to which US government agencies monitor the end use of assistance provided to foreign governments varies. Furthermore, specific measures of how programs are contributing to overall counternarcotics goals have yet to be established.

- Officials from all agencies generally agreed that no single organization was in charge of antidrug activities in he cocaine source countries or in the transit zone. US officials in Colombia stated that they were unsure who had operational control over their activities and questioned which agency could best provide that control.
- An official of the acknowledged that staffing constraints had limited progress in developing some type of leadership of US counter drug programs.
- The US Interdiction Coordinator, a position that was established in 1993, does not have specific roles and mission authority established for it. Coordinator officials stated that their ability to coordinate activities was limited because of the lack of funds, expertise, and authority over agencies involved.

Finally, the effectiveness of US international drug control programs depends in large measure on the willingness and ability of foreign governments to combat the drugs in their country. The extent and direction of host-country action often vary over time. Recent actions by the government of Colombia, such as the incarceration of several senior members of the Cali Cartel, are positive steps, but continued commitment is needed. For a variety of reasons, foreign governments are not always willing to fully participate in counternarcotic efforts. Even when they are willing, they often lack the necessary resources.

Extensive corruption in some countries further weakens the host country actions to combat the drug trade.[5]

SO WHAT

Until the time of the announcement of the selection of General Barry McCaffrey as the new drug czar, the Clinton Administration appeared to have paid only lip-service to the drug issue. McCaffrey could tip the scales in favor of the president's bid for a second term. With the drug and law enforcement issues second only to the economy in the upcoming election, the General could provide the leadership for the creation of a new drug policy. What is unclear is whether or not the a reelected President Clinton would support the hard decisions that will have to be made—after the election.

Comments by Speaker of the House Newt Gingrich—who as a junior legislator stated that "the US Army should be in every country simultaneously wiping out the drug trade"—to the effect that those who traffic in large amounts of drugs should face the death penalty, suggest that the battle of words may soon again be joined.[6] The findings and recommendations of a seventeen member Republican committee which is due out at the end of March 1996 should provide the fuel to fire new election-year debate.

But caution is in order.

Past debates have been mostly smoke. What did happen—and will probably happen again—is best described by Senator John McCain. Responding to the continuing failure of the government to create a realistic drug strategy, he said that:

It is all too easy to talk of a war on drugs, involve our military in an antidrug program, pour billions into the effort, and then disguise a lack of success with reassuring rhetoric. Wars, however, are not political games, they are not exercises in political imagery, and they cannot be won with rhetoric or false measures of success.The measures of success that are being made public have virtually no practical meaning. For example, efforts to assist seizures are measured in terms of the amount of drugs seized, with no effort to relate such data to the percentage of total drugs that get through, or to whether the seizures have any meaningful impact on the main smuggling networks.

Constant reference made to the street price of drugs seems to be impressive to those in the media who have never bothered to consider the meaning of such data, but law enforcement officers who exaggerate the importance of their seizures by describing the value of their seizures in street prices are indulging in little more than publicity stunts. Smugglers do not pay street prices. They do not measure losses in street prices. In most cases, the major smugglers have paid just a small fraction of the so-called street price for the drugs that are seized, and see such losses as a minor cost of doing business. Another equally meaningless measure of capability is to report the number of detections, arrests, or intercepts, with no attempt to relate this to the number of successful crossings or actual convictions, or whether such actions have any real effect on the flow of drugs.[7]

Sharing the Secrets provides a body of descriptive material which will enable serious public discussion to begin on national drug policy and strategy. The simple fact remains that the United States cannot have a national policy comparable to its commitments unless it has the means to form such a policy and to base it upon the best possible knowledge of the facts and circumstances.[8]

Appendix

SOUTHWEST NEW MEXICO
RESERVE, SILVER CITY, DEMING, HURLEY, MIMBRES

Gender

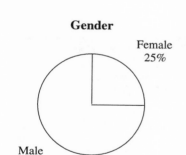

Female
25%

Hispanic
50%

Male
75%

Ethnic

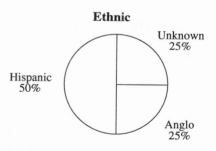

Unknown
25%

Anglo
25%

Drug Type

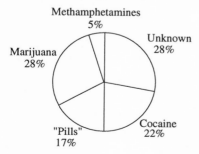

Methamphetamines
5%

Unknown
28%

Marijuana
28%

Cocaine
22%

"Pills"
17%

With only 10 tips, no solid
statistical basis may be drawn.

Miscellaneous Information	
Meth Lab	0
Marijuana Plantation	0
Weapon Involved	1/8%
Prior Arrest of Suspect	4/33%
Informant ID	3/33%
Links	1/2
Chains	0
Businesses	1

I-25 SOUTH COMMUNITIES
ISLETA, LOS LUNAS, BOSQUE FARMS, BELEN, TRUTH OR
CONSEQUENCES, SOCORRO, LAS CRUCES

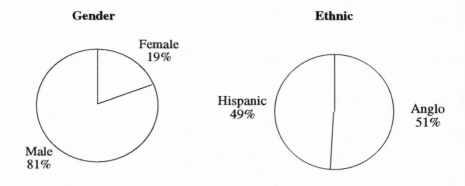

Gender

Female 19%

Male 81%

Ethnic

Hispanic 49%

Anglo 51%

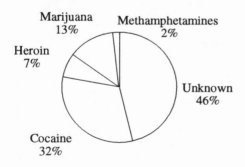

Drug Type

Marijuana 13%

Methamphetamines 2%

Heroin 7%

Unknown 46%

Cocaine 32%

Miscellaneous Information	
Meth Lab	0
Marijuana Plantation	0
Weapon Involved	5/13%
Prior Arrest of Suspect	7/18%
Informant ID	18/48%
Links	1/2
Chains	0
Businesses	0

SOUTH SANDOVAL COUNTY AND NM 44 NORTH
ALAMEDA, RIO RANCHO, BERNALILLO, JEMEZ SPRINGS, CUBA

Gender

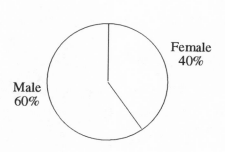

Female
40%

Male
60%

Ethnic

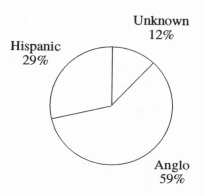

Unknown
12%

Hispanic
29%

Anglo
59%

Drug Type

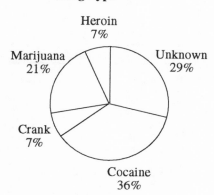

Heroin
7%

Marijuana
21%

Unknown
29%

Crank
7%

Cocaine
36%

Miscellaneous Information	
Meth Lab	1
Marijuana Plantation	0
Weapon Involved	13/19%
Prior Arrest of Suspect	19/28%
Informant ID	14/18%
Links	8/18
Chains	
Businesses	3

Not enough tips to form a solid statistical base. No discernible links or patterns.

I-40 EAST AND SOUTHEAST NEW MEXICO COMMUNITIES TIJERAS, EDGEWOOD, MANZANO, ESTANCIA, VAUGHN, CLOVIS, ROSWELL, ALAMAGORDO, CLOUDCROFT, RUIDOSO, TULAROSA, ARTESIA, CARLSBAD

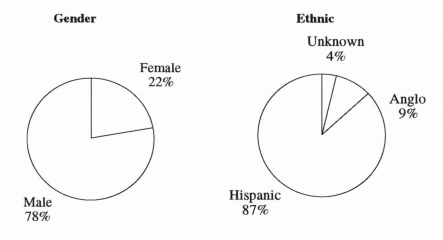

Gender

Female
22%

Male
78%

Ethnic

Unknown
4%

Anglo
9%

Hispanic
87%

Drug Type

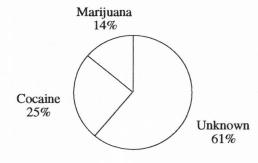

Marijuana
14%

Cocaine
25%

Unknown
61%

Miscellaneous Information	
Meth Lab	0
Marijuana Plantation	1
Weapon Involved	5/8%
Prior Arrest of Suspect	3/11%
Informant ID	9/33%
Links	1/3
Chains	0
Businesses	3

While this area produced 33 tips, we do not feel that there is enough information to speak to the area with any conviction. The number of tips were sparse from Roswell and the far southeast corner. Without a solid series of tips, neither a local or regional picture can be drawn.

I-40 WEST AND NORTHWEST NEW MEXICO COMMUNITIES
LAGUNA, GRANTS, BLUEWATER, GALLUP, NAVAJO, FARMINGTON

Gender

Ethnic

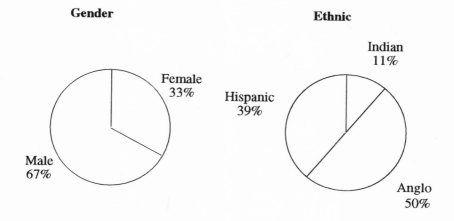

Drug Type

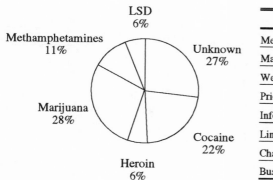

Miscellaneous Information	
Meth Lab	0
Marijuana Plantation	0
Weapon Involved	2/11%
Prior Arrest of Suspect	3/16%
Informant ID	1/17%
Links	2/4
Chains	1/8
Businesses	3

This area did not have enough tips to build a valid statistical workup.

NORTHWEST ALBUQUERQUE

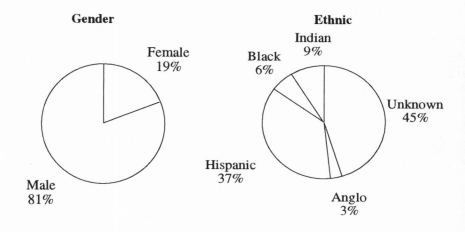

Gender

Female
19%

Male
81%

Ethnic

Indian
9%

Black
6%

Unknown
45%

Hispanic
37%

Anglo
3%

Drug Type

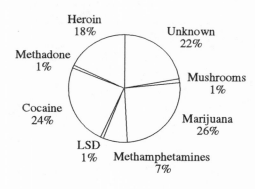

Heroin
18%

Methadone
1%

Cocaine
24%

LSD
1%

Methamphetamines
7%

Unknown
22%

Mushrooms
1%

Marijuana
26%

Miscellaneous Information	
Male Age	32
Female Age	24
Meth Lab	2
Marijuana Plantation	0
Weapon Involved	7/11%
Prior Arrest of Suspect	14/22%
Informant ID	10/17%
Links	2/5
Chains	3/10
Businesses	13

Northwest Albuquerque has a "feel" similar to the Northeast part of the city. We have a sense of many small players.

SOUTHEAST ALBUQUERQUE

Gender

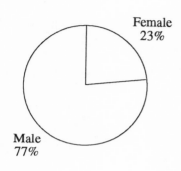

Female
23%

Male
77%

Ethnic

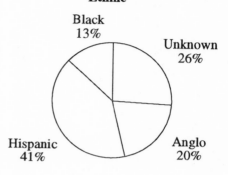

Black
13%

Unknown
26%

Hispanic
41%

Anglo
20%

Miscellaneous Information	
Male Age	32
Female Age	31
Meth Lab	1
Marijuana Plantation	0
Weapon Involved	13/19%
Prior Arrest of Suspect	19/28%
Informant ID	14/18%
Links	8/18
Chains	
Businesses	3

Drug Type

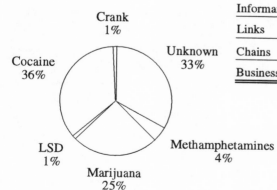

Crank
1%

Cocaine
36%

Unknown
33%

LSD
1%

Methamphetamines
4%

Marijuana
25%

SOUTHWEST ALBUQUERQUE

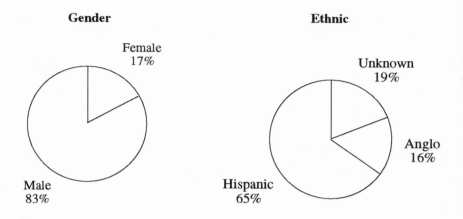

Gender

Female
17%

Male
83%

Ethnic

Unknown
19%

Anglo
16%

Hispanic
65%

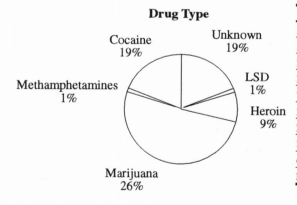

Drug Type

Cocaine
19%

Methamphetamines
1%

Unknown
19%

LSD
1%

Heroin
9%

Marijuana
26%

Miscellaneous Information	
Male Age	31
Female Age	30
Meth Lab	1
Marijuana Plantation	0
Weapon Involved	25/22%
Prior Arrest of Suspect	28/24%
Informant ID	28/23%
Links	9/26
Chains	1/9
Businesses	17

NORTHEAST ALBUQUERQUE

Gender

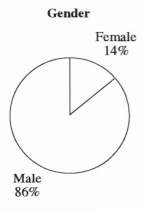

Female
14%

Male
86%

Ethnic

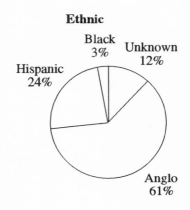

Black
3%

Unknown
12%

Hispanic
24%

Anglo
61%

Drug Type

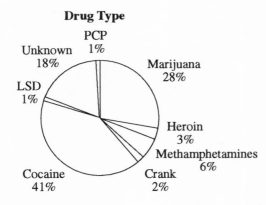

PCP
1%

Unknown
18%

Marijuana
28%

LSD
1%

Heroin
3%

Methamphetamines
6%

Cocaine
41%

Crank
2%

Miscellaneous Information	
Male Age	28
Female Age	30
Meth Lab	3
Marijuana Plantation	0
Weapon Involved	14/9%
Prior Arrest of Suspect	30/20%
Informant ID	28/23%
Links	15/30
Chains	5/18
Businesses	10

Northeast Albuquerque has a different "feel" from other parts of the city. While a sizable number of links and chains were developed, this area does not appear to have the "hot spots" or strips of activity to the degree that is found in other areas of the city. The "sense" of this area is that it is not close knit.

Notes

INTRODUCTION

1. Angelo Codevilla, *Informing Statecraft: Intelligence for a New Century* (New York: The Free Press, 1992), p. xiii.

2. Sherman Kent, *Strategic Intelligence for American World Policy* (Princeton N.J.: Princeton University Press, 1949), p. 201.

3. Jerome K. Clauser and Sandra M. Weir, *Intelligence Research Methodology: An Introduction to Techniques and Procedures for Conducting Research in Defense Intelligence* (State College, Penn.: HRB-Singer, 1975; prepared for the Defense Intelligence School), p. 295.

4. Kent, p. vii.

5. Ibid., p. viii.

6. Ibid., p. 3.

7. Ibid.

8. Ibid., p. viii.

9. To date there has been no single, comprehensive definition of OSINT. This definition is an attempt to flesh out the skeleton and offer up a strawman for argument.

10. Kent, p. 182.

11. Ibid., p. 201.

12. Ibid.

13. Willmoore Kendall, "The Function of Intelligence," *World Politics*, Vol.1, July 1949, p. 548.

14. Big "I" has traditionally been used to refer to national/strategic intelligence. Little "i" refers to law enforcement intelligence.

15. Bruce D. Berkowitz and Allen E. Goodman, *Strategic Intelligence for American National Security* (Princeton, N.J.: Princeton University Press, 1989), p. 4.

16. Kent, p. 3.

17. Abram N. Shulsky, *Silent Warfare: Understanding the World of Intelligence* (Washington, D.C.: Brassey's, 1991), p. 10.

CHAPTER 1: THE NEW INTELLIGENCE ENVIRONMENT

1. George S. Pettee, *The Future of American Secret Intelligence* (Washington, D.C.: Infantry Journal Press, 1946), p. vii.

2. Sherman Kent, *Strategic Intelligence for American World Policy* (Princeton, N.J.: Princeton University Press, 1949), pp. vii-viii.

3. See Ray Cline, *Secrets, Spies, and Scholars: The Blueprint of the Essential CIA* (Washington, D.C.: Acropolis Books, 1976), for full coverage.

4. Pettee, p. 67.

5. Ibid., pp. 108-109.

6. Kent, p. 80.

7. Ibid.

8. Ibid., p. 91.

9. Rod Paschal, *LIC 2010-Special Operations & Unconventional Warfare in the Next Century* (Washington, D.C.: Pergamon-Brassey's, 1990), p. 21.

10. Patrick Brogan, *The Fighting Never Stopped: A Comprehensive Guide to World Conflict Since 1945* (New York: Vintage Books, 1990), p. viii.

11. Alvin Toffler, *Powershift* (New York: Bantam Books, 1990), p. 372.

12. Robert Gates, "The Future of American Intelligence," an address to the Intelligence Community, December 4, 1991.

13. Paula L. Scalingi, "US Intelligence in an Age of Uncertainty," *Washingon Quarterly*, Winter 1992, p. 147.

14. William Pfaff, Op-Ed, *Albuquerque Journal*, February 18, 1991, p. 9.

15. *Armed Forces Journal*, May 1992, p. 8.

16. *American Intelligence Journal*, Winter/Spring 1992, p. 25.

17. Robert D. Steel, "Open Source Intelligence Clarifies Global Threats," *Signal*, September 1992, p. 66.

18. Gregory R. Copely, "The Medium or the Message," *Defense & Foreign Affairs*, October 15, 1991, p. 2.

19. Robert D. Steele, "Applying the New Paradigm: How to Avoid Strategic Intelligence Failures in the Future," *American Intelligence Journal*, Autumn 1991, p. 43.

20. J. F. Holden-Rhodes and Peter A. Lupsha, "Horsemen of the Apocalypse: Gray Area Phenomena and the New World Disorder," *Journal of Low Intensity Conflict and Law Enforcement*, Autumn 1993, pp. 212-226.

21. Ibid., p.1.

22. Holden-Rhodes, Working Notes (hereafter WN), March 1992.

23. Pettee, pp. 70-71.

23. WN, April 1993.

24. Phillip B. Davidson, *Secrets of the Vietnam War* (Novato, Calif.: Presidio Press, 1990), p. 6.

25. WN, April 1992.

26. WN, Sandia National Laboratory, April 1995. It has been suggested with credence that DOE and Intelligence are mutually exclusive.

27. Eliot A. Jardines, Interview with Dr. Joseph Markowitz, Director of the Community Open Source Program Office, *Open Source Quarterly*, January-March and April-June 1996. Special thanks to Captain Jardines for an advanced copy of the *OS Quarterly* and his key role in creating the *OSQ*.

28. Ibid.

29. Ibid.

CHAPTER 2: IN SEARCH OF A COMMON GROUND: THE QUEST FOR COUNTER DRUG INTELLIGENCE

1. *National Drug Control Strategy* (Washington, D.C.: Government Printing Office, 1995), p. 77 (hereafter *NDCS* 95).

2. Peter A. Lupsha, *The Quest for a Comprehensive Drug Policy*, unpublished manuscript, p. 30.

3. John W. Fisher, "Can Intelligence Win a War on Drugs? The National Drug Intelligence Strategy and Efforts for a 'Drug Free America,'" seminar paper, given at the Defense Intelligence College, Defense Intelligence Agency, December 1988, p. 13.

4. *The Role of Intelligence* US Congress, (Washington, D.C.: Government Printing Office, 1992), p. 7.

5. Fisher, p. 15.

6. Raphael Perl, November 9, 1988, Congressional Research Service.

7. Lupsha, p. 30.

8. Lupsha, p. 6.

9. Policy and Program Development, *International Narcotics Matters Report* (Washington, D.C.: US Department of State, 1992).

10. *NDCS* 95, p. 44.

11. *National Drug Control Strategy* (Washington, D.C.: Government Printing Office, 1990), pp. 89-90.

12. *NDCS* 95, p. 82.

13. Author's visit to South Florida HIDTA, May 23-26, 1995.

14. National Institute of Justice figures, provided by Tony McDonald, Middle Atlantic Great Lakes Organized Crime Law Enforcement Network, June 1995.

15. Drawn from excerpts from House Appropriations Committee, Judiciary Subcommittee Hearings, March 9, 1995.

16. Conversations with author, December 1995.

17. Memorandum from NDIC to FBI HQ's, December 12, 1994. This was another attempt to force the issue as to just what the misson of NDIC is. The memo noted that "an important first step was to reaffirm that the mission of the NDIC is, primarily, to produce multi-source organizational analyses of illicit drug trafficking organizations."

18. In my estimation the products that NDIC has produced address the right topics, covers them with good forecasting and of the greatest importance—they can be shared—with state and local law enforcement.

19. A "force multiplier" is a termed coined by the DoD to describe the results of a device or innovation that is touted to equal more than its normal output, i.e., a synergistic action or activity.

20. This is certainly the sense that has been expressed to me over the past 6 years—"you can't get there from here."

21. This is my experience, gleaned throughout my research.

22. Mary C. Lawton, Counsel for International Policy, US Department of Justice, AFCEA Conference, October 1989.

23. Office of Technology Assessment, 1987.

24. *DoD's Role in Drug Interdiction* (Washington, D.C.: Government Accounting Office, 1992), p. 23.

CHAPTER 3: THE NATIONAL DRUG CONTROL STRATEGY: THE INTELLIGENCE AGENDA

1. David Musto, *The American Disease: Origins of Narcotics Control* (New York: Oxford University Press, 1987), p. 13.

2. Douglas Clark Kinder, "Bureaucratic Cold Warrior: Harry J. Anslinger and Illicit Narcotics Traffic," *Pacific Historical Review,* Vol. 50, May 1981, pp. 169-191.

3. William O. Walker III, *Drug Control in the Americas* (Albuquerque: University of New Mexico Press, 1981), p. 193.

4. Kinder, p. 183.

5. Jefferson Morley and Malcom Byrne, "The Drug War and National Security: The Making of a Quagmire, 1969-1973," *Dissent,* Winter 1989, p. 39.

6. Edward J. Epstein, A*gency of Fear: Opiate and Political Power in America* (New York: G.P. Putnam's Son's, 1977). p. 21.

7. Morley and Byrne, p. 39.

8. Ibid., pp. 41-42.

9. *Federal Drug Control Strategy* (Washington, D.C.: Government Printing Office, 1976), p. 49.

10. Ibid., p. 51.

11. Ibid.

12. Ibid.

13. Steven Wisotsky, *Breaking the Impasse in the War on Drugs* (Westport, Conn.: Greenwood Press, 1986) p. 3.

14. *GI NARCS: A Syllabus of the Military's Role in Counternarcotics*, Ridgeway Center, University of Pittsburg, Alternative Uses of the Military Working Group, April 1991, pp. 6-7.

15. *National Drug Control Strategy* (Washington, D.C.: Government Printing Office, 1990), cover letter.

16. Ibid., pp. 87-90.

17. Ibid.

18. Ibid.

CHAPTER 4: THE THREAT

1. US Army, FM 30-5, COMBAT INTELLIGENCE, p. 68.

2. Sherman Kent, *Strategic Intelligence for American World Policy* (Princeton, N.J.: Princeton University Press), 1949, p. 3.

3. William Drohan, *The 1984 Cocaine Surprise: Drugs Declare War on the United States*, unpublished paper, Defense Intelligence Agency, 1989; NNICC Narcotics Intelligence Estimate, 1984, p. 25. (Drohan's paper was, and is, a vital piece in any drug intelligence research. In spite of its present and future value, it has been completely ignored by the intelligence community.)

4. Drohan, p. 34; NNICC Narcotics Intelligence Estimate, December 1978, p. 6.

5. NNICC, December 1978, p. 5, and NNICC, December 1984, p. 6.

6. Drohan, p. 34.

7. *Federal Drug Control Strategy* (Washington, D.C.: Government Printing Office, 1976), p. 49.

8. Drohan, p. 29.

9. Ibid., p. 30.

10. Paul Eddy, Hugo Sabogal, and Sara Walden, *The Cocaine Wars* (New York: Bantam Books, 1988) p. 26.

11. Ibid., p. 27.

12. Drohan, p. 32.

13. Eddy, Sabogal, and Walden, p. 30.

14. Drohan, p. 30.

15. *National Drug Control Strategy* (Washington, D.C.: Government Printing Office, 1989), p. 86.

16. "The Kingdom of Cocaine," *The New Republic*, November 21, 1989, pp. 27-28.

17. J.F. Holden-Rhodes and Peter A. Lupsha, *Plata o Plomo*, Los Alamos National Laboratory CD Intel Team working paper, July 1991, p. 7.

18. Ibid.

19. Ibid.

20. Ibid., p. 4.

21. Ibid., p. 9.

22. "Kingdom of Cocaine," p. 28.

CHAPTER 5: THE MILITARIZATION OF THE WAR ON DRUGS

1. General Sir John Hackett, *The Profession of Arms* (New York: Macmillan Publishing Company, 1983), p. 9.

2. *Military Cooperation with Civilian Law Enforcement Officials Act*, US Code Chapter 18, sections 371-373, (1981).

3. *Narcotics Digest*, June 15, 1991, p. 2.

4. *Federal Drug Interdiction Efforts Need Stronger Central Oversight*, GGD-83-52, (Washington, D.C.: Government Accounting Office, June 13, 1983).

5. During this time frame, drug-laden aircraft frequently flew north in groups that in some cases consisted of 20 aircraft. In one documented case in Mexico, 30 drug aircraft were detected flying in a rough "formation." Just prior to the Grenada invasion, radar screens in Barbados "lit-up" with approximately 20 "bogeys." A panic ensued as no one knew where the aircraft came from. Not a few folks suggested that they were Russian. (The scare reached well up the US chain of command). I believe they were airborne narcos who just happened on the scene at the wrong moment.

6. AP Wire Service, September 28, 1984.

7. For more details on this schism, see George C. Schultz, *Turmoil and Triumph, My Years as Secretary of State* (New York: Macmillan Publishing Company, 1993), Chapter 29.

8. Peter Reuter, *Sealing the Borders: The Effects of Increased Military Participation in Drug Interdiction* (Santa Barbara, Calif.: RAND, 1987), preface.

9. Ibid., p. 32.

10. Ibid., p. 45.

11. Ibid., p. 46.

12. Ibid.

13. *Washington Post*, May 13, 1989, p. 1.

14. Ibid., p. 1.

15. Ibid.

16. *Air Force Times*, October 2, 1989.

17. *Army Times*, July 5, 1989.

18. Holden-Rhodes, Working Notes (hereafter WN), January 1992.

19. National Defense Authorization Act of 1989.

20. Ibid., p. 3.

21. ULTRA secret is in reference to the Allies breaking of the German Enigma Code during World War II. ULTRA enabled the Allies to break almost all German signal traffic. The security that accompanied ULTRA was of the highest nature. After the war similar

stringent security measures were applied to other types of intelligence. Unfortunately this obsession was carried to extremes and intelligence never made its way to all potential customers.

22. In a sense, "stove piping" was a response to undo the excessive lack of intelligence caused by the ULTRA/green door syndrome. Unfortunately this attempt to "pipe" it to all customers failed to work.

23. *American Intelligence Journal*, Spring-Summer 1991, p. 22.

24. *Defense News*, April 13, 1992.

25. WN, July 1991. From 1990-1992, I served as a special advisor to the New Mexico National Guard for special operations and counter drug intelligence. During that time, in addition to deploying to the field with them on selected counter drug operations, I conducted a survey of their activities. It became clear that aircraft crossed the New Mexico-Mexico border with virtual impunity. On several occasions, Guard units contacted C_3I West to report suspicious aircraft. The responses indicated that C_3I West could not "see" below a certain altitude—something the airborne narcotraficantes had discovered early on. Reports of multiengine aircraft were frequent, single engine aircraft were commonplace, and on at least one occasion a "military-type bomber" (thought to be a B-24) came over the border at 200-plus knots, skimming the piñon, 20 feet off the deck.

26. Thomas Donnelly, Margaret Roth, and Caleb Baker, *Operation Just Cause: The Storming of Panama* (New York: Lexington Books, 1991), pp. 2-3.

27. Ibid., p. 12.

28. Ibid., pp. 23-24.

29. Ibid., p. 33.

30. See Donnelly et al. for a more detailed account. It appears that General Woerner was "double-crossed."

31. Donnelly et al., p. 37.

32. Major James Nicholson, conversation with author, July 15, 1993.

33. Donnelly et al., p. 365.

34. Ibid., p. 366.

35. Ibid., pp. 366-367.

36. *Armed Forces Journal*, September 1992, p. 10.

37. Ibid., p. 10.

38. Ibid.

39. Ibid., pp. 11-12.

40. WN, June 30, 1992.

41. Ibid.

42. The reference to "rogue elephant" is drawn from the Church Commitee Report of 1974 that referred to the CIA as an agency out of control. In the case of DDD this was true.

43. WN, July 1993.

44. US Southern Command Counter Drug Wargaming System, Developmental Game, Executive Summary, May 30, 1992.

45. It was of great interest to tie together the comments of the WIAG players with previous policy and strategic statements that they had made. From these comments, it was easy to see from whence came the "Alice in Wonderland" mentality that pervades the wars on drugs thinking in Washington.

46. WN, July 1994.

47. Ibid.

48. The scope of this book required that I briefly mention the role of the National Guard. In reality they deserve a book unto themselves. The intelligence support of the Texas National Guard to state and local law enforcement was some of the best "intel" work that I have ever

seen. The California National Guard's operational intelligence production is also superb. Their support to law enforcement proved that the narcotraficantes can be "channelized" and set up for the kill— just after they cross the US/Mexico border. Under the inspired guidance and imagination of Major General Edward Baca (newly appointed Chief of the National Guard Bureau), the New Mexico National Guard wrote the book on supply and demand support. Designated as an Air Defense unit, the troops took on the "grunt" missions with enthusiasm and drive. Working from the "boot-heel" of New Mexico—where the summer temperatures reach 120 degrees—to the mountainous regions in the northern part of the state—where the highways became landing strips for drug-laden aircraft—the guard troopers did, and continue to do, a professional job. Guided "up front" by Lt. Col. Barry Stout, and Major Dana Carden, the NMNG could field a unit for a mission within hours—Standard Operating Procedure. They put the regulars to shame, showing how CD support could and should be done.

49. *American Intelligence Journal*, p. 40.

50. Ibid., p. 42.

51. David Kahn, *Clausewitz and Modern Strategy* (London: Frank Cass Publishing, 1986), p. 117.

52. *Impact of DoD's Detection and Monitoring of Cocaine Flow* (Washington, D.C.: Government Accounting Office, June 1993).

53. The Andean Drug Intiative, Committee on Foreign Relations, United States Senate, February 20, 1992.

CHAPTER 6: THE SOUTH WEST BORDER: LA FRONTERA

1. Lawrence A. Gooberman, *Operation Intercept* (New York: Pergamon Press, 1974), p. 1.

2. Ibid., p. 2.

3. *Newsweek*, September 22, 1969, p. 37.

4. Gooberman, p. 3.

5. Ibid., pp. 2-4.

6. Terence E. Poppa, *Drug Lord: The Life and Death of a Mexican Kingpin* (New York: Pharos Books, 1990), p. 6.

7. Ibid., p. 218.

8. Peter A. Lupsha, *Drug Lords and Narco-Corruption: The Players Change but the Game Continues*, draft paper, December 1991, p. 3.

9. Ibid., pp. 14-15.

10. James Rudolph, *Mexico: A Country Study* (Washington, D.C.: Government Printing Office, 1985).

11. Ibid.

12. J. F. Holden-Rhodes, "Counter Drug Intelligence on the South West Border," *American Intelligence Journal*, Spring 1991, p. 18.

13. Holden-Rhodes, Working Notes (hereafter WN), SWB LEAs, Fall 1991.

14. Ibid.

15. *National Drug Control Strategy* (Washington, D.C.: Government Printing Office, February 1991), p. 102.

16. *South West Border Drug Control Strategy* (El Paso, Texas: Operation Alliance, 1990), p. 7.

17. *National Drug Control Strategy* (Washington, D.C.: Government Printing Office, 1995), pp. 83-84.

18. *Border Control: Drug Interdiction and Related Activities Along the Southwestern US Border* (Washington, D.C.: Government Printing Office, September, 1988).

19. WN, NG/LEAs.

20. For an excellent example of corruption on the SWB, see Randy Fitzgerald, "A Whistle-Blower's Ordeal," *Readers Digest*, June 1994, pp. 73-79.

21. South West Border Law Enforcement Computer Capabilities and Information/Intelligence Management and Exchange Study, (1990).

22. Ibid.

23. J. F. Holden-Rhodes, *Counter Drug Technology Assessment*, Los Alamos National Laboratory (1991).

24. WN, SWB Seminar, El Paso, Texas, May 28, 1991.

25. WN, conversation with New Mexico HIDTA members, November and December 1995.

26. *Narcotics Control Digest*, September 12, 1991, p. 10.

27. *South West Border Drug Control Strategy*, (El Paso, Tex.: Operation Alliance, 1990), p. 10.

28. Ibid.

29. WN, SWB Seminar Notes, May 1991.

30. David L. Hood, *Southwest Border Seizures: The New Mexico Corridor, January 1989–November 1989. An Analysis of Seizures Reported to Operation Alliance by U.S. Border Patrol and U.S. Customs Service* (New Mexico Department of Public Safety, Special Investigations Division, Criminal Information and Analysis Bureau, Santa Fe).

31. WN, Dona Ana County Sheriff's Office, 1990-1993.

32. *South West Border Drug Control Strategy*, (El Paso, Tex.: Operation Alliance, 1990), p. 32.

33. *Albuquerque Journal*, March 27, 1995.

34. Ibid.

35. WN, Federal Reserve/Banking Institutions, July 1995.

36. James Rudolph, pp. 283-284.

37. See "Mexico," Chapter 7 of this book for an in-depth account of the corruption and its impact.

38. Poppa, p. 267.

CHAPTER 7: GETTING IT RIGHT: OPENING THE BOOK TO THE RIGHT PAGE

1. Sherman Kent, *Strategic Intelligence for American World Policy* (Princeton, N.J.: Princeton University Press, 1949), p. 201.

2. George S. Pettee, *The Future of American Secret Intelligence* (Washington, D.C.: Infantry Journal Press, 1946), p. 3.

3. Willmoore Kendall, *The Function of Intelligence* (New York: Global Affairs, 1949), p. 546.

4. Lawrence Livermore National Laboratory, 1991. This statement was made by an LLNL spokesman after a number of articles—the elements of which were classified—appeared in the open press, having been drawn from open sources. This dilemma will become more and more prevelant as the information revolution continues to be deluged with open source information that was never before accessible.

5. Admiral William Studeman, Deputy Director of Intelligence, Central Intelligence Agency, comments at the 1st National Open Source and National Competitiveness Symposium, McLean, Virginia, November 5, 1991.

6. Red Team/CD Intelligence Team, Los Alamos National Laboratory, drawn from La Empresa Coordindora Colombiano, March 1992.

7. The issue of "capture" versus "surrender" is unclear. Seeking to curry favor with the government, traficantes have in the past allowed their entry into government hands to be

"colored" so as to appear to have been a "capture."

8. La Empresa Coordinadora Colombiano.

9. The visit of Prime Minister John Major during may 1994, underscores the importance of the oil fields. Above all else, Colombia must find a way to secure the area from guerrilla forces so that production can take place.

10. *Christian Science Monitor* (hereafter *CSM*), February 2, 1996, p. 2; and, Knight-Ridder Wire Service, February 18, 1996.

11. *CSM*, p. 2.

12. Ibid.

13. Ibid.

14. *CSM*, January 24, 1996, p. 6.

15. Westlaw, 1995, 944422, Presidential Determination No. 95-15, p. 18. (Hereafter Westlaw).

16. *Trend Analysis: Drugs in the Western Hemisphere*, December 1, 1993-May 30, 1995 (Placitas, N.M.: Praetorians Ltd.) p. 21. (Hereafter *TA*)

17. Ibid.

18. Westlaw, p. 18.

19. Ibid.

20. Ibid.

21. Ibid.

22. *Albuquerque Journal* (hereafter *AJ*), March 13, 1994, p. A-21.

23. *TA*, p. 21.

24. Ibid., p. 8.

25. Ibid., p. 19.

26. Ibid., p. 20.

27. Ibid., pp. 21-22.

28. Ibid., p. 25.

29. *Washington Post* (hereafter *WP*), April 8, 1994, p. 24.

30. *Death Beat: A Colombian Journalist's Life Inside the Cocaine Wars* (New York: Harper Collins, 1994), pp. 85-136.

31. *TA*, p. 1.

32. Duzan, pp. 279-280.

33. Ibid., p. 137.

34. National Narcotics Intelligence Consumers Committee, *The NNICC Report: 1994 The Supply of Illicit Drugs to the United States* (Washington, D.C.: Drug Enforcement Administration, 1995), p. 21. (Hereafter NNICC-94)

35. *CSM*, February 8, 1996, p. 14.

36. Ibid.

37. Ibid.

38. *AJ*, January 29, 1996, p. A-2.

39. NNICC-94, pp. 16-17.

40. *TA*, p. 41.

41. NNICC-94, p. 18.

42. *TA*, p. 52.

43. Westlaw, p. 17.

44. Ibid., p. 23.

45. *TA*, p. 51.

46. NNICC-94, p. 15.

47. Ibid.

48. Ibid.

49. *Newsweek*, May 31, 1992, p. 37.

50. Gordon McCormick of the Naval Post Graduate School argues that Sendero is still active in 90 of the 183 Peruvian departments in 1994.

51. Reuters Wire Servce, December 21, 1995.

52. Holden-Rhodes, Working Notes (hereafter WN), January 1995.

53. *The Economist*, September 17-23, 1994, p. 26.

54. *The Economist*, May 7, 1994, p. 50.

55. *TA*, p. 57.

56. *TA*, p. 56.

57. *TA*, p. 63.

58. *AJ*, December 18, 1995, p. 2.

59. Reuters Wire Service, December 21, 1995.

60. Westlaw, p. 3.

61. *TA*, p. 21.

62. *Newsweek*, January 14, 1996, p. 41.

63. *TA*, p. 21.

64. Ibid., pp. 22-23.

65. Ibid., p. 24.

66. *CSM,* February 8, 1996, p. 14.

67. *TA*, p. 24.

68. Westlaw, p. 5.

69. Ibid., p. 5.

70. *The Economist*, April 7, 1994.

71. Westlaw, p. 15. This is a government-generated figure. Using open sources, I estimate that in 1989, 80 tons passed through the country, which by 1992 had risen dramatically to 500 tons, minimum. Much of this was bound for Europe by the Venezuelan-Italian connection.

72. *TA*, p. 21.

73. Westlaw, p. 15.

74. Ibid.

75. Ibid., p. 17.

76. NNICC-94, p. 22.

77. Westlaw, p. 23.

78. Ibid., p. 22.

79. Ibid.

80. *Newsweek*, January 14, 1996, p. 39.

81. Ibid.

82. NNICC-94, p. 23.

83. *CSM*, February 7, 1996, pp. 1, 14.

84. NNICC-94, p. 14.

85. *Time*, February 26, 1996, p. 46.

86. *TA*, p. 52.

87. Ibid.

88. NNICC-94, p. 14.

89. *Time*, February 26, 1996, pp. 46-47.

90. Ibid.

91. Ibid., and NNICC-94, p. 13.

92. NNICC-94, p. 7.

93. Westlaw, pp. 4-5.

94. NNICC, pp. 12-13.

95. Ibid.

96. Ibid.

97. Ibid., and *TA*, p. 50. Again, there is a disparity in the "numbers." The figures from the *Trend Analysis* are drawn from onsite journals.

98. Knight-Ridder Wire Service, December 17, 1995.

99. NNICC-94, p. 12.

100. Ibid., p. 14.

101. *Time*, February 26, 1994, p. 46.

102. Ibid., p. 48.

103. Ibid.

104. Ibid.

105. Thanks to Russ Holland, chief analyst at Joint Task Force 5 for the maritime update. Working with Randy Layland, Russ and the other analysts at JTF-5 are the unsung heroes of maritime intelligence. Responsible for not only tracking cocaine in the western hemisphere, they "reach-out" to the Golden Triangle, where they track opium and heroin as they make their way to the United States. Their former boss, Admiral John Linnon (now at the 1st Coast Guard District in Boston) is one of a hand full of flag officers who really understand the drug business. Not afraid to put it all on the line to make his case, Admiral Linnon—like General John Pickler, formerly of JTF-6, now with the 4th Infantry Division—makes the difference.

106. *Washington Times*, April 7, 1994, p. 13.

107. Joint Publications Research Service (JPRS), Narcotics, US Government (hereafter JPRS-N) January 1994.

108. JPRS-N, April 1994.

109. Westlaw, p. 13.

110. *TA*, p. 26.

111. Ibid.

112. *TA*, p. 25.

113. JPRS-N, June 1994.

114. NNICC-94, p. 11.

115. *TA*, p. 26.

116. Westlaw, p. 29.

117. *TA*, p. 28.

118. Ibid.

119. *Barricada International*, No. 370, February 1994, p. 8.

120. JPRS-N, April 1994.

121. *TA*, p. 28; NNICC-94, p. 4.

122. WN, Belize, 1994, 1995.

123. NNICC-94, p. 10.

124. Hearings, Options for United States Policy Towards Guatemala, Committee on Foreign Affairs, US House of Representatives, July 17, 1990.

125. J. F. Holden-Rhodes, *The New Thirty Years War*, unpublished paper, (Political Science Department, University of New Mexico, 1991), p. 17; CERI-GUA, 1989-1993 (newsletter); Major James Nicholson conversations with author, July 1993.

126. *The New Thirty Years War*, p. 17.

127. NNICC-94, p. 10.

128. Ibid.

129. NNICC-94 and INSCR figures result from the deliberate melding for certain purposes. They are almost always in close agreement.

130. Holden-Rhodes, *The New Thirty Years War*, p. 33.

131. Unknown source.

132. JPRS-N, June 1994.

133. *TA*, p. 30.

134. *AJ*, June 1, 1994, p. 2.

135. *TA*, p. 39.

136. Ibid., p. 40.

137. Ibid., p. 42.

138. *Time*, October 17, 1994, p. 24.

139. *TA*, p. 47.

140. Ibid., pp. 39-40. In the first sixteen months of the Salinas administration, it appeared that the government was really making headway against drug trafficking. Some 345 drug trafficking organizations were said to have been broken and some 40 metric tons of cocaine and cocaine base were seized. On March 15, 1990, "El Padrino," Felix Gallardo, was sentenced by a Mexican court to a prison sentence of 300 years.

In early October 1990, Javier Coello Trejo, an assistant attorney general, directed the antinarcotics police to a ranch in Chiapas near the Guatemalan border where they seized 5.75 tons of pure cocaine. It was the largest seizure of this type in Mexican law enforcement history. Then, on October 15, Coello Trejo authorized a raid in Chihuahua that seized 3 aircraft and 6 tons of cocaine (pura and basica). Within hours of this raid, the traditional pattern of narco-corruption asserted itself. Javier Coello Trejo was suddenly appointed Attorney General for Consumer Affairs, a post of little significance in Mexico. The official announcment stated that the move was a promotion. It appears that those aggressive raids, or perhaps the US seizure of 3.85 tons of cocaine on October 5, 1990 in a propane truck (in the United States) belonging to the untouchable Zaragosa family of Juarez, was too much for the traffickers who applied enough pressure to have Coello Trejo ousted. Operations of this type would not happen again during the Salinas administration. In retrospect, things had moved out of government hands by this time. It will be interesting to learn, as events further unroll, to what degree and at what point in time the three drug mafia's in Mexico "seized" power.

141. Ibid., p. 35.

142. Ibid.

143. Ibid., p. 38.

144. *AJ,* Februrary 18, 1996, p. B-4.

145. Ibid., March 21, 1996, p. 2.

146. *CSM*, November 2, 1994, p. 9.

147. *TA*, p. 43.

148. Ibid., p. 38.

149. Ibid., p. 43.

150. Ibid., pp. 43-45.

151. Ibid., p. 30.

152. WN. It is with great caution that I use this figure. What makes me believe that it is close to the mark is the knowledge that over the past 6 years, we have dramatically underestimated both the amount of cocaine produced and the profits accrued therefrom.

153. *TA*, p. 30.

154. Reuters Wire Service, January 15, 1996.

155. *San Francisco Chronicle* (Wire) (hereafter *SFC*), February 27, 1996.

156. Ibid.

157. Ibid.

158. *AJ*, January 19, 1996, p. 2.

159. WN. This information came from a confidential source who has been 99.99% accurate in the past. I do not take such information lightly, and I reference it only after

attempting to corrobarate the information through other sources. I believe that such an event did take place and that within 6-9 months, the specific details will be forthcoming.

160. Reuters Wire Service, December 19, 1996.

161. Committee on Foreign Affairs, Andean Drug Strategy, Hearing before the Senate Committee on Western Hemisphere Affairs, February 26, 1991, p. 1.

162. Committee on Foreign Affairs, Subcommitee on Terrorism, Narcotics, Intelligence Operations, Andean Drug Initiative, February, 1992, p. 72.

163. Ibid., pp. 1-2.

164. Ibid., p. 14.

165. Ibid., pp. 68-69.

166. Ibid., p. 69.

167. Ibid., p. 37.

168. Ibid., p. 38.

169. Ibid., p. 39.

170. Ibid., p. 40.

171. Kent, p. 7.

172. *National Drug Control Strategy* (Washington, D.C.: Government Printing Office, September 12, 1989), p. 93. (Hereafter *NDCS*)

173. NNICC-92, p. iii.

174. *International Narcotics Control Strategy Report* (Washington, D.C.: Government Printing Office, 1992), p. ii. (Hereafter *INCSR*)

175. NNICC-92, p. iii.

176. Ibid.

177. *INCSR*, p. 11.

178. Ibid., p. 8.

179. WN, February, 1992.

180. NNICC-94, p. 16.

181. WN. I attended the QPWG meetings in 1991, 1992, 1993. It is still unclear to me today, why the "numbers" from those meetings were—and still are—classified. The narcotraficantes know what they lost. How does it aid them if they know that we know? It strikes me that this is another example of mindless classification to protect someone's "6" (6 is military jargon that refers to covering one's backside).

182. Ibid.

183. Ibid.

184. Major (now Lt. Col.) James Nicholson, chief, Analytical Support Team (AST), US Southern Command, May 1992.

185. Eliot A. Cohen and John Gooch, *Military Misfortunes: The Anatomy of Failure in War* (New York: Vintage Books, 1991). These three themes run through the text.

186. Why the LANL team was selected to to perform this task is still unclear to me. On the one hand we could be counted upon to complete any task in short order—something the SouthCom staff sections did not appear to do well, or often.

187. WN, July 1993. In retrospect, I suspect that we were assigned the task with a specific set of findings already in the minds of SouthCom. If we completed the task and came up with the "school-solution" then any adverse reaction to the findings could be blamed upon us. To even think about multi-division augmentation from the production countries was absurd and patently dangerous. This, however, was where the SouthCom mentality was under General George Joulwan.

188. Mike Levine, *Deep Cover* (New York: Dell Books, 1991), p. 78.

189. Drug Enforcement Administration, DEA Strategic Management System (FFS:190-01), February 26, 1991.

190. WN. Drawn from conversation with a senior DEA analyst on September 16, 1994. Not so affectionately known as "Trooper 1"—a reference to his state trooper mentality—it was soon clear that the new administrator had been appointed to see to the draw-down of DEA forces overseas, something that the old-timers viewed with revulsion. Constantine wanted to get the DEA back "where it belonged," making busts in the cities of the United States.

191. WN, October, 1991.

192. General Barry McCaffrey, comments to the Heritage Foundation on January 14, 1996.

193. WN, Joint Task Force 4, November 1993.

194. Alvaro Vargas Llosa, *The Madness of Things Peruvian: Democracy Under Siege.*

195. WN, National War College, After Action Report, June 1992. This episode was extremely embarrassing for all of us. We had alerted a number of colonels from the S-5 and S-6 as to the impending engagement. It simply didn't register with them. I still don't understand why heads didn't roll. During my tenure as Team Chief at LANL, I never saw anyone fired for failing to perform at SouthCom.

196. "Clinton's Phony Drug War," *American Spectator,* February 1994, pp. 40-44.

197. WN, July, 1995.

198. Comments from a LANL staffer who worked with SouthCom staff during 1994. He noted that General McCaffrey was abusive to his general officer staff directors (S-2, S-3), frequently dressing them down during staff meetings in a manner that the observer considered to be degrading. One general officer literally did hand-stands down the passageway on his last day of duty under McCaffrey.

199. I use this term with the utmost respect. It is a descriptor that I personally prize. It is drawn from Tom Clancy's book, *Without Remorse.* General Mc Caffrey is most certainly worthy of the title of predator. Reference here is to the last two sentences of Clancy's work (my italics).

Recon Marines, they'd all volunteered to become Marines first—there were no draftees here—then done so again to join the elite within the elite. There was a slightly disproportionate representation of minorities, but that was only a matter of interest to sociologists. These men were Marines, first, last, always, as alike as their green suits could make them. Many bore scars on their bodies, because their job was more dangerous and demanding than that of ordinary infantrymen. They specialized in going out in small groups, to look and learn or to kill with a high degree of selectivity. Many of them were qualified snipers able to place an aimed shot in a particular head at four hundred yards, or a chest at over a thousand, if the target had the good manners to stand still for the second or two needed for the bullet to cover the longer distance. *They were the hunters. Few had nightmares from their duties, and none would ever fall victim to delayed-stress syndrome, because they deemed themselves to be predators, not prey, and lions know no such feelings.*

Lt. Col. Jim Nicholson summed up the situation that exists within the CD community at a briefing at INSCOM:

When you do counterdrug work, be prepared to engage people of low repute, negotiate around conspiratorial riff-raff and lowlifes, duel with treacherous minds and sidestep skullduggery at every turn. If you successfully do this, then your next step will be to take on the drug dealers.

It will take a predator to successfully fight the counter drug community—before the fight against the traficantes ever begins.

200. Hearst Wire Service, February 27, 1996.

201. Ibid.

202. Ibid.

203. Ibid.

204. Heritage Foundation comments, January 11, 1996.

205. *SFC*, February 26, 1996.

206. Comments from LANL staffer in regards SouthCom lack of contact with law enforcement agencies in Panama. January 1996.

207. Hearst Wire Service, February 27,1996.

208. See David Hood, *Southwest Border Seizures: The New Mexico Corridor* (New Mexico Department of Public Safety, Santa Fe, December 1989). Also, see Trevor Armbrister, "Our Drug-Plgued Mexican Border," *Readers Digest*, January 1996, pp. 53-58, for a concise picture of the situation today.

209. Philadelphia Inquirer Wire Service, February 25, 1996.

210. Conversation with DEA, Albuquerque, November, 1995.

211. Malcolm M. Feeley and Austin D. Sarat, *The Policy Dilemma: Federal Crime Policy and the Law Enforcement Assistance Administration, 1968-1978* (Minneapolis: University of Minnesota Press, 1980), p. 23.

212. New Mexico Crimestoppers Commission, *Drugs in New Mexico: The First Report*, study prepared by BMC Ltd, J. F. Holden-Rhodes and Gavin Holden Rhodes, June 1990.

213. Ibid.

214. I was part of the New Mexico group.

215. Ibid.

216. WN, July 1991. Shortly after my second visit to EPIC, and following what I thought was a postive discussion about the value of competitive intelligence analysis with Ed Heath, I was informed by the EPIC publications section that "Mr. Heath does not want any documents or reports released to you." I learned shortly thereafter from his deputy that I was not to be allowed to visit EPIC in the future—as long as Heath was in command. Known to insiders as the "dinosaur," Heath left EPIC during the fall of 1994 and went to Washington were he was "held" by the DEA until his retirement shortly thereafter.

217. James Thompson, *Rolling Thunder: Understanding Policy and Programs Failure* (Chapel Hill: The University of North Carolina Press, 1980), p. 27.

218. Pettee, p. 23.

219. For the best treatment of interest-based policy, see Alan Tonelson, "What is the National Interest," *Atlantic Monthly*, July 1991, pp. 35-52.

220. Grant F. Wardlaw, *Intelligence and the International Narcotics Problem: A Framework for Considering Options for the Future*, report prepared for the Defense Intelligence College, Defense Intelligence Agency, Washington, D.C., January 1990, p. 72.

221. *NDCS*, 1991, p. 9.

222. Feeley and Sarat, p. 35.

223. *NDCS*, 1991, p. 10.

224. James Q. Wilson, *Thinking About Crime* (New York: Random House, 1985), p. 6.

225. Wardlaw, p. 72.

226. Ibid.

227. Ibid.

228. Aaron Wildavsky and Jeffrey Pressman, *Implementation* (Berkeley: University of California Press, 1979), p. 11.

229. Ibid.

230. Richard Elmore, *Encyclopedia of Policy*, (New York: Houghton Mifflin Com-

pany,1988), p. 25.

231. Feeley and Sarat, p. 34.

232. Thompson, p. 31.

233. Colin S. Gray, *War, Peace, and Victory: Strategy and Statecraft for the Next Century* (New York: Simon and Schuster, 1990), p. 344.

234. Thompson, p. 31.

235. Gray, p. 348.

236. Naval Institute Proceedings, June 1992, p. 94.

237. WN, November 1991.

238. AP Wire Service, December 19, 1995.

239. Pacific Gateway/Port of Tacoma brochure, Summer 1993, pp. 14-15.

240. WN, June 1991.

241. Phillip B. Davidson, *Secrets of the Vietnam War* (Novato, Calif.: Presidio Press, 1990), p. 6.

242. Alfred C. Maurer, Marion D. Tunstall, and James M. Keagle, *Intelligence: Policy and Process* (Boulder, Colo.: Westview Press), 1985, p. 54.

243. David Heilbroner, "Is It Police Work or Plunder?" *Readers Digest*, April 1995, pp. 181-188.

EPILOGUE: TURNING POINTS

1. Sherman Kent, *Strategic Intelligence for American World Policy* (Princeton, N.J.: Princeton University Press, 1949), pp. 39-68.

2. The failure of the cotton crop in Bolivia in 1972—the seed money for which was provided by Alliance for Progress dollars—caused a group of Bolivian businessmen to turn to coca as a cash crop. Thus began the coca industry. By 1980, Bolivia had become the first narcocracy.

3. It is absolutely critical that the United States stay engaged with Mexico. Traditionally the safety valve in times of trouble south of the border, the US can and must play a role in assisting Mexico to move beyond the present crisis. The same holds true with US /Colombian relations. The engagement must be of a much different nature than what has been the norm over the past 23 years. Unfortunately, pressure is building to isolate the US from Mexico. Senator Dianne Feinstein put it very succinctly, "Increased commerce is not worth increased drug trafficking." (See Trevor Armbrister, "Our Drug-Plagued Mexican Border," *Readers Digest*, February 1996, pp. 53-58.)

4. Matthew Robinson, "Another Shot in War on Drugs," *Investors Business Daily*, September 11, 1995 p. 1. (Hereafter *IBD*)

5. Joseph E. Kelley, National Security and International Affairs Division, *Observations of US International Drug Control Effort*, General Accounting Office, August 1, 1995. It is of some interest to note the findings of a 1994 GAO report on the transit zone: The supply of illegal drugs reaching the United States via Central America continues virtually uninterrupted despite years of US drug interdiction efforts. Traffickers are now using sea and overland routes to move drugs, and the ability of Central American nations to combat the problem remains limited due to a variety of factors, including lack of resources and government corruption.

6. *IBD*, p. 2.

7. Senator John McCain, *Narcotics Digest*, Washington, D.C., June 1993, pp. 7-8.

8. George S. Pettee, *The Future of American Secret Intelligence* (Washington, D.C.: Infantry Journal Press), p. 3.

Glossary

ADNET	Anti-Drug Network
AOR	Area of Responsibility
AWACS	Airborne Warning and Control System
BATF	Bureau of Alcohol, Tobacco, and Firearms
BORTAC	Border Patrol Tactical Unit
BP	Border Patrol
C3	Command, Control, and Communications
C_3I Center	USCS or Joint USCS/USCG facility that is the focal point for detecting and interdicting drug smugglers
C4	Command, Control, Communications, and Computers
CD	Counter drug
CDO	Counter drug operations
Chapare	Bolivia's most important coca-growing area, encompassing the provinces of Chapare, Carrasco, and Tiraque in Cochabamba department
CHCL	Cocaine Hydrochloride (cocaine)
CI	Counterintelligence
CIA	Central Intelligence Agency
CINC	Commander-in-Chief
CN	Counternarcotics
CNC	Counter Narcotics Center operated by the CIA
COMINT	Communications Intelligence
CONUS	Continental United States
D&M	Detection and Monitoring
DAO	Defense Attache Office (US embassies)
DDN	Defense Data Network

DEA	Drug Enforcement Administration
DF	Direction Finding
DIA	Defense Intelligence Agency
DIRECO	Direccion de Reduccion de Cultivos de Coca, the Coca Reduction agency in Bolivia, under the Bolivian Ministry of Agriculture
DLEA	Defense Law Enforcement Agency
DoD	Department of Defense
DOJ	Department of Justice
DOS	Department of State
DESNET	Defense Integrated Secure Network
El Conducto	The conduit, the primary sea, air, and land routes north from Colombia through which cocaine is transported
ELINT	Electronic Intelligence
EMERALD	Prototype AIS for counter drugs
EPIC	El Paso Intelligence Center
EW	Electronic Warfare
FAA	Federal Aviation Administration
FARC	Fuerzas Armadas Revolucionarias de Colombia, the Revolutionary Armed Forces of Colombia, Colombia's largest guerrilla group
FBI	Federal Bureau of Investigation
FBIS	Foreign Broadcast Information Service
GSR	Ground Surveillance Radar
HIDTA	High Intensity Drug Trafficking Area
HUMINT	Human Intelligence
IMINT	Imagery Intelligence
INM	Bureau of International Narcotics Matters
INS	Immigration and Naturalization Service
IRS	Internal Revenue Service
ITAC	Intelligence Threat Analysis Center
JCS	Joint Chiefs of Staff
JIC	Joint Intelligence Center
JTF	Joint Task Force
JVIDS	Joint Visually Integrated Display System
La Empresa	La Empresa Coordinadora, the loose confederation of drug trafficking families or mafias that come together to do business
LAN	Local Area Network
LP	Listening Post
MAS	Muerte a Los Secuestradores, or Death to Kidnappers, a vigilante organization founded by Medillin traffickers in 1981
MOU	Memorandum of Understanding
NDCS	*National Drug Control Strategy*

NDIC	National Drug Intelligence Center
NG	National Guard
NORAD	North American Aerospace Defense Command
NORTIC	NORAD Tactical Intelligence Center
NPIC	National Photographic Interpretation Center
NSA	National Security Agency
ONDCP	Office of National Drug Control Policy
OP	Observation Post
OPCON	Operational Control
OPSEC	Operational Security
OSINT	Open Source Intelligence
PAN	Party of National Action, largest opposition party in Mexico
pasta basica	Basic paste, the results of mixing coca leaf and chemicals to form a paste that is then subject to further processing at a laboratory into finished cocaine.
PGR	Office of the Attorney General (Mexico)
PJF	Federal Judicial Police (Mexico)
PRI	Party of Institutionalized Revolution, the ruling party of Mexico
SCI	Sensitive Compartmented Information
SCIF	SCI Facility
Sendero Luminoso	Shining Path, Peru's largest guerrilla organization
SIGINT	Signals Intelligence
SOUTHCOM	US Southern Command, located at Quarry Heights, Panama
TAT	Tactical Analysis Teams, located at embassies
UHV	Upper Huallaga Valley, the main coca-growing area in Peru, encompassing parts of San Martin and Huanuco departments
UMOPAR	Unidad Movil de Partrullaje Rural, the name given to rural mobile patrol units in Bolivia and Peru
USCG	United States Coast Guard
USCS	US Customs Service
USMS	US Marshals Service

Selected Bibliography

BOOKS

Andrade, Dale. *Ashes to Ashes: The Phoenix Program and the Vietnam War.* Lexington, Mass.: Lexington Books, 1990.

Armstrong, Scott J. *Long-Range Forecasting from Crystal Ball to Computer.* New York: John Wiley & Sons, 1985.

Bamford, James. *The Puzzle Palace.* New York: Penguin Books, 1982.

Berkowitz, Bruce D., and Goodman, Allan E. *Strategic Intelligence for American National Security.* Princeton, N.J.: Princeton University Press, 1989.

Bozeman, Adda B. *Strategic Intelligence & Statecraft: Selected Essays.* Washington, D.C.: Brassey's, 1992.

Brogan, Patrick. *The Fighting Never Stopped: A Comprehensive Guide to World Conflict Since 1945.* New York: Vintage Books, 1990.

Bueno de Mesquita, Bruce. *The War Trap.* New Haven, Conn.: Yale University Press, 1981.

Builder, Carl H. *The Masks of War: American Military Styles in Strategy and Analysis.* Baltimore, Md.: Johns Hopkins University Press, 1989.

Burrows, William E. *Deep Black Space Espionage and National Security.* New York: Berkley Books, 1988.

Candlin, Stanton A. H. *Psycho-Chemical Warfare.* New Rochelle, N.Y.: Arlington House, 1973.

Clancy, Tom. *A Clear and Present Danger.* New York: Berkley Books, 1990.

Clauser, Jerome K., and Weir, Sandra M. *Intelligence Research Methodology.* Washington, D.C.: HRB-Singer, 1976.

Cline, Ray. *Secrets, Spies, and Scholars: The Blueprint of the Essential CIA.* Washington, D.C.: Acropolis Books, 1976.

Cline, Ray. *Comparing Foreign Intelligence: The U.S., the USSR, the U.K. and the Third World.* London: Pergamon-Brassey's International Defense Publishers, 1988.

Codevilla, Angelo. *Informing Statecraft: Intelligence for a New Century.* New York: Free Press, 1992.

Davidson, Phillip B., Lt. Gen. USA (ret.). *Secrets of the Vietnam War.* Novato, Calif.: Presidio Press, 1990.

de Gramont, Sanche. *The Secret War Since World War II*. New York: G.P. Putnam's Sons, 1962.

Donnelly, Thomas, Roth, Margaret, and Baker, Caleb. *Operation Just Cause: The Storming of Panama*. New York: Lexington Books, 1991.

Duzan, Maria Jimena. *Death Beat: A Colombian Journalist's Life Inside the Cocaine Wars*. Translated and edited by Peter Eisner. New York: HarperCollins Publishers, 1994.

Eddy, Paul, with Hugo Sabogal and Sara Walden. *The Cocaine Wars*. New York: Bantam Books, 1989.

Epstein, Edward J. *Agency of Fear: Opiates and Political Power in America*. New York: G.P. Putnam's Sons, 1977.

Feeley, Malcolm M., and Sarat, Austin D. *The Policy Dilemma: Federal Crime Policy and the Law Enforcement Assistance Administration*. Minneapolis: University of Minnesota Press, 1980.

Freemantle, Brian. *The Fix*. New York: Tom Doherity Associates, 1986.

Gentry, John. *Lost Promise: How CIA Analysis Misserves the Nation*. Lanham, Md.: University Press of America, 1993.

Global Outlook 2000: An Economic, Social, and Environmental Perspective. United Nations Publications, 1990.

Godson, Roy. *Intelligence Requirements for the 1980's: Elements of Intelligence*. New Brunswick, N.J.: National Strategy Information Center, Inc., 1983.

Gray, Colin S. *War, Peace, and Victory: Strategy and Statecraft for the Next Century*. New York: Simon and Schuster, 1990.

Hackett, General Sir John. *The Profession of Arms*. New York: Macmillan Publishing Company, 1983.

Hannah, Norman B. *The Key to Failure*. New York: Madison Books, 1987.

Hillsman, Roger. *Strategic Intelligence and National Decisions*. Glencoe: The Free Press, 1956.

Johnson, Loch K. *A Season of Inquiry: Congress and Intelligence*. Chicago: Dorsey Press, 1988.

Johnson, Loch, and Inderfurth, Karl F. *Decisions of the Highest Order: Perspectives on the National Security Council*. Pacific Grove, Calif.: Brooks/Cole Publishing Company, 1988.

Kam, Ephraim. *Surprise Attack*. Cambridge: Harvard University Press, 1988.

Katz, Samuel K. *Soldier Spies: Israeli Military Intelligence*. Novato, Calif.: Presidio Press, 1992.

Kent, Sherman. *Strategic Intelligence for American World Policy*. Princeton, N.J.: Princeton University Press, 1949.

Kipling, Rudyard. *Kim*. New York: Bantam Books, 1983.

Kirsch, M. M. *Designer Drugs*. Minneapolis: CompCare Publishers, 1986.

Lee, Rensselaer W. III. *The White Labyrinth: Cocaine and Political Power*. New Brunswick, N.J.: Transaction Publishers, 1989.

Levine, Michael. *Deep Cover*. New York: Dell Books, 1991.

Mabry, Donald J. *The Latin American Narcotics Trade and U.S. National Security*. Westport, Conn.: Greenwood Press, 1989.

MacDonald, Scott B. *Dancing on a Volcano*. New York: Praeger Publishers, 1988.

Malamud-Goti, Jaime. *Smoke and Mirrors: The Paradox of the Drug Wars*. Boulder, Colo.:Westview Press, 1992.

Martin, John M., and Romano, Anne T. *Multinational Crime: Terrorism, Espionage, Drug and Arms Trafficking*. Newbury Park, Calif.: Sage Publications, 1992.

Maurer, Alfred C., Tunstall, Marion D., and Keagle, James M., eds. *Intelligence: Policy and Process*. Boulder, Colo.: Westview Press, 1985.

Meyer, Herbert E. *Real-World Intelligence*. New York: Weidenfeld & Nicolson, 1987.

Mills, James. *The Underground Empire: Where Crime and Govenments Embrace*. Garden City, N.J.: New York, Doubleday Company, 1978.

Musto, David. *The American Disease: Origins of Narcotics Control*. New York: Oxford University Press, 1987.

O'Neil, Bard E. *Insurgency and Terrorism Inside Modern Revolutionary Warfare*. New York: Brassey's, 1990.

Oseth, John M. *Regulating U.S. Intelligence Operations: A Study in Definition of the National Interest*. Lexington: University Press of Kentucky, 1985.

Pettee, George S. *The Future of American Secret Intelligence*. Washington, D.C.: Infantry Journal Press, 1946.

Pressman, Jeffrey L., and Wildavsky, Aaron. *Implementation*. Berkeley: University of California Press, 1979.

Ra'Anan, Uri. *Hydra of Carnage*. Lexington, Mass.: Lexington Books, 1986.

Record, Jeffrey. *Beyond Military Reform: American Defense Dilemmas*. Washington, D.C.: Pergamon-Brassey's, 1988.

Rowe, Dennis. *International Drug Trafficking*. Chicago: The University of Illinois at Chicago, 1987.

Schroeder, Richard C. *The Politics of Drugs: An American Dilemma*. Washington, D.C.: Congressional Quarterly, Inc. Press, 1980.

Scott, Peter Dale, and Marshall, Jonathan. *Cocaine Politics: Drugs, Armies, and the CIA in Central America*. Berkeley: University of California Press, 1991.

Seabury, Paul, and Codevilla, Angelo. *War Ends and Means*. New York: Basic Books, 1989.

Shulsky, Abram N. *Silent Warfare: Understanding the World of Intelligence*. Washington, D.C.: Brassey's, 1991.

Simpkin, Richard E. *Race to the Swift: Thoughts on Twenty-First Century Warfare*. London: A. Wheaton & Co., 1985.

Smith, Myron J. *The Secret Wars: A Guide to Sources in English. Volume I: Intelligence, Propaganda and Psychological Warfare, Resistance Movements, and Secret Operations, 1939–1945*. Santa Barbara, Calif.: ABC-Clio Press, 1980.

Smith, Myron J. *The Secret Wars: A Guide to Sources in English. Volume II: Intelligence, Propaganda and Psychological Warfare, Covert Operations, 1945-1980*. Santa Barbara, Calif.: ABC-Clio Press, 1981.

Smith, Myron J. *The Secret Wars: A Guide to Sources In English. Volume III: International Terrorism, 1968-1980*. Santa Barbara, Calif.: ABC- Clio Press, Ltd., 1980.

Smith, Peter H. Smith. *Drug Policy in the Americas*. Boulder, Colo.: Westview, Press, 1992.

Staley, Sam. *Drug Policy and the Decline of American Cities*. New Brunswick, N.J.: Transaction Publishers, 1992

Thompson, James Clay. *Rolling Thunder: Understanding Policy and Program Failure*. Chapel Hill: The University of North Carolina Press, 1980.

Treverton, Gregory F. *Covert Action: The Limits of Intervention in the Postwar World*. New York: Basic Books, 1987.

Tully, Andrew. *The Secret War Against Dope*. New York: Coward, McCann & Geoghegan, 1973.

Von Clausewitz, Carl. *On War*. Edited with an introduction by Anatol Rapoport, Baltimore: Penguin Books, 1968.

Walker, William O. III. *Drug Control in the Americas*. Albuquerque: University of New Mexico Press, 1981.

Wildavsky, Aaron, and Pressman, Jeffrey. *Implementation*, Berkeley, Calif.: The University of California Press, 1979.

Wilson, James Q. *Thinking About Crime*. New York: Random House, 1985.

Wisotsky, Steven. *Breaking the Impasse in the War on Drugs*. Westport, Conn.: Greenwood Press, 1986.

REPORTS & PAPERS

Army Science Board, Summer Study. *Use of Army Systems and Technologies in Counter-Narcotics Efforts*. August 2, 1990.

Aspin, Les, Rep. Chairman, House Armed Services Committee. *An Approach to Sizing American Conventional Forces for the Post-Soviet Era*. January 1992.

Cathcart, James A. Col., USMC. *And That Goes for Domestic Wars TOO!: The Weinberger Doctrine and Domestic Use of the Military*. Carlisle Barracks, Penn.: US Army War College, March 31, 1989.

"Counternarcotics Intelligence Analysis." Defense Intelligence College. 1990.

Cox, Robert. *Counter Drug Report*. Ft. Leavenworth: US Combined Arms Command, Training. 1991.

Defense Technical Information Center. *Counternarcotics Technical Report*. March 1989.

Dehoust, Walter F. LtCol., USMC. *The Use of Conventional Military Forces for Drug Interdiction*. Newport, R.I.: US Naval War College, 1988.

Department of Defense. *Integration of Command, Control, Communications and Technical Intelligence into an Effective Communications Network for Drug Interdiction*. Report to Congress. May 1989.

Dickens, Homer Q. Lt. Col., *The Role of the Reserve Components in the War on Drugs*. Carlisle Barracks, Penn.: US Army War College, March 31, 1989.

Document of Cartagena. Washington, D.C.: Government Printing Office, February 1990.

Dodge, Lowell. Director, Administration of Justice Issues. *The Department of Justice's Efforts to Compile State Crime Statistics*. Washington, D.C.: General Accounting Office, April 1990.

Drug Enforcement Administration. *The Illicit Drug Situation in the United States and Canada,1987-1986*. Washington, D.C.: Government Printing Office, February 1987.

Drug Interdiction: Funding Continues to Increase but Program Effectiveness Is Unknown. Washington, D.C.: Government Printing Office, December 1990.

Drug Interdiction Operation Autumn Harvest: A National Guard-Customs Anti-Smuggling Effort. Report to Congressional Requesters. Washington, D.C.: General Accounting Office, June 1988.

Dziedzic, Michael J., Lt.Col., USAF. *The Emerging Inter-American Drug Control Regime: Prospects and Limitations*. US Air Force Academy, 1991.

Final Report. *Technology Initiatives Game 90*. Newport, R.I.: US Naval War College, June 24-29, 1990.

Flynn, Ronald B. Lt. Col. *The National Guard Drug Interdiction Mission: A Circumvention of Posse Comitatus?* Carlisle Barracks, Penn.: US Army War College, April 2, 1990.

Fortier, A. *War on Drugs*. House Armed Services Committee. Washington, D.C.: Government Printing Office, April 1990.

Harris, William H. Jr., Major, U.S. Army. *Are Counternarcotics Operations a Viable Mission for U.S. Army Special Operations Forces?* Ft. Leavenworth: Command and General Staff College, June 1989.

Hearing before the Select Committee on Narcotics Abuse and Control House of Representatives. Washington: D.C.: Government Printing Office, December 10, 1990.

Holden-Rhodes, J. F., and Rhodes, Gavin H. "Crackdown: The First Report— Drugs in New Mexico." New Mexico Crime Stoppers Commission, June 1990.

Hood, David L. *Southwest Border Seizures: The New Mexico Corridor, January 1989– November 1989. An Analysis of Seizures Reported to Operation Alliance by U.S. Border Patrol and U.S. Customs Service.* New Mexico Department of Public Safety, December 1989.

Lupsha, Peter A. *Drug Lords and Narco-Corruption: The Players Change but the Game Continues.* University of New Mexico, 1991.

Money Laundering: The U.S. Government Is Responding to the Problem. Washington, D.C.: General Accounting Office, May 1991.

The National Drug Strategy Status Report. *Hearing before the Select Committee on Narcotic Abuse and Control.* October 1990.

Narcotics Traffickers Intelligence Operations in CONUS (U). DOS 2400-65290, May 1990.

Office of National Drug Control Policy. Science and Technology Committee, Office of Supply Reduction. *Law Enforcement Agency Technical Requirements for Review by Federal Research and Development Facilities.* February 1990.

Office of National Drug Control Policy. *Science and Technology Committee Workshop for Matching Federal R&D Capabilities with Law Enforcement Agency Requirements.* Washington, D.C.: ONCIP, August 1990.

Redway, H. Jonathan. *Drug Testing Police Personnel: A Discussion Paper.* Washington, D.C.: Police Forum, 1989.

Rice, Paul Jackson, Col., JAGC. *New Laws and Insights Encircle the Posse Comitatus Act.* Carlisle Barracks, Penn.: US Army War College, May 26, 1983.

Simmons, O.W., Lt. Col., USA. *The Reasoned Drug War Role for the Military.* Newport, R.I.: US Naval War College, 1989.

Southwest Border Law Enforcement Computer Capabilities and Information/Intelligence Management Exchange. El Paso, Tex.: Operation Alliance, April 1991.

Texas National Guard. *Suspect Information Resource Center.* San Antonio, Tex.: Texas Narcotic Control Program/Texas National Guard, 1991.

Tritchler, William K. Maj. USMC. *Employment of the U.S. Armed Forces and the War on Drugs.* Quantico, Va.: Marine Corps Command and Staff College, 1987.

US Commander-in-Chief, Southern Command. *Counterdrug Wargaming and Simulation Initiative.* Draft ROC & Information Brief. June 10, 1991.

US Department of Energy National Laboratory Consortium. *Integrated Analytic/Computer Models To Support National Counter Narcotics Activities.* October 23, 1991.

US House of Representatives, Committee on Foreign Affairs House of Representatives. *Andean Drug Strategy.* Hearing before the Subcommittee on Western Hemisphere Affairs. February 1991.

US Department of Justice. *Federal Drug Data for National Policy.* Washington, D.C.: Government Printing Office, April 1990.

US Department of Justice, Drug Enforcement Administration, Office of Intelligence. *Illicit Drug Wholesale/Retail Price Report—United States: January-March, 1990.* Washington, D.C.: DEA, 1990.

US Department of Justice, Drug Enforcement Administration. *Worldwide Heroin Situation Report—January 1990.* Washington, D.C.: DEA, January 1990.

US Department of Justice, Drug Enforcement Administration. *Worldwide Cocaine Situation—1990.* Washington, D.C.: DEA, 1990.

US Department of State, Bureau of International Narcotics Matters. *International Narcotics Control Strategy Report.* Washington, D.C.: DOS, March 1990.

US Department of the Treasury. *Southwest Border Drug Control Strategy.* July 1990.

US Senate. *Senate Select Committee to Study Governmental Operations with Respect to Intelligence Activities, Final Report, Vol.1, Foreign and Military Intelligence,* 94th Congress, 2d session, No. 94-755. Washington, D.C.: Government Printing Office, 1976.

US Sentate. *Review of the National Drug Control Strategy: Hearing before the Committee on the Judiciary United States Senate.* First Session. Washington, D.C.: Government Printing Office, October 1989.

US Senate. *Review of the Second National Drug Control Strategy. Hearing before the Committee on the Judiciary United States Senate.* First Session. Washington, D.C.: Government Printing Office, December 1989 and February 1990.

US Southern Command, Analytical Support Team, J-Z. *After Action Report.* May 1992.

Wardlaw, Grant F. *Intelligence and the International Narcotics Problem: A Framework For Considering Options for the Future.* Report prepared for the Defense Intelligence College, Defense Intelligence Agency. Washington D.C.: DIA, January 1990.

War on Drugs: Information Management Poses Formidable Challenges. Washington, D.C.: Government Printing Office, May 1991.

The White House. *The National Drug Control Strategy.* 1989-1995.

Zadareky II, Joseph T. Col, USAF. *National Drug Policy: Fact or Fiction.* Newport, R.I.: US Naval War College, 1986.

UNPUBLISHED PAPERS/INTERNAL DOCUMENTS

Drohan, William. *The 1984 Cocaine Surprise: Drugs Declare War on the United States.* Defense Intelligence Agency, 1989.

Rhodes, Gavin Holden. *INSCR & INM Report.* George Washington University, 1992.

BRIEFINGS AND TRIP REPORTS

Holden-Rhodes, J. F., CDT/Los Alamos National Laboratory. *Trip Report: Southwest Border Seminar IV.* May 1990.

Holden-Rhodes, J. F., Lt. Col., Infantry, USAR, 405th Military Intelligence Detachment (S). *Report/Review of NMNG Drug Interdiction Operations.* February 1990.

Holden-Rhodes, J. F., Lt. Col., Infantry, USAR, Intelligence Command, *Trip Report: Forces Command.* April 1991.

Holden-Rhodes, J. F., Lt. Col., Infantry, USAR, 405th Military Intelligence Detachment (S). *Counterdrug Information: Manzano Mountains East of Albuquerque.* July 1991.

2nd Army Counternarcotics Conference. January 1991.

Southwest Border Seminar III. Albuquerque, New Mexico: January 1991.

ARTICLES

"Apoyo a la Cultura." *Caretas* (January 1991), p. 8.

Bagley, Bruce Michael. "US Foreign Policy and the War on Drugs: Analysis of a Policy Failure." *Journal of Interamerican Studies and World Affairs,* Vol. 1 (1989), pp. 189-239.

Bosarge, Betty B. "Laboratory Spearheads Drug Control Strategy for Border." *Narcotics Control Digest,* Vol. 20, No. 26 (December 19, 1990), pp. 1, 7-8.

Capaccio, Tony. "Lindsay's War on Drug Planes." *Defense Week,* Vol. 11, No. 4 (January 22, 1990), p. 7.

Capaccio, Tony. "Army Leaders Differ on Using Troops to Battle Drug Lords." *Defense Week,* Vol.10, No. 42 (October 23, 1989), p. 10.

"Como se Llego al Video." *Caretas* (February 1991), pp. 28-33.

Cowan, William V., "Melting the Snowman: Communications and the Counternarcotic

Threat." *Signal* (December 1989), pp. 27-32.

"Drug Interdiction: The Nation's Air War on Drugs Takes Off." *Aviation Week & Space Technology* (February 1990), p. 32

Ehrenfield, Rachel. "Narco-Terrorism and the Cuban Connection." *Strategic Review* (Summer 1988), pp. 34-41

"El Buen Paso." *Caretas* (October 1990), pp. 17-18, 83.

"El Precio del Deber." *Caretas* (January 1991), pp. 34-36.

"Embestida Roja." *Caretas* (October 1990), pp. 29, 83.

Fuss, Charles M., Jr. "Lies, Damn Lies, Statistics, and the Drug War." *Proceedings* (December 1989), pp. 65-69.

Gorriti, Gustavo A. "How to Fight the Drug War." *The Atlantic Monthly* (July 1989), pp. 70-76.

Hude, James C. "National Guard, Law Enforcement Agencies Team Up in War on Drugs." *Armed Forces Journal* (September 1989), pp. 22-23.

Lane, Dennison D., Col., and Weisenbloom, Mark, Lt. Col. "Low-Intensity Conflict in Search of a Paradigm." *International Defense Review* (January, 1990), pp. 35-39.

Marshall, Eliot. "A War on Drugs With Real Troops?" *Science,* Vol. 241 (July 1, 1988), pp. 13-15.

Morales, Waltraud Q. "The War on Drugs: A New US National Doctrine." *Third World Quarterly,* Vol. 11 (July 1989), pp. 147-189.

"Motor del Desarrollo." *Caretas* (January 1991), pp. 2-3.

Narcotics Control Digest (November 7, 1990), pp. 9-10.

"1991: Debut Sangriento." *Caretas* (January 1991), pp. 26-29.

"Peliculina Sangrienta." *Caretas* (February 1991), pp. 34-35.

"Presos Cantando." *Si* (February 1991), pp. 10-13.

"Protegiendo el Ahorro." *Caretas* (January 1991), pp. 4-7.

Raezer, Timothy A. "Needed Weapons in the Army's War on Drugs: Electronic Surveillance and Information." *Military Law Review,* Vol. 116 (Spring 1987), pp. 1-65.

"Reformando la Redforma." *Caretas* (January 1991), pp. 15-18, 88.

Robinson, Clarence A., Jr. "Fighting the War on Drugs." *Signal* (December 1989), pp. 35-40.

Rubio, Marcial. "Hacia Un Nuevo Orden Social." *Debate* (May/June 1990), pp. 17-19.

Silva Ruete, Javier. "1978-1988: Entre las Crisis." *Debate* (May/June 1988), pp. 8-10.

Steele, Robert David. "Applying the New Paradigm: How to Avoid Strategic Intelligence Failures in the Future." *American Intelligence Journal* (Autumn 1991), pp. 32-37.

Temple, Herbert R., Lt. Gen., US Army, and Steward, Walter L., Lt. Col., US Army. "The National Guard in the War on Drugs." *Military Review* (March 1990), pp. 41-48.

Toffler, Alvin & Heidi. "War, Wealth, and a New Era in History." *World Monitor* (May 1991), pp. 46-52.

"29 de noviembre, 1990, Una nueva masacre Senderista." *Caretas* (December 1990), pp. 26-32.

"Violencia '87." *Caretas* (December 1987), pp. 28-31.

"Vivito y Coleando." *Si* (February 1991), pp. 5-9.

"What to Do About Drugs." *Fortune* (June 1988), pp. 37-41.

"Y que con los DD.HH." *Caretas* (December 1990), pp. 32-32A.

Index

About the Author

J. F. HOLDEN-RHODES is a former serving Officer in the U.S. Marine Corps and U.S. Army where he held Reconnaissance, Infantry, Special Forces and Intelligence positions. He was appointed as a Post-Doctoral Fellow at Los Alamos National Laboratory, and also served as Member of Laboratory Staff, Sandia National Laboratories. He is presently an Adjunct Professor at the University of New Mexico where he teaches and writes in the areas of Intelligence, National Security, and Military History.

ISBN 0-275-95454-4

90000>

EAN

9 780275 954543

HARDCOVER BAR CODE